History of Computing

The *History of Computing* series publishes high-quality books which address the history of computing, with an emphasis on the 'externalist' view of this history, more accessible to a wider audience. The series examines content and history from four main quadrants: the history of relevant technologies, the history of the core science, the history of relevant business and economic developments, and the history of computing as it pertains to social history and societal developments.

Titles can span a variety of product types, including but not exclusively, themed volumes, biographies, 'profile' books (with brief biographies of a number of key people), expansions of workshop proceedings, general readers, scholarly expositions, titles used as ancillary textbooks, revivals and new editions of previous worthy titles.

These books will appeal, varyingly, to academics and students in computer science, history, mathematics, business and technology studies. Some titles will also directly appeal to professionals and practitioners of different backgrounds.

Gerard Alberts • Jan Friso Groote

Editors

Tales of Electrologica

Computers, Software and People

 Springer

Editors
Gerard Alberts (iD)
Department of Mathematics
University of Amsterdam
Amsterdam, The Netherlands

Jan Friso Groote (iD)
Computer Science
Eindhoven University of Technology
Nuenen, The Netherlands

ISSN 2190-6831   ISSN 2190-684X   (electronic)
History of Computing
ISBN 978-3-031-13035-9   ISBN 978-3-031-13033-5   (eBook)
https://doi.org/10.1007/978-3-031-13033-5

This Springer imprint is published by the registered company Springer Nature Switzerland AG
The registered company address is: Gewerbestrasse 11, 6330 Cham, Switzerland

Preface

Electrologica is a legend in the Dutch history of computing. Founded in 1956 it was the first Dutch computer manufacturer. The company built the Electrologica X1 and X8 computers based on the pioneering work at the Center for Mathematics and Computer Science in Amsterdam. The X8 was in every sense the culmination of the ingenuity of its time. It represented a breakthrough towards general availability of computing power for scientific research. On March 24, 2018, we celebrated the exhibition of the Electrologica X8 at the Rijksmuseum Boerhaave in Leiden by a small symposium. This book is dedicated to this event.

In the 1950s and 1960s, computers were exceptional. The computing machines surviving from this time are large, clunky, and impressive. They evoke recollections with those, the few, who worked with them. The remnants inspire the imagination of the rest of us mortals who never even came close to these large contraptions. They allow to imagine how such machines performed their calculations, as every wire and every transistor is still clearly visible, which is inconceivable for modern equipment. They give presence to history. Most importantly, such old computers give historical context to our digital, algorithmic, and information age.

The presentation of computer heritage is worthy of a celebration because so little is preserved. Of the unique machines from the 1950s and the few dozens of later installations from the 1960s, mainly bits and pieces remain. To our knowledge, only a single copy of the Electrologica X1 is preserved. Great was the joy when a copy of its second product, the Electrologica X8, appeared to have survived in the depots of the Kiel computer museum. We commend the Stichting Electrologica for extending its care to this installation when the Kiel museum decided to deselect it and swiftly organize its transport to the Netherlands. We praise Stichting Electrologica for its wisdom to not only take this extraordinary piece of heritage home but on top of that make it possible for Rijksmuseum Boerhaave to put it on exhibit. There, it found a fitting place among the microscope of van Leeuwenhoek and the pendulum clock of Huygens.

At the symposium of March 24, 2018, a number of speakers, most of them early pioneers of computing, joined in the dedication of this exhibit.

Fig. 1 The X8 console catching dust in the stores of the Computermuseum der Fachhochschule Kiel, 2006

Ton van Helvoort, *Een fluwelen revolutie: De computerisering van de weten-schappen*
Gerard Alberts, *Computerbouw in Nederland van academie naar onderneming*
Paul Klint, *Software zonder geheugen*
Frans Kruseman Aretz, *Het Mathematisch Centrum, ALGOL 60 en de Electro-logica X8*
Willem van der Poel, *De commissie Z8*
Dirk Dekker, *Dekker's algorithme voor wederzijdse uitsluiting*
Gauthier Van Den Hove, *The birth of semaphores in the Electrologica X8*
Ernst-Günter Hoffmann, *The adventure of developing a FORTRAN Compiler in the 1960s*
Dirk van Delft, *De reis van de X8 naar Rijksmuseum Boerhaave*

As an interlude, Lambert Meertens en Dick Grüne were interviewed as former users of the Electrologica machines at the Mathematical Center. Ernst-Günter Hoffmann brought from Kiel the original FORTRAN Compiler handbook. We thank them for their presentations at this very unique event.

Two contributions were published in Dutch in *Studium* 12 (1–3) 2019: Gerard Alberts, "Computerbouw in Nederland: ondernemende academici en bedachtzame industriëlen," pp 48–69. Ton Van Helvoort, "Computergebruikers aan de Groningse universiteit: pendule of torsie tussen centraal en decentraal?" pp 70–90.

The present book offers an English edition of a number of the talks from 2018. In addition Huub de Beer provides an overview of the design of the machines and

Fig. 2 Parts of the X8 on exhibit at Rijksmuseum Boerhaave, March 24, 2018

the policy decisions at Electrologica. René van Dantzig reports on the use of the X8 in nuclear physics research, and Lambert Meertens shares his recollections of musical composition with the aid of the X8 computer. This is not the final book on the Dutch computer manufacturer Electrologica. But it gives a nice insight in early Dutch computing and the entrepreneurial and research activities in the form of a number of stories by authors who were either involved or who are highly engaged with this remarkable period.

We are grateful to Dirk van Delft, the parting director of Rijksmuseum Boerhaave, for taking up computer heritage as the final commitment of his museum career. It has been a great pleasure for us to work with Dirk van Delft of Boerhaave and CWI's Paul Klint to organize the symposium. We thank the team of Boerhaave for the smooth organization and operation of the day. We enjoyed a wonderful and most engaged audience.

Amsterdam, The Netherlands   Gerard Alberts
Eindhoven, The Netherlands   Jan Friso Groote
February 2022

Contents

Chapter 1
Electrologica, a Gem

Gerard Alberts
Korteweg-de Vries Institute for Mathematics, University of Amsterdam,
Amsterdam, The Netherlands

Abstract This chapter introduces the main subject of our book, the computer manufacturer Electrologica. It offers a survey of the state of historiography of this subject in the Netherlands and introduces the contributions to this volume.

1.1 Electrologica Is a Gem in the History of Dutch Computing

Logic per electrons, isn't that a fascinating idea. The play on words conveyed enough of the progressive spirit of the postwar years to make it to the name of a new enterprise, Electrologica. In their 1955 meetings Jojo Engelfriet and Aad van Wijngaarden had unleashed great ambitions. The immediate result was the founding of an enterprise which did, in fact, grow to manufacture computers in series. More than creating a production facility, they grounded a company culture which resonated long after Electrologica had been assimilated into Philips-Electrologica. Annual parties, amazingly breaking with the environment of the frugal fifties, resonate in reminiscences shared among former employees. The core of the company culture was a belief that nothing was unthinkable. Or in a more specific sense, anything technical reason could think of could be imposed on matter. The prowess of reason expressed in its name was at the heart of the company culture. Logic would dictate the course of electrons. It made Electrologica a strong and courageous enterprise. By the same token, the implicit disdain for the muddy materiality of technics, and of commerce, was its Achilles' heel.

The rationalism under discussion here is intrinsically connected to the very idea of an automatic computer. Being the expression of a strong belief in reason makes the story of Electrologica a gem in the history of computing in the Netherlands. The company was linked to special events in adjacent fields. It was connected to the emerging concept of semaphores and the algorithm of mutual exclusion. It was connected to the Dutch reception of ALGOL and the Dijkstra-Zonneveld compiler, and later to the THE-multiprogramming system. In the field of nuclear physics the Electrologica machines allowed frontline research in three-dimensional particle detection. In art it served computer-aided musical composition. Perhaps surprising but not unusual for computers in 1950s was the involvement with design. The Electrologica X1 was a well-designed machine, even if it came with a divergent set of peripherals. The Electrologica X8 was truly exquisite in its design. The bouquet of these stories is on offer in the following chapters. The present book takes stock of the historiography of Electrologica, the enterprise, the machines, their software, and their use.

1.1.1 Organizing Research

Leading mathematicians founded a national institute for mathematical research in 1946. In doing so they followed their growing social awareness of the 1930s. The only untypical thing about the Dutch mathematicians in this case was that they were first, earlier than the physicists and other disciplines, in setting up a system of organized research. Large scale investment in, and organization of, research was a typical reflection of the warfare experience. Yet, computing was not among the major topics of strategic interest in 1945. It did not appear among the fields of prime interest noted by Vannevar Bush, in his report to the president of the USA, Science, *the endless frontier*, nor was the construction of computing machinery surrounded by high levels of military secrecy or confidentiality.

For the Dutch mathematicians in their immediate postwar initiative, the expressed motivation lay not so much in the war experience but in the economic and cultural distress of the interbellum. David van Dantzig had been among the few who, against the grain, succeeded in pushing their career to a professorship in the 1930s. Once he did in 1938, he made a sharp turn toward putting mathematics at the service of society. He effectively shifted his interest from topology to statistics. He was joined by Hans Schouten, a well-established professor of differential geometry, who in 1938–1939 judged that it was time for true engineering mathematics. In Groningen, Jan van der Corput, senior professor of number theory, had been organizing debates on the societal role of mathematics. He mobilized intellectuals, maths teachers, in particular, in a tenor opposite to Hardy's 1939 outcry, *A mathematician's apology*. Jurjen Koksma was the young and ambitious professor of mathematics at the Free University. Together, with the support of scholars from adjacent fields, they founded the Mathematical Center on February 11, 1946. And the Dutch government subventioned, as did the city of Amsterdam.

In absence of experience in advanced computing, the four of them did act on their societal ambition and decided there should be a computing department at the newly founded institute. "Computing department" was what they wrote, there was not even a Dutch expression for it.

They found Adriaan van Wijngaarden ready to lead the department, "Rekenafdeling"—in English publications curiously translated to "Computation Department." Unlike the ambitious mathematicians, Aad van Wijngaarden did know what scientific computing was. Trained at the Delft polytechnic, he did have experience in what was sometimes called "practical mathematics," or in the words of Douglas Hartree "numerical analysis": laying out, organizing, and executing procedures for the computation of advanced technical problems. The clue was to not only perform the tedious calculations without error, but more importantly to design new schemes of calculation that were deemed fitting for untried technical challenges.

1.1.2 Mathematical Culture

The ambitious setting of research in mathematics and Van Wijngaarden's experience in advanced calculations produced a special mix. First, it made Van Wijngaarden bend over to the mathematicians, working with them in projects, e.g. nibbling on the edges of the classic problem of Fermat's last theorem. A second trait, of even deeper impact, was that the work on computing and machinery was positioned as a work of mathematical nature. Van Wijngaarden had been trained and had taken his doctor's degree in engineering, but on the extremely mathematical side of it. In Delft he matured in the study of rational mechanics and aerodynamics. It presented a natural context for embarking in lengthy and tedious calculations. The rationalist worldview implicit in scientific engineering went well with the Amsterdam environment of a mathematical research institute and in fact allowed him to present the computing department's projects as mathematical. It worked both ways. The Mathematical Center did not hesitate to embrace the work of the Computation Department as its own. And the department in its choices for the substance and strategies of research would naturally follow a preference for mathematically toned topics. Van Wijngaarden readily identified as such, "if as a mathematician you want to create something, of course you want it to be a thing of beauty."[1] Indeed, the presumption of elegance was an argument in the design of computers and in the work on programming languages. A mathematical esprit pervaded the work of the computation department and gave a special twist to the gradual adoption of the idea of programming and, even further, of programming languages.

International cooperation gave an impulse in the same direction. A bigger international conference on automatic computers was held in Darmstadt, Germany, in 1955. Formally convening on automatic calculators, the main topic at the gathering turned out to be the exchange of experience in programming and the brainstorm on how to create better programs. Most of the Europeans in the field of advanced computation had lived their first hands-on experience in programming in the mathematical laboratory of Cambridge University, where the EDSAC, from its dedication in May 1949, was the object of an annual summer course. The Darmstadt conference took the discourse to a new level.

From the conference, Van Wijngaarden en Dijkstra took home the concept of "superprogram" elevating programming to a higher level of abstraction. By 1958 they

---

[1] This and the following quote are from: Alberts, G., and P.C. Baayen. 1987a. Ingenieur van taal. Interview met A. van Wijngaarden. In *Zij mogen uiteraard daarbij de zuivere wiskunde niet verwaarloozen*, eds. Alberts G., F. van der Blij, and J. Nuis, 276–288. Amsterdam: CWI.

got on board of the international, transatlantic Algol initiative, on creating an algorithmic language, with a strong German-Swiss input. And of course, getting recursion included in the definition of the Algol language, that is allowing self-referential procedures in programming, was a "matter of decency" to Van Wijngaarden and to his pupil Edsger Dijkstra. Dijkstra had joined the Mathematical Center in the spring of 1952 as a research assistant commissioned to "the programming of the ARRA"—the ARRA meant to be the institute's first computer. Dijkstra rose to the occasion of being the first programmer and Van Wijngaarden's prime pupil. In the field of programming he developed new concepts and took his PhD on Communication with an automatic computer, 1959.

When the Algol language was agreed upon in January 1960, the challenge was to make it work on the computer, in the Dutch case on the Electrologica X1 of the Mathematical Center. Making it work meant to write a superprogram translating programs written in Algol into instructions executable on the machine: a "translator" or "compiler."

Dijkstra and his colleague Jaap Zonneveld set out to meet the challenge. The way they did it impressed the world. In construing a translator for programs written in Algol, Dijkstra broke new grounds for compiler construction, "eye-opening" in the words of Brian Randell. Dijkstra got there very much in defiance of the good advice by Van Wijngaarden. Dijkstra took his own path in disregard of the experience in compiler writing offered by Harry Huskey, whom Van Wijngaarden had organized to come over from California in support of Dijkstra, Zonneveld, and their team. They preferred to follow their own reason, and in doing so they indeed strongly emulated Van Wijngaarden's style of work, his rationalism, and his boldness to follow one's mind in new directions. Even in novel fields of programming and the programming of programming, a mathematical culture governed the work of the Rekenafdeling at the Mathematical Center. It was this culture that was passed on to computer construction and to the company Electrologica (Fig. 1.1).

1.1.3 Owning Electrologica

Johannes J. Engelfriet had earned his credentials in contributing to novel approaches in actuarial science, insurance mathematics. He was a follower of David van Dantzig in introducing the concept of mathematical model in his field. However quantitative in nature the field of insurance already was, Engelfriet was among the group of scholars who helped to mathematize it even further. The Mathematical Center lent strong, but indirect, support to the establishment of extraordinary professorship in actuarial science. In 1948, Engelfriet and his colleague C. Campagne were called to occupy the chair, next to their role as managers of insurance companies. Their initiatives were deployed in close vicinity of the Mathematical Center and they fully shared the atmosphere of postwar ambitions. Jojo Engelfriet thus came in as no stranger, when he addressed Van Wijngaarden with the request that the Rekenafdeling build him an automatic calculator. It was a recurring request. And finally in 1955

Fig. 1.1 Electrologica advertising its pride in producing a Dutch computer X1

Van Wijngaarden sold him not one machine, but the complete workshop and the expertise for the production.

The resulting company Electrologica was Van Wijngaarden's, in that it straightforwardly continued his ambitions for the Rekenafdeling to embark on the construction of computing machinery. It was Engelfriet's enterprise in that it more than fulfilled his eagerness to be at the forefront of the new developments in automation. Engelfriet

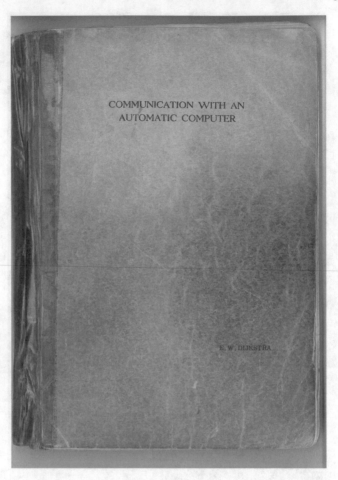

Fig. 1.2 A perused copy of Edsger Dijkstra's dissertation, showing the signs of its intense use as a manual

was the the owner, chairing over his colleague Anton Dek and Aad van Wijngaarden in Electrologica's supervisory board. The board of the Mathematical Center was proud to have given birth to a new enterprise, and so was the Center's national funding agency, ZWO.

Edsger Dijkstra had been involved in the design of the computers constructed at the Mathematical Center all along. He led the development of the basic research program. For him the agreement with the designers of the electronics felt like a contract. His dissertation *Communicating with an automatic computer* expressed the programming facilities of the Electrologica X1 computer under construction in such detail that it read like a reference guide and programming manual. Well-worn copies could be found at the X1 desk (Fig. 1.2). Electrologica, or at least the X1 machine, was Dijkstra's. In recognition of his involvement, the company had an extra run of the book printed.

Bram Loopstra and Carel Scholten had from scratch led the design of the ARRA and ARMAC computers of the Mathematical Center and now moved along to become the managers of the company. Of course, Electrologica was their factory.

Upon the mere announcement of the X1 computer, the Dortmund Mathematische Beratungs- und Programmierungsdienst GmbH, a Hoesch subsidiary, wanted to "own" it and offered to be the sales representative for Germany. Instead, Electrologica opened a German branch, its head Dr E. Hort joining the management with Loopstra and Scholten.

Computing Centers of the universities agreed with Electrologica to join efforts in coding programs for the new machines. In the absence of a software department in the Electrologica company during the first years, they, as the prime users, appropriated the machine. When the next machine, the X8, was developed, a further coalition of academic users formed a committee to create its system software, the committee Z8—pronounced "Zacht," Dutch for "soft" as in software. They could make the machine work.

They all owned Electrologica, the company, its branches, the computer, the production facility, the code. The founders, the facilitators, the managers, the supervisors, the constructors, the programmers, they were all highly engaged. All taking a share in the proud ambitions, possessed as they were with the new technology, they were all "owners." From its inception, Electrologica floated on a cushion into the world.

1.2 State of the Art

The gem in the history of Dutch computing, of early Dutch computing, has been studied. The ultimate study of Electrologica has not been done. And the present book only takes stock of the current state of the historiography.

1.2.1 The Company

The first to test the water of Electrologica's history was Ben Gales in his book on the bicentenary of AEGON insurance company.[2] That is because Engelfriet's insurance company NILLMIJ merged and merged again into the conglomerate AEGON. The most impressive and to this day most comprehensive study of Electrologica as a business was done by Dirk de Wit, making it a major case-study in his dissertation, *The shaping of automation*.[3]

---

[2] Gales, B.P.A. 1986. *Werken aan zekerheid: een terugblik over de schouder van AEGON op twee eeuwen verzekeringsgeschiedenis*, 238–241. 's-Gravenhage: AEGON Verzekeringen.

[3] Wit, D. de. 1994. *The shaping of automation. A historical analysis of the interaction between technology and organization, 1950–1985*, Hilversum: Verloren; Wit, D. de. 1997. The construc-

More specifically under the aspect of innovation the company has been studied by Jan van den Ende and Onno de Wit, and by Dick Manuel and Willem Hulsink.[4] Philips company and its efforts to step into the computer industry have been studied from various angles. Company historian Ivo Blanken devotes sections to Philips' own efforts and the relation to Electrologica.[5] Jan van den Ende, Nachoem Wijnberg, and Albert Meijer offer a thorough interpretation of the company strategy.[6] Gerard Alberts, in his present contribution, builds on these to further detail the relation between the board of Philips and the founders of Electrologica. Adriënne van den Bogaard studies the Philips Physics Laboratory, the NatLab.[7]

The common trait of these studies of the company is that they all look from the outside in. By contrast, Huub de Beer searched the AEGON archives in order to find the considerations and decisions on the boardroom table and on the engineer's desk. His interpretation of the intimate details appears here in Chap. 3 in English for the first time.

1.2.2 The Mathematical Center

De Mathematical Center side of the story has been the recurring subject for the present author. The first run in 1987[8] did present oral history, interviews with Aad van Wijngaarden and with the women computers, who had performed most of the calculating work in the 1950s, but little on Electrologica. More comprehensive studies followed by Gerard Alberts with Huub de Beer, on Mathematical Center and Electrologica, and by Gerard Alberts and Bas van Vlijmen on the culture of

---

tion of the Dutch computer industry: The organisational shaping of technology. *Business History* 39(3):81–104.

[4] Wit, O. de, en J. van den Ende. 2000. The emergence of a new regime: Business management and office mechanisation in the Dutch financial sector in the 1920s. *Business History* 42(2):87–118; Wit, O. de, e.a. 2002. Innovative junctions. Office Technologies in the Netherlands, 1880–1980. *Technology and Culture* 43:50–72; Dick Manuel. 2004. Caleidoscoop van de informatietechnologie in Nederland, 1946–2004, In *Ondernemen in netwerken. Nieuwe en groeiende bedrijven in de informatiesamenleving*, edited Wim Hulsink, Dick Manuel en Erik Stam, 35–51. Van Gorcum.

[5] Blanken, I.J. 2002. *Een industriële wereldfederatie; Geschiedenis van Koninklijke Philips Electronics N.V., Deel 5* Zaltbommel. De Europese Bibliotheek; 153 ff; 347 ff.

[6] Ende, J. van den, N. Weinberg, and A. Meijer. 2004. The influence of Dutch and EU government policies on Philips' information technology product strategy. In Coopey (2004a), *Information technology*, 187–208.

[7] Alberts, G. 2019. Computerbouw in Nederland: ondernemende academici en bedachtzame industriëlen. *Studium* 12(1–3):48–69; Reworked in this volume, Chap. 2; Bogaard, Adriënne van den. 2007. De bijdrage van Philips (Research) aan de informatietechnologie in Nederland vanuit het perspectief van kenniscirculatie, 1945–2010. Eindhoven: Stichting Historie der Techniek [rapport vooronderzoek].

[8] Alberts G., F. van der Blij, and J. Nuis, eds. 1987c. *Zij mogen uiteraard daarbij de zuivere wiskunde niet verwaarloozen*. Amsterdam: CWI.

pioneering in computing in the 1950s.[9] Provided with relevant archives and oral history, historians might return to further stories of the company culture and look if there was in fact continuity from the Mathematical Center's Computing Department to Electrologica.

1.2.3 Software, Language, and ALGOL

The history of software has been a focus of the Amsterdam history of computing all along, including the history of programming languages. Particularly revealing is the study of the transition when such techniques came to be called a language. In this vein the Mathematical Center and Electrologica have been studied repeatedly under the aspect of history of software.

In 2005 Adriënne van den Bogaard and Gerard Alberts organized a colloquium on the state of historiography of Electrologica. The inspiration has been kept alive to this day. Huub de Beer, and later David Nofre and Karel van Oudheusden joined the team. Adriënne van den Bogaard took the lead in a project at the Stichting Historie der Techniek resulting in *De eeuw van de computer*, 2008. History of computing internationally shifted its focus from the machines to computers and their users, and so did Van den Bogaard and Alberts in their special issue of *Studium, computers en hun gebruikers*, shedding a new light on the practices at Mathematical Center and Electrologica.[10]

Broadening the perspective to users and co-construction of technology laid the groundwork for Soft-EU, the international project *Software for Europe*, led by Gerard Alberts. In fact, "Electrologica's software: co-entrepreneurship and the emergence of a Dutch software industry" was the Dutch branch of the Collaborative Research Project Software for Europe. In turn, Soft-EU was one of four projects in the European Science Foundation EUROCORES programme *Inventing Europe: technology and the making of Europe, 1850 to the present* (2007–2011). And within the history of software with a focus on Europe and transatlantic relations, a keen interest in the

---

[9] Alberts, G., H.J.M. Bos, and J. Nuis, eds. 1989. *Om de wiskunde. Stimulansen voor toepassingsgerichte wiskunde rond 1946*. Amsterdam: CWI; Alberts, Gerard. 1998a. *Jaren van berekening. Toepassingsgerichte initiatieven in de Nederlandse wiskunde-beoefening 1945–1960*. Amsterdam: Amsterdam University Press; Alberts, G. 2006. De geboorte van de Nederlandse informatica in Londen – Aad van Wijngaarden. *Informatie* 48(1): 46–50; Alberts, Gerard, and Huub T. de Beer. 2008a. De AERA. Gedroomde machines en de praktijk van het rekenwerk aan het Mathematisch Centrum te Amsterdam, *Studium* 2, 101–127. Amsterdam: Amsterdam University Press; Beer, H. de (2008) Electrologica, Nederlands eerste computerindustrie. *Informatie* Informatie 50(10):30–37; Alberts, Gerard, and Bas van Vlijmen. 2017. *Computerpioniers: het begin van het computertijdperk in Nederland*. Amsterdam: Amsterdam University Press.

[10] Bogaard, Adriënne van den. 2008b. Stijlen van programmeren 1952–1972. In *Computers en hun gebruikers*, 128–144; Bogaard, Adriënne van den, and Gerard Alberts. 2008c. Inleiding, in Adriënne van den Bogaard and Gerard Alberts (eds), *Computers en hun gebruikers, een halve eeuw computergeschiedenis in Nederland* (special issue) *Studium* 1–2:1–16; Bogaard, A. van den, H. Lintsen, F. Veraart en O. de Wit. 2008d. *De eeuw van de computer. Geschiedenis van de informatietechnologie in Nederland* Deventer: Kluwer/Stichting Historie der Techniek.

programming language ALGOL and its implementations was only natural. David Nofre and Karel van Oudheusden, also known as Edgar Daylight, joined the project.[11] Adriënne van den Bogaard and Karel van Oudheusden discerned various "styles" of programming. Van Oudheusden captured the intrepid culture of early programmers in the USA mirroring themselves to the "space cadets" from the comics, "traveling for unknown destinations."

The local tradition of working with computers at the Mathematical Center and at Electrologica beautifully illustrates the hesitant steps in early programming. It reflected the gradual realization that programming was a layered activity. Programming involved not just the automation of calculation but also automating the automation. By the mid-1950s, this aspect of working with computers came to be called "autocoding" or "automatic programming." Van Wijngaarden and Dijkstra took the notion of "superprogram" home from the 1955 Darmstadt conference. In the local Amsterdam lore that was a major step in making the layered aspect of programming explicit. Further steps followed and something like a local style of thinking about programming evolved. Notions like compiler, language, and the more general idea of "software," rather than "autocoding," gained currency, also in the Netherlands. A local curiosity was that "operating system," a notion coined at IBM labs in 1958, made it to the Netherlands slowly. In the famous Dijkstra-Zonneveld compiler of 1960, the operating functions still were an integral part of the compiler, internally vaguely distinguished as the "housekeeping" part of the compiler. In a series of reports Frans Kruseman Aretz has detailed the history of the Electrologica operating systems when they did become separate entities: PICO, MICRO, and MILLI.[12]

In the details of the local history, the gradual adoption of the metaphor of "language" in programming was observed. Gerard Alberts, David Nofre, and Mark Priestley further elaborated this observation and the impact of the language metaphor on early software.[13]

---

[11] Cf. the archived ToE website, the programme *Inventing Europe: technology and the making of Europe, 1850 to present.* Strassbourg: ESF, 2007, and its links to the Final report 2011.

[12] Kruseman Aretz, Frans E.J. 1974. Doelstellingen en achtergronden van de operating systems PICO, MICRO en MILLI. *Informatie* 16:672–678; Kruseman Aretz, Frans E.J. 2013. *On the design of two small batch operating systems 1965–1970.* CWI report SwAT, Centrum Wiskunde & Informatica, Amsterdam.

[13] The ALGOL-, and Electrologica-related output of Soft-EU include: David Nofre. 2010. Unraveling Algol: US, Europe, and the creation of a programming language, *Annals for the History of Computing* 32(2):58–68; Alberts, G. 2014a. Algol culture and programming styles; guest editor's introduction, algol culture and programming styles. *IEEE Annals for the History of Computing* 36(4):2–5, special issue; Alberts, G., ed. 2014a. Algol culture and programming styles. *IEEE Annals for the History of Computing* 36(4), special issue; Alberts, G., and E. Daylight. 2014c. Universality versus locality: the Amsterdam style of ALGOL implementation. *IEEE Annals for the History of Computing* 36(4): 52–63; Nofre, D., M. Priestley, and G. Alberts. 2014. When technology became language: the origins of the linguistic conception of computer programming, 1950–1960. *Technology and Culture* 55(1):40–75; Edgar G. Daylight. 2016. De werking van de geest. In *De geest van de computer,* edited Eric Berkers and Edgar G. Daylight, 23–55. Utrecht: Matrijs; David Nofre. 2021. The politics of early programming languages: IBM and the algol project. *Historical Studies in the Natural Sciences* 51(3):379–413.

Not only the Mathematical Center but also the university computing centers engaged in developing software for the Electrologica X1. For the X8 such cooperation was somewhat formalized in the committee Z8. One would want to know through further historical research, how Electrologica led these efforts, or did not lead, and when it was that the company organized a software department within its own ranks.

1.2.4 The Dijkstra-Zonneveld Compiler

In this early Dutch history of programming no one was more influential than Edsger Dijkstra. Mathematical Center, Electrologica, ALGOL, and software were all connected through Dijkstra's work. His dissertation and his consecutive work with Jaap Zonneveld on the Algol compiler for the X1 computer broke new ground for compiler construction. Called to a professorship in Eindhoven, Dijkstra, with a new team around him, developed the THE-multiprogramming system, allowing multitasking by the X8 computer. No wonder Dijkstra's work is an issue of keen interest to historians. Adriënne van den Bogaard compared Dijkstra's to Van der Poel style of programming. Invaluable groundwork for historians was done by Frans Kruseman Aretz editing and detailing Dijkstra's and his own work on Algol compilers in the 1960s.[14] Independently, Huub de Beer in Eindhoven, Gauthier van den Hove in Namur, and Karel van Oudheusden in Amsterdam wrote their MSc theses on the Dijkstra-Zonneveld compiler for the X1. Van den Hove went on to write his PhD dissertation on the same subject. Further historical interpretations may be expected. One may hope the THE-multiprogramming system will be the subject of similar historical scrutiny.

1.2.5 Industrial Design and Cold War

In all, the historiography of Electrologica has been strong on the side of emerging computer science, biased by the perspective of the computer manufacturer appearing as an exploit of academic research. Also, several studies take Electrologica under the aspect of innovation. The company as an enterprise flourishing and surviving in the 1950s and 1960s has been touched only superficially. An overview of its locations and its German branch has not been composed. Little is known of the details of its

---

[14] Kruseman Aretz, Frans E.J. 2003. *The Dijkstra-Zonneveld ALGOL 60 compiler for the Electrologica X1*. CWI Report SEN-N301. Centrum voor Wiskunde en Informatica. Amsterdam, The Netherlands; Kruseman Aretz, Frans E.J. 2006. Progress in ALGOL 60 implementation: two successive MC systems compared, unpublished note, November 23; Kruseman Aretz, Frans E.J. 2008. *A comparison between the ALGOL 60 implementations on the Electrologica X1 and the Electrologica X8*. CWI report SEN-E0801, Centrum Wiskunde & Informatica, Amsterdam; Hove, G. van den. 2019. *New insights form old programs, the structure of the first ALGOL 60 system*. PhD thesis. University of Amsterdam.

management. Provided further archival sources, a head-on history will certainly pay off.

Fig. 1.3 The cabinet knobs and the machine parts pending by the table legs reveal Wim Rietveld's industrial design. The X8 at the NatLab, Philips Physics Laboratory, 1972

What appears as a curious detail at first, may well offer an entry to deeper insight, namely the design of the machines. If the X1 was remarkable in its design, the X8 presented a masterpiece of industrial design by Wim Rietveld. It posits Electrologica on the leading edge of modern industry in postwar times (Fig. 1.3).

Electrologica may in Dutch context appear as a gem, in comparison to other European countries, the firm was hardly an exception. First, many European countries saw initiatives of research into mathematics and engineering, including the development of computing machinery. The Mathematical Center was no exception in setting up organized research, be it in universities, academies, or new institutes. The Swedish committee for mathematical machines and the German program to fund experimental calculation devices are just two examples of the European trend of organizing research in this field in service of the common good of science and engineering. A perspective of postwar reconstruction will serve well to compare all such endeavors.

Second, some of the initiatives grew into efforts to manufacture computers in series. The Manchester university computer construction was adopted by Ferranti. The Mathematical Center's constructions morphed into Electrologica. In Copenhagen Regnecentralen remained Regnecentralen, being the exception of staying inside an academic institute while preparing computer construction in series.[15]. They

---

[15] Klüver, Per Vingaard. 1999. From research institute to computer company: Regnecentralen 1946–1964. *IEEE Annals of the History of Computing* 21(2):31–43; Klüver, Per Vingaard. 2003.

all seemed to think they were competing with each other and with the established electronic industry. The attempted transitions all saw the contrast between academic research culture, conceived as serving the public cause, and the particular interest of a private enterprise. None survived the innate conflict of business cultures. It takes a Cold War perspective on this part of their histories to observe and compare how governments on a national scale and in international cooperation would at once support newly founded industries and at the same time withhold and leave their fate to the market. If the present book is a snapshot of the history of Electrologica, both a comparative European perspective and a Cold War perspective on Electrologica's history will be in place.

1.3 On Offer

The present volume offers views on the backgrounds of the Mathematical Center culture, specifics on the history of the work on software that went into Electrologica and two use cases of the X8 machine.

Struck by the difference in perspective between the founders of the firm Electrologica in their boyish entrepreneurial spirit and the board of the Philips corporation in its well-informed and prudent decision making, Gerard Alberts in Chap. 2 takes a slightly distantiated look at Philips and the fate of Electrologica. Chapter 3 is Huub de Beer's tour of the Electrologica boardroom and engineer's desk. It offers not only the internal discussions on new types of computers and their innards but also a listing of where these machines went.

Paul Klint, in Chap. 4, invites the reader in the opposite direction. Fully engaging in the Dutch traditions of software he shows the national hall of fame from the inside.

Technology transfer, modernization, and the welfare state: Regnecentralen and the making of governmental policy on computer technology in Denmark in the 1960s. In *History of nordic computing*, edited Bubenko, Janis, John Impagliazzo, and Arne Sølvberg, 61–77. Boston, MA: Springer; Lavington, Simon. 1980. *Early British computers: The story of vintage computers and the people who built them*. Bedford: Manchester University Press; Lavington, Simon. 2011. *Moving targets. Elliott-automation and the dawn of the computer age in Britain, 1947–1967*. London: Springer; Lavington, Simon. 2019. *Early computing in Britain: Ferranti Ltd. and government funding, 1948–1958*. Cham: Springer; Mounier-Kuhn, Pierre-Eric. 2010. *l'Informatique en France; de la seconde guerre mondiale au Plan Calcul*. Paris: PUBS; Mori, Elisabetta. 2019. Coping with the "American Giants". *IEEE Annals of the History of Computing* 41(4):83–96; Paju, Petri, and Helena Durnova. 2009. Computing close to the iron curtain. Inter/national computing practices in Czechoslovakia and Finland, 1945–1970. *Comparative Technology Transfer and Society* 7(3):303–322; Paju, Petri, and Thomas Haigh. 2016. IBM rebuilds Europe: The curious case of the transnational typewriter. *Enterprise & Society* 17(2):265–300; Paju, Petri and Thomas Haigh. 2018. IBM's tiny peripheral: Finland and the tensions of transnationality. *Business History Review* 92:3–28; Petersson, Tom. 2008. Private and public interests in the development of the early swedish computer industry. Royal Institute of Technology, CESIS – Centre of Excellence for Science and Innovation Studies. In *Working Paper Series in Economics and Institutions of Innovation* 1; Petersson, Tom. 2005. Facit and the besk boys: Sweden's computer industry (1956–1962). *IEEE Annals of the History of Computing* 27(4):23–30; Petzold, Hartmut. 1992. *Moderne Rechenkünstler. Die Industrialisierung der Rechentechnik in Deutschland*. München: Beck.

As software does not go without memory his is a plea for historical awareness, "Software without memory."

In the next two chapters Frans Kruseman Aretz and Dirk Dekker serve history first hand. Frans Kruseman worked with, developed and preserved compilers and operating systems for the Electrologica computers. He relates how he joined the Mathematical Center and was drawn more and more to the core tasks of getting the systems to work, a field of work which he then took as the subject of scientific study. It is from that vantage point that Kruseman has started to look back and has taken care to preserve and study the compilers and operating systems developed and implemented by Dijkstra, by himself and by others. Over the past decades he has edited and explained the systems and made them accessible to further historical study. The present Chap. 5 is more than a fitting overview. It rounds up a series of reports crucially contributing to the history of computing in the Netherlands, "The Mathematical Center, ALGOL 60 and the Electrologica X8."

It is well known, but poorly documented, how Dirk Dekker crucially contributed to Edsger Dijkstra's work on programming the process of cooperating processors. Dijkstra went on to develop his ideas and results on describing parallel processes. He has always paid tribute to Dekker's contribution, but Dekker himself never published it. Until now, posthumously. On offer is Dekker's recollection and his recent update of the algorithm, Chap. 6, "History of Dekker's Algorithm for mutual exclusion."

Two use cases of the X8 conclude the present volume, one on the processing of measurement data in nuclear physics and the second on computer-aided musical composition. In the 1960s at IKO, the Instituut voor Kernfysisch Onderzoek in Amsterdam, René van Dantzig was a member of a team in nuclear physics exploring three-dimensional detection of particles. They called their project BOL, like Dutch for "sphere." If that was not enough of an experiment by itself, an X8 computer was installed to control and coordinate two DEC PDP8 computers. What made the case for computing fascinatingly historical, was that it involved the programming of a system to make three processors work together smoothly. While computer industry was struggling with time sharing and interfering processes, and while Dijkstra was developing a practice and a theory of parallel processes elsewhere in the Netherlands, within the BOL project local solutions were found and implemented for the task: Wammes. Van Dantzig looks back in Chap. 7, "The Electrologica X8 and the BOL detector—Networking, programming, time-sharing and data-handling in the Amsterdam nuclear research project 'BOL'."

The Mathematical Center esprit of trying the computers on new things offered young Lambert Meertens the freedom to follow his passion and explore the potential of programmable electronic computers. In fact he was one of the first in the Netherlands to explicitly use the expression and wander the lanes of "Artificial Intelligence." Inspired by an IFIP, International Federation of Information Processing Societies, prize contest, he set out to program the X8 to assist in musical composition. The old X1 computer at the Mathematical Center, still available as a printer driver, was programmed to print the score. A commendation by the jury ensued, and publications with colleague Leo Geurts and composer Louis Andriessen,[16] and a record—a vinyl recording of the composition played by a human string quartet. Appended to his story is a translation of a talk Lambert Meertens gave at the time, plus the algorithm as it was written at the time: Chap. 8, "An early experiment in algorithmic composition."

---

[16] Andriessen, Louis, Leo Geurts, and Lambert Meertens. 1969. Componist en computer. *De Gids* 132:304–311.

Chapter 2
Philips and the Fate of Electrologica

From Single Computer Construction to Manufacturing

Gerard Alberts

Korteweg-de Vries Institute for Mathematics, University of Amsterdam,
Amsterdam, The Netherlands

Abstract It seemed as if in the Netherlands in postwar years initiatives to construct computers were bound to be absorbed by established industry. Indeed Electrologica, the firm emerging from the mathematics research institute Mathematical Center, did find its end as Philips-Electrologica. But this was not because either Philips Industries or Electrologica would have wanted this outcome.

In fact, there was not just this one, but a plethora of initiatives to build computers. Similarly, on the market side, several industrial enterprises did purchase an automatic calculating machine. Between the two there was no easy match. Most ideas brought to the fore with sparkling enthusiasm never made it to the stage of production, not even those which had resulted in a prototype computing machine. PTT researcher Willem van der Poel's computer design, called ZEBRA, was taken into production by Stantec in Newport (Wales) only after frustrating refusals by PTT itself, by Zuse KG in Germany and by Philips. Philips also declined to join in a venture by the Mathematical Center and NILLMIJ life insurance company to set up Electrologica.

It was not out of ignorance that Philips Industries evaded the participation in a Dutch computer industry. Both at the level of research and at the level of business policy and strategy, Philips knew what was going on. No single entity in Dutch society was better informed than the board of Philips Industries. And it acted rationally according to all this knowledge. It played on a global level and would have its agreements with partners at the same level. In this case IBM was the partner and the agreement was that IBM purchased its components from Philips in exchange for Philips' abstinence in the market of computer manufacturing. Even after the agreement had expired Philips was hardly interested in joining in a "national" industry. If it did finally purchase the remnants of Electrologica, it did so to appropriate the expertise accumulated there.

Finally, not only a view of Philips' own rationality in business strategies but also a view on the context of the Cold War with its characteristic relations between the hegemonic US and the European states helps to better understand the fate of Electrologica and the logic of it ending in Philips-Electrologica.

© The Author(s), under exclusive license to Springer Nature Switzerland AG 2022   17
G. Alberts, J. F. Groote (eds.), *Tales of Electrologica*, History of Computing,
https://doi.org/10.1007/978-3-031-13033-5_2

2.1 Introduction

Electrologica would build and supply computers. In the context of Dutch computer manufacturing where so many things did not occur, the founding and continued existence of this enterprise was something to be noted. Computer manufacturing was a field of entrepreneurial academic enthusiasts and prudent entrepreneurs. The Netherlands was so small that those involved all knew each other. Some played a role on both the academic and the entrepreneurial sides, incidentally some changed sides. Yet, only by exception would scientists and entrepreneurs truly join efforts. Too often their collaboration failed; one side not positioning itself where the other expected it to be. Philips-Electrologica was such an exception. Or was it?[1]

2.2 Calculating Machines in the Postwar Innovation Spirit

Innovation initiatives popped up in the immediate postwar years in such fields as advanced engineering, automation, and instrumentation. In the early days of 1947 the board of Philips Industries would engage in a debate on "machines without workers." Later, the board commissioned a strategic reconnaissance committee to follow up with reflections on "Philips and thinking machines." The "light bulb manufacturer in the south," kept itself well informed, ... and did not move.[2] In the west of the country, in Delft, as early as 1945 young engineer ir. J. Woldringh brought up the idea of a central production facility for instrumentation. Woldringh's employer was TPD, Technical-Physical Service, a shared agency of the Technical University Delft and the National Agency for Applied Research. Even though no such factory was created, TPD did in the 1950s go on to construct a wide range of installations for computing, control, and measuring.[3]

Following a suggestion by the Delft professor of fluid dynamics Jan Burgers, the Delft University Fund during the cold days of the first winter after the war sent

---

[1] The present chapter is a translation appearing here for the first time in English of Alberts, G. 2019. Computerbouw in Nederland: ondernemende academici en bedachtzame industriëlen. *Studium* 12(1–3):48–69. It is in part based on research with Bas van Vlijmen: Alberts, Gerard, and Bas van Vlijmen. 2017. *Computerpioniers: het begin van het computertijdperk in Nederland*. Amsterdam: Amsterdam University Press. It continues on earlier work with Huub de Beer: Alberts, Gerard, and Huub T. de Beer. 2008a. De AERA. Gedroomde machines en de praktijk van het rekenwerk aan het Mathematisch Centrum te Amsterdam, *Studium* 2, 101–127. Amsterdam: Amsterdam University Press. The work of Huub de Beer in 2007–2008 en of Bas van Vlijmen in 2014–2017 was in part supported by the foundation PAOi, Stichting Fonds Post Academisch Onderwijs in de Informatica.

[2] In the postwar culture, government agencies and news agencies would prudently avoid any suggestion of free publicity and allude to Philips as "a light bulb manufacturer in the south," "een gloeilampenfabriek in het zuiden des lands."

[3] In Dutch "Technisch-Physische Dienst TH-TNO." Cf. page 105 of Alberts, Gerard. 1998b. Optimaal regelen. In *De opkomst van de informatietechnologie in Nederland*, ed. E. van Oost e.a., 103–117. Amsterdam: Amsterdam University Press.

out a dozen young engineers to tour the universities and research institutes of the United Kingdom in order to report on the latest in their fields of engineering science. Adriaan van Wijngaarden, a doctor of engineering sciences since December 1945, made the trip to cover the fields of mechanics and naval engineering. On February 18, 1946, while still in London he wrote to his supervisor Cornelis Biezeno, also his thesis supervisor, that he had noted so many a novelty on "mathematical machines," that he had decided to report on the subject separately. Thus, the first seeds for a Dutch computer science were sown in a London hotel room.

Again in Delft, the University Fund financed a project submitted by physics professor for optics, Bram van Heel, and mathematics professor Dick de Bruijn aiming at the development of an automatic calculation device for optical calculations. Moreover the annual prize contest of the very same Fund in 1948, following a suggestion by Dick de Bruijn, called for an essay on the possibilities of modern computing devices in relation to pure mathematics. All these may have been niche initiatives, taken together they built up a postwar scenery of broad interest in modern computing machinery. And Philips Industries were never at great distance, yet the corporation did not move. Electrologica sprang from academic circles and ended up as a part of Philips. Still, if during the decade of Electrologica's existence as an independent enterprise, Philips refrained from action, this was not caused by lack of knowledge or lack of entrepreneurial vision.

2.3 The English Tour

Among the scientists in 1945 eager to organize research systematically, in the Netherlands the mathematicians were, perhaps surprisingly, the first to have their plans installed. On February 11, 1946, the Mathematical Center was founded and part of the prospective institute in Amsterdam was to be a "Computing Department." Jan van der Corput chaired the management of the institute and Cornelis Biezeno figured in the board of trustees.

It was not through his supervisor that Van Wijngaarden was introduced to the Center's management, but rather through Ralph Kronig—of electron spin fame. Kronig had attended Van Wijngaarden's reporting on the English tour and conveyed a recommendation to his friend Van der Corput. The young doctor had meanwhile found a job at the National Aeronautical Laboratory but was happy to be convinced by Van der Corput to join the Center and build up a Computing Department: "It was the offer of freedom; I could spread my wings and travel to familiarise myself with the new field." Starting on January 1, 1947, he spent the best part of the year in the UK and the USA, getting acquainted with the people in Cambridge (UK), Teddington, Manchester and Cambridge (Massachusetts) and Princeton.[4] Judging

---

[4] Alberts, G. 2006. De geboorte van de Nederlandse informatica in Londen – Aad van Wijngaarden. *Informatie* 48(1): 46–50; Alberts, G., and P.C. Baayen. 1987a. Ingenieur van taal. Interview met A. van Wijngaarden. In *Zij mogen uiteraard daarbij de zuivere wiskunde niet verwaarloozen*, eds. Alberts G., F. van der Blij, and J. Nuis, 276–288. Amsterdam: CWI.

from his talks and reports, he had absorbed every detail and cautiously moved towards the construction of "Automatic Digital Machines." Sweeping statements and grand claims were strikingly absent from his publications.[5] Between trips he briefly returned to Amsterdam in the Summer of 1947 and hired two students of physics to be his research assistants in building computing machinery. Carel Scholten and Bram Loopstra stayed on. They spent their hours in the fall studying the literature Van Wijngaarden had left them with, publications on the principles of a differential analyzer.

Upon Van Wijngaarden's return, the differential analyzer, and with it the interest in analog technology, was put to the side. Van Wijngaarden had spent his time at Harvard with Howard Aiken and in Princeton with John von Neumann, Herman Goldstine and, in particular, Julian Bigelow, and now firmly put his bets on digital automatic machinery. From his tour he took home two concepts, one based on electronic technology, the other in a more modest fashion on the electromechanics of relay technology.

The AERA concept, Automatische Electronische Rekenmachine Amsterdam, continuing on the Princeton and Cambridge (UK) examples, would be a long shot for the team of beginners. Instead he decided to take the inspiration from the Harvard relay machine and more or less copy the ARC machine, he had witnessed under construction in London with Donald Booth at Birkbeck College. Booth had reached major innovations in storage technology, developing a workable magnetic memory drum and like Van Wijngaarden had been traveling to the USA in 1947. ARC stood for Automatic Relay Calculator; ARRA for Automatische RelaisRekenmachine Amsterdam.[6] By 1950 a working prototype would print a table. However, the problem of getting the slower but reliable electromechanical relays to genuinely cooperate with the faster technology of a memory drum was never really solved, neither in London, where Booth after the 1948 inauguration of his ARC abandoned the relay technology altogether and saved his magnetic drum, nor in Amsterdam, where Van Wijngaarden's team muddled through to the day of dedication in 1952, before giving up.

The Computation Department of the Mathematical Center was surrounded by institutes and individuals most eager to help. When the whole of the Center comprised one room in a former school building, Jacob Clay, member of the board of trustees next to Biezeno, offered working space in his Physics Laboratory. From the side of Philips Physics Laboratory one of its directors would serve the board of trustees, first Balthasar van der Pol, known for the VanderPol-equation, later Hendrik Casimir, of "Casimir effect" fame. Casimir enjoyed receiving the Amsterdam computer developers in the Eindhoven Physics Lab and offering them novel electronic parts, and

[5] Cf. page 247 of Wijngaarden, Adriaan van. 1949a. Algemeen overzicht moderne rekenmachines. *Nederlands Tijdschrift voor Natuurkunde* 15:243–254; Wijngaarden, Adriaan van. 1948. Principes der Electronische Rekenmachines, Mathematisch Centrum, Rekenafdeling, CR 3, Cursus Februari 1948; Wijngaarden, Adriaan van. 1949b. Practisch rekenen. In *Eerste Nederlandse Systematisch Ingerichte Encyclopaedie*, Vol IV, 104–112. Amsterdam: ENSIE.

[6] JMC47. *Jaarverslag Stichting Mathematisch Centrum* [Annual Report Foundation Mathematical Center] (1947).

special plugs, that might be of use for the ARRA. In the UK, from the dedication of the EDSAC in Cambridge in May 1949 onwards, Maurice Wilkes would organize an annual *Summer school* in Cambridge allowing his colleagues from across Europe to acquire their first experience in working with an automatic computer. Loopstra was welcomed for weeks of internship in the Cambridge Mathematical Laboratory and was given access to the wiring schedules of the EDSAC machine. Howard Aiken in Cambridge Massachusetts promoted his Harvard machines and showed interest in acquiring assignments to construct copies for European institutes. In short, patrons were queuing at the door of the Center. But Van Wijngaarden let his team choose its own ways—with sometimes surprising choices like building the ARRA calculator without a clock.

On the occasion of opening a new building for the Mathematical Center, planned for June 21, 1952, the Computation Department decided to showcase its calculator. During the Spring the wiring was completely resoldered but the performance showed little improvement. The Minister of Education and the Lord Mayor of Amsterdam pushed the button to set the machine in operation. It duly produced a table of random numbers; the Netherlands had entered the computer age.[7]

The remaining material construction failed to present a useful apparatus and the Computation Department prepared for the construction of the second machine.

Outside the Netherlands another Dutch engineer dedicated his career to the development of computing machinery. Gerrit A. Blaauw had finished his studies in Electrical Engineering in Delft, then moved to the USA and graduated again to be well prepared to apply for a PhD project with Howard Aiken at Harvard. Starting with the Harvard Mark I, or IBM ASCC, in 1943 Aiken had supervised the consecutive construction of calculating machines, Mark III in 1950 and Mark IV in 1951. Blaauw obtained his PhD in April 1952 on his share of the design of the Harvard Mark IV, namely the operation of the background storage and the sequencing unit of the processor.[8] Returning to the Netherlands, as required by the fellowship that had allowed him to study, Gerrit Blaauw was advised by Aiken to join the team at Mathematical Center.

The expectations, raised by the public event of the Computation Department inaugurating its ARRA, had to be met at some point and indeed these were met smoothly, through the arrival of Blaauw. "Oh yes, approximately twenty minutes," Scholten replied with a smile when asked whether it took him and Loopstra long to be convinced by Blaauw's ideas and expertise. Van Wijngaarden and Blaauw had been in contact from 1949. While Van Wijngaarden had declined Aiken's suggestion conveyed by Blaauw to construct a copy of the Harvard machine for the Dutch, it was on Wijngaarden's request that Blaauw brought a suitcase filled with diodes and other electronic parts which were not readily available in the Netherlands.

Blaauw brought the suitcase, experience in computer construction, lessons from Aiken and, perhaps most importantly, an engineering style of working. To foster a

---

[7] Alberts and de Beer (2008a), AERA.

[8] Blaauw, Gerrit A. 1952. *The application of selenium rectifiers as switching devices in the Mark IV calculator*. Dissertation, Harvard University (Mass.).

systematic way of working Blaauw had design forms printed for the department.[9] The new machine was built up out of pluggable parts, avoiding the need to solder in case of replacement for repair or maintenance. Inherited straightly from Aiken was the principle of using standardized proven technology for the components, since their novel combination would present enough of a challenge by itself. Because of those expectations to be met, the new machine was called ARRA, like the first one. Van Wijngaarden left no room to doubt or criticize his team. He did not blink and wrote in the Annual Report on 1952:

> Research continued into electronic calculators. In particular, the issue was addressed how the parts of a relays-machine may fruitfully be replaced by faster, less vulnerable, and therefore better operable, electronic parts. The results give rise to the development of a schedule to overhaul the ARRA.[10]

Of course the Annual Report did not explain that the schedule comprised the full dismissal of the first machine, to shove it to the wall, and start from scratch. That was Van Wijngaarden exercising his micro-politics in writing the annual report, always covering his team.

2.4 The Harvest of 1953

By the end of 1953 the new ARRA was completed and it was in daily operation from early 1954. Now that there was a functioning ARRA, others started wanting one too, from J.H. Greidanus of Fokker Aircraft Industry to J.J. Engelfriet of NILLMIJ insurance company. Meanwhile other computers had been put into operation in the Netherlands, in Delft, in The Hague, in Amsterdam, in Eindhoven.[11]

Bram van Heel was a part-time professor and an entrepreneur in optical industry. His wish was to automate the calculation of optical trajectories of lenses. On the project he set up in cooperation with Dick de Bruijn, a very young professor of mathematics at the Technical University, Willem van der Poel, a student of physics, was appointed as a research assistant. Van der Poel designed and constructed the first version of the ARCO, Automatische RelaisCalculator voor Optische berekeningen, and took his Engineering degree on the subject in 1950. Two further students brought the machine to its final state in 1952. The ARCO was nicknamed Testudo, Latin for tortoise, as a play of words on its slow pace; it did function to the satisfaction of the optics engineers for almost a decade. When graduated, Van der Poel in turn was hired by Leen Kosten, head of the Mathematical Department of PTT's Central Laboratory

---

[9] Gerrit Blaauw, personal communication, June 24, 2015.

[10] JMC52 (1952); the full text in Dutch reads: "De research over electronische rekenmachines werd onderwijl voortgezet. Met name werd aandacht besteed aan de vraag op welke wijze de onderdelen ener relaismachine met vrucht zouden kunnen worden vervangen door snellere en tevens minder kwetsbare, dus beter in bedrijf te houden, electronische onderdelen. De hierbij behaalde resultaten geven aanleiding tot de opzet van een schema ter revisie van de ARRA".

[11] For more on Van der Poel, PTT, BPM/Shell, Fokker see: Alberts and Van Vlijmen (2017), Computerpioniers. This article adds the reference to Fortune and further backgrounds from the Philips and AEGON archives.

in The Hague. Kosten himself had taken his PhD a decade before on the design of a traffic simulation machine, an analog model to study the congestion of telephone traffic. Van der Poel and Kosten went on to build an electronic digital calculator for PTT, PTERA, PTT's Eenvoudig Rekenapparaat, or "PTT's Simple Computing Device." It was put in to use in April 1953 with a small celebration. Simplicity was the key notion for Willem van der Poel in all of his work on computers. Following PTERA he designed ZEBRA, Zeer Eenvoudig Binair RekenApparaat, Very Simple Binary Computing Device.

Royal Dutch Shell Oil Company and its Dutch branch BPM, Bataafsche Petroleum Maatschappij, cherished a long tradition of experimenting with processes and their control, the cracking process of crude oil, in particular. In postwar years it built an experimental production facility close to the Delft Technical University. Its biggest laboratory, however, was in Amsterdam: KSLA, Koninklijke-Shell Laboratorium Amsterdam. Simulators and analog instrumentation were built in house; digital computers were purchased. In 1951 KSLA decided to invest in computer technology. It ordered a Ferranti Mark 1* in Manchester, which was delivered in Amsterdam in 1953 and inaugurated in 1955.

For Philips Physics Lab 1953 was the year to embark on the construction of a computer in house. *Fortune* magazine of November 1946 carried a cheerful article on "The automatic factory" and a more sobering essay "Machines without workers." It was the pessimistically toned second piece that was translated and multiplied by typing carbon copies for Philips' board of directors, in early 1947, with an introduction to the theme by Van Sluiters (Fig. 2.1).[12]

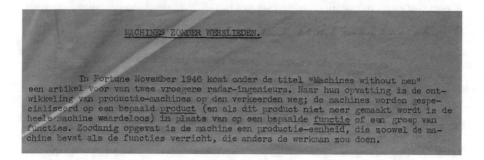

Fig. 2.1 Typescript translation of an article in the magazine *Fortune* from 1946, as distributed among Philips board members in January 1947. The translation "Machines zonder werklieden" of "Machines without workers," mistakenly referred to the original as "Machines without men"

Shortly after, in 1951, the board requested a permanent reconnaissance committee, the Quo Vadis-commissie, to prepare a discussion on "Philips and thinking machines." The board and the departmental managers engaged in lively debate. Talks were given on "Philips and thinking machines," "Philips and thought-machines,"

---

[12] Philips Company Archives folder 81 'Mechanisatie 1'.

"Electronic computing and control." *Automation* was a recurring theme in board meetings. Board member M. Lopes Cardozo even had a survey conducted inside Philips to produce a rough estimate of the impact of electronic calculators on employment—he confidentially reported the findings to Jan Tinbergen, director of the national planning agency, CPB.[13] Yet another Quo Vadis meeting on January 1955 was introduced by J.M. Unk, director of the laboratory of PTI, the Hilversum branch Philips Telecommunication Industry, speaking on "Information processing machines, computers and automation." It was but the prelude to a year buzzing with conferences, study trips, reconnaissance tours on "electronic computers and electronic aids in manufacturing."[14] Debates were far reaching, but only rarely touched upon the computer as a product in its own right. Down in the real world the Physics Laboratory kept hesitating to get involved with computers until finally in 1953 Casimir's colleague Rinia made way for Wim Nijenhuis to create a team and within the experimental setting of the lab incept the construction of an automatic calculator, producing in 1956 the PETER, Philips Experimental Binary Electronic Calculator.

Nowhere in the Netherlands was the enthusiasm for automatic calculators more lively than in the boardroom of the NILLMIJ insurance company, the Netherlands Indies Life Insurance and Annuities Society which had just before merged with Life Insurance Company "Arnhem."[15] In particular, its manager J.J. Engelfriet had his mind set on the idea of a computer. Jojo Engelfriet had brought innovative ideas to the field of insurance mathematics and from 1949 held an extraordinary chair in actuarial science at the University of Amsterdam. In his eagerness to automate calculations, among other things the calculations of the annual reserve by legal requirement, he in 1953 ordered for NILLMIJ a Bull Gamma 3. The Gamma 3 was a punched card installation, with vacuum tubes. It presented computing capacity, in that each sequence of instructions, it would be equipped with a plugboard. It offered a storage capacity of 7 words. In the context of an insurance company and its primary need for data processing, however, it was not quite a practicable machine.[16] Engelfriet knew Van Wijngaarden well and had commissioned the Computation Department of the Mathematical Center to do the required annual calculation of the "mathematical reserve." Engelfriet did so for the sake of having his calculations done at a research institute; Van Wijngaarden accepted the work, which was fully uninteresting from the perspective of mathematical research, to cherish the good relations. Engelfriet had even before purchasing the Bull Gamma 3 made the inquiry whether the Center would construct a computer for his company. Once the Bull was installed, Jan Berghuis, one of the employees from Van Wijngaarden's team, spent a couple of months in secondment to NILLMIJ to compose the plugboards, in fact to "program" the machine.

Johan Greidanus had been Van Wijngaarden's colleague at the National Aeronautical Laboratory and had moved on in 1952 to become manager of aircraft develop-

---

[13] Letter ir. M. Lopes Cardozo to J. Tinbergen, October 14, 1954; PCA folder 81 'Mechanisatie 1'.
[14] PCA folder 81 'Mechanisatie 1'.
[15] NILLMIJ, Nederlandsch Indische Levensverzekerings en Lijfrente Maatschappij and Levensverzekeringsmaatschappij Arnhem.
[16] Interview Anton W. Dek, by G. Alberts and H.T. de Beer, January 8, 2008.

ment at Fokker Aircraft Industries. From his new position, in 1954, he was able to negotiate the delivery of an automatic computer, of course with Van Wijngaarden's team "because they were really excellent." The FERTA, Fokker Electronic Calculating Device Type ARRA, was completed in 1955 and installed by Gerrit Blaauw and Edsger Dijkstra in close cooperation. When Greidanus got his FERTA delivered, Engelfriet returned to the Center and wanted the same. This time negotiations came to a standstill. Continuing to produce computers for external parties began to take on the appearance of manufacturing and that could not be the commitment of a research institute. In Dutch context this was not considered appropriate. Engelfriet tried a new initiative and embed the computer construction in a broader coalition of Bull, Philips, Mathematical Center, NILLMIJ and the investment group Nederlandsche Handelsmaatschappij, but he failed to get the parties moving.[17]

The harvest of 1953 at various fields was considerable and triggered further expectations. Steps towards industrial manufacturing in series were not within easy reach.

2.5 Towards Production in Series, the ZEBRA Story

Philips, although never far off, carefully avoided getting involved. Conversely everybody had an eye on Philips. The electronics company, the "light bulb manufacturer in the south," was well informed but did not move. It declined both Engelfriet's initiative and the offer to take up production of PTT's ZEBRA design for a computer. Willem van der Poel and Leen Kosten had finished the design for the ZEBRA in 1955 inside the Mathematical Department of PTT's Central Laboratory. When PTT itself would not take it from laboratory to production, they expected to find a welcome at Philips Industries. Indeed, this was what Unk wanted. J.M. Unk, of Philips Telecommunication Industry, who held an extraordinary chair in Delft, was an influential inventor and strategist inside the corporation. Unk was impressed by Van der Poel's design and believed he could set up a production line at the Philips PTI division in Hilversum. PTI and PTT had made major steps towards cooperation, when in the end the company board vetoed taking it into production.

Konrad Zuse, the German computer manufacturer, traveled to The Hague and briefly entered into negotiations with Van der Poel, but no agreement was reached. The Nederlandsche Röntgen-Apparatenfabriek in Delft, a Woldringh-like enterprise in the field of instrumentation, prepared an offer to start constructing the machine, but never even received an answer from PTT.

Finally, Standard Electric made a viable offer, through its Dutch branch NSEM, Nederlandse Standard Electric Maatschappij. NSEM showed interest, together with its parent company in Belgium, Bell Telephone Manufacturing Company, and the sister company in England, STC or Stantec, Standard Telephones and Cables Ltd.

---

[17] Extract from a letter of J. Engelfriet to A.W. Dek, March 24, 1954, "Extract uit brief van de directie te 's-Gravenhage (w.g. J. Engelfriet) aan Hr. Dek d.d. 24 Maart 1954," p. 1. AEGON company archives, folder 251, X.046.1:658.564.

These companies could refer to experience in the construction of large calculating installations, Bell constructing the *Machine mathématique IRSIA-FNRS* in Antwerp, and STC in England unsuccessfully manufacturing a machine of its own design.[18] A notable detail: the Antwerp machine was a copy of the Harvard Mark IV, the machine of Gerrit Blaauw. PTT, NSEM, and STC sat around the table and agreed that STC would manufacture computers of PTT-design and PTT would purchase a number of these. Technical details were discussed with Kosten and Van der Poel. As STC was impressed by Van der Poel's ideas, agreement in technicalities was easily reached. It helped that Van der Poel's work was a logical design, leaving the realization in large part and without restrictions to STC. The only real hurdle was in the realm of patents. Van der Poel wished to submit his work as a doctoral dissertation and was thereby implicitly claiming the design as his proper work. A compromise was reached, leaving to STC the rights outside of the Netherlands and to PTT inside. Patents were submitted jointly by PTT and STC on December 23, 1955, naming W.L. van der Poel, H.H. Clement and J. Rice as the inventors.[19] STC in cooperation with NSEM elaborated the ZEBRA design to an actual machine and took responsibility for the production and marketing. STC would pay PTT 2% of the ZEBRA sales. The agreement between PTT, STC, and NSEM towards the manufacturing of *Stantec ZEBRA* was signed on December 7, 1955.[20] Thus a production in series was finally realized, albeit not in the Netherlands but in Newport, Wales, in the Stantec facilities.

The ZEBRA events were strictly speaking none of Engelfriet's business. Still he judged it his duty to make an appeal to Philips on its policy in these matters. The Mathematical Center would not make him a computer, Philips and other partners did not show up in his effort to create a consortium, and now he witnessed the PTT-design going abroad. Where was computer manufacturing to start in the Netherlands? From his vantage point it was a rational for PTT, being a state owned company for public service, to not enter the industrial production of calculating machinery, but where was Philips! He approached Casimir to get answers; to no avail.

By contrast, the talks between Engelfriet and Van Wijngaarden after the first refusal took a different turn. Even if Van Wijngaarden had met with little opposition to constructing and delivering an ARRA-like machine to Fokker Aircraft, nor to the investment for the purpose, he was clearly out of line with the ethos of a research institute. It was in his own interest to elevate Engelfriet's request for one machine to the

---

[18] Correspondence NSEM to the general manager of PTT, March 10, March 18, 1955. PTT Archives: NL-HANA, Staatsbedrijf PTT, 1955–1988, inv.nr. 4103; R.J. Ord-Smith. 1988. Memories of forty years with computers. In *Vooruitgang, bit voor bit. Liber Amicorum ac Collegarum bij het afscheid van Prof.dr.ir. W.L. van der Poel 26 oktober 1988*, edited Pronk, C. and W.J. Toetenel, 30–34. Delft: Delftse Universitaire Pers, in particular, pages 31–32; Udekem-Gevers, Marie d'. 2011. *La machine mathématique IRSIA-FNRS (1946–1962)*. Bruxelles: Académie Royale de Belgique.

[19] Poel, W.L. van der, H.H. Clement, and J. Rice. 1958. Patent Specification GB802,745: Improvements in or relating to Electrical Digital Computers. Submitted December 23, 1955, awarded October 8, 1958.

[20] Heads of agreement dated the 7th day of December 1955 between Netherlands Postal and Telecommunication Services (PTT), Standard Telephones and Cables Limited (STC) and Nederlandsche Standard Electric Maatschappij N.V. (NSEM) Relating to Computers. PTT Archives: NL-HANA, Staatsbedrijf PTT, 1955–1988, inv.nr. 4103.

higher level of creating production facilities for computers. What the Mathematical Center had to contribute to that higher level was its construction team, the workshop, and its expertise. NILLMIJ could provide the capital investment. The Center's management and board of trustees were really charmed with the prospect of seeing the industrial production of computers lifted out of the research institute. In particular, the delegate of its main funder ZWO, the National Research Agency, judged it an elegant solution to what might have grown into a future clash of commitments. This time Engelfriet could convey to Casimir not a message of general concern but a pressing request to jump the wagon of a new entrepreneurial initiative. The men did have a conversation, and Casimir made it unequivocally clear that Philips Industries was not interested in the adventure.

Now it was Reinoud's turn to raise protest. H. Reinoud, PTT's general manager, phrased his dismay with Philips' stance as explicitly as his position would allow. In a brief contribution, late 1956, and a review, March 1957, in *Economisch Statistische Berichten* he refrained and stated that this was not the place to discuss the desirability of a European or even a Dutch industry for the manufacturing of computers. A special issue of the same journal prepared for October 1957 on the Application of Automation—*Toepassing der Automatisering* with contributions by Kosten, Engelfriet, Van Wijngaarden—challenged Reinoud to speak out and confront the reader with the question of Philips' participation. The question might rise why "this enterprise, which seems destined to establish a computer industry for office and industrial purposes, appears completely absent in this field." Rumor had reached him that the reason was that Philips was supplier of electronic parts to a major manufacturer in the field. If that were the case then "for Philips [...] it was rational under the given circumstances [...]." What read like a note of understanding, Reinoud finished off with a quote by William Whyte, management guru and editor of *Fortune*, telling American business that this was not a time for complacency, but for bold innovation.[21]

For Philips, however, the rationality of its refrain was more than the incidental observation of good relations with its buyer IBM. The rationality was company policy and had a name, the Loupart doctrine, named after Othon Loupart, long time serving member of the board and the creator of the international sales organization. Loupart's strategic doctrine was for an enterprise to maintain good relations with its milieu and to leave space for buyers, for suppliers and, most importantly, for competitors.[22] The

[21] *Economisch Statistische Berichten* was *the* venue for debates among economists and policy makers. The confronting question in Dutch: De vraag kon rijzen waarom "deze onderneming, die als het ware aangewezen lijkt voor het vestigen van een computer-industrie voor administratieve en industriële doeleinden, op dit gebied tot nu toe verstek heeft laten gaan." Reinoud, H. 1956. Over de produktie en toepassing van elektronische administratiemachines. *Economisch-statistische berichten* 41(2020):193–196; Reinoud, H. 1957a. De recente ontwikkeling van elektronische administratiemachines. *Economisch-statistische berichten* 42(2098):728–732, cf. specifically page 731; Reinoud, H. 1957b. Een Nederlandse industrie van elektronische reken- en administratiemachines? *Economisch-statistische berichten* 42(2103):843–845, specifically page 845; Whyte, W.H. 1956. *The organisation man*. New York: Simon and Schuster.

[22] Blanken, I.J. 2002. *Een industriële wereldfederatie; Geschiedenis van Koninklijke Philips Electronics N.V., Deel 5* Zaltbommel. De Europese Bibliotheek, cf. pages 155–156.

milieu envisaged by Loupart's strategic view was the world of big manufacturers of lightbulbs, tv sets, and electronics, far from the startups in exciting products on a national scale. The responsibility for national entrepreneurship or national champions of which Engelfriet and Reinoud would remind Philips Industries, and Casimir of the PhysicsLab, in particular, was a vanishing entity in the face of the responsibilities the corporate board of Philips perceived within its strategic view.

Engelfriet, taken less than seriously in his appeal to Philips, now had a clear view of what to do. In their ongoing talks both he and Van Wijngaarden fully embraced the challenge. At the insurance companies he was leading, he organized support for sufficient investment to be combined with the expertise from the Mathematical Center to create an enterprise for the production of computers, Electrologica. Followed a year of intense talks and negotiating details in order to convince the boards of the companies, of the Center and of ZWO. As a result NILLMIJ was to create a subsidiary company, to which the construction team would be transferred in stages. In return the Center was to be compensated and to share in the profits. The agreement between Mathematical Center, NILLMIJ and Electrologica was passed on June 25, 1956.[23] Meanwhile the computer construction team hurried to finish off what could be done for the Mathematical Center, before devoting all its efforts to Electrologica. Within the same year 1956, the ARMAC, Automatische Rekenmachine MAthematisch Centrum, was completed and installed.

With the investments from the side of NILLMIJ into the new company, the construction team made its transfer while simultaneously growing from 20 to over 60 employees. While still in the building of the Center, the team finished the first prototype of an Electrologica machine. The design for the as yet unknown machine bore codename x, as is wont among mathematicians. The name stuck: Electrologica X1. It was finished in 1958 and installed in the premises of NILLMIJ in The Hague.[24] Further copies were constructed in Electrologica's new production facilities in the southern outskirts of Amsterdam. Thus it was at Willem Fenengastraat 31 in Amsterdam that a series of computers were manufactured in the Netherlands.

At considerable pace the 1953 scene of building, purchasing, and installing singular automatic calculators had shifted to manufacturing a series of computers. Everyone eyed Philips, but that corporation was out, playing on a different field. Production reached series in two cases, for ZEBRA at Stantec in Wales; for the machines stemming from the Mathematical Center inside the Netherlands at the newly founded enterprise Electrologica.

---

[23] Minutes of the 16th meeting of the Board of Trustees: 'Notulen der 16e Curatorenvergadering van het Mathematisch Centrum op Dinsdag 7 februari 1956 in het gebouw van het M.C., 2e Boerhaavestraat 49, p. 6, Noordhollands Archief: Archief van de Stichting Mathematisch Centrum, 1946–1980, inv. nr. 4.

[24] A last improvement of the ARMAC, late 1958, concluded machine construction at the Computation Department. During the first two months of 1959 the Department performed all of its automated computing on the NILLMIJ copy of the X1. It combined using ARMAC and traveling to that machine in The Hague for the rest of the year. By the end of 1959 the Mathematical Center had its own X1 machine installed.

Fig. 2.2 Aad van Wijngaarden, Bram Loopstra, Carel Scholten, and Johannes Engelfriet played crucial roles in laying the foundations and the further growth of Electrologica

2.6 Electrologica

Van Wijngaarden would back his people. Bram Loopstra and Carel Scholten had been his computer makers ever since 1947, so now they went on to be the managers of Electrologica. Jojo Engelfriet, his colleague Anton Dek, and Aad van Wijngaarden served at the management board (Fig. 2.2). From that position they did interfere frequently with the executive management—as if it was their favorite toy. Practically the managers and staff moved in with the NILLMIJ offices in The Hague, while the construction team at first remained in Amsterdam at Fenengastraat. The programmers were the last to move, floating between Mathematical Center and Electrologica. Later, office and production facilities were reunited in a new building in Rijswijk, a suburb of The Hague, inaugurated in 1964 by Prince consort Bernhard.

The machine Electrologica X1 expressed coherence of design. Materially it was a wild composition of parts, covered by cabinets and desks of in-house design. The fast memory was made in house from ferrite core purchased from Philips. The punched card reader and sorter were of Bull manufacture; the electric typewriter and other parts of IBM. Perhaps the mixed lot of parts was a remnant reflection of Engelfriet's earlier efforts to get all parties involved. Still, with some elements visibly tagged Bull and IBM, the visual impression was decisively Electrologica, with its white black-framed cabinets. When opened the cabinets revealed what was proudly dubbed "tulip fields," tightly packed ranges of small size standardized pluggable elements in primary colors.

The design for the X1 machine was done in one year, in 1957, and after another year the first copy for NILLMIJ was finished. In the meantime no less than nine orders had come in. A surprisingly large portion of the orders came in from Germany, through Dipl.-Ing. Hans Konrad Schuff, director of the Mathematische Beratungs- und Programmierungsdienst GmbH, Mathematical Consultation and Programming Service in Dortmund. MBP was a subsidiary of Hoesch AG, founded February 26, 1957, a very early software firm. Schuff had heard about the Electrologica X1 and signaled his interest.[25] Schuff's colleague acted more vigorously and presented himself as a sales representative for Germany. Instead Electrologica responded by establishing a German branch in 1959, Electrologica GmbH for sales and maintenance at German buyers, lead by Dr E. Hort (Fig. 2.3). The initial six orders for an X1 were followed by another eleven—nine of which were actually delivered. As the first order was considered to be of primordial importance for entering the German market, the X1 order of the Mathematische Beratungs- und Programmierungsdienst was swiftly fulfilled, even skipping extensive tests. In all, 35 X1 installations were delivered, 15 of which in Germany.[26]

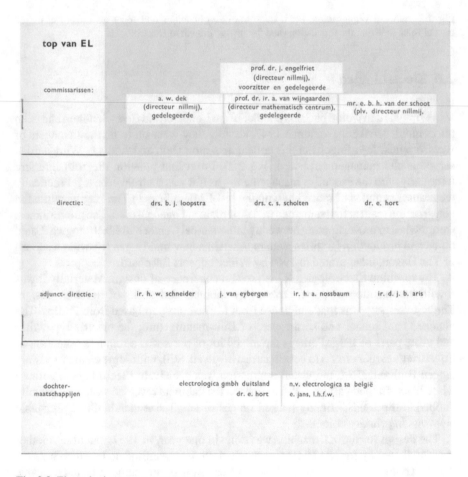

Fig. 2.3 Electrologica company structure

---

[25] Interview Dek (cf. note 16); N.V. Electrologica, Annual Report 1960 ('s-Gravenhage), 5. AEGON company archives: folder 165, X.003.055.5.

[26] Minutes of the meeting held April 16, 1959: Notulen van de vergadering gehouden op Donderdag 16 April 1959 ten kantore van de Nillmij te 's-Gravenhage, 1. AEGON company archives: folder 171, X.008.13.053.7 G.

The X1 design with all its parts from various suppliers involved a ragbag of decisions to be made on purchasing versus in house development and on prioritizing some parts over others. Compared to that the decisions on programming and software were really complicated. Loopstra and Scholten had worked in the closest of cooperations with Edsger Dijkstra, who like them had joined the Mathematical Center as a research assistant "for the programming of the ARRA" in March 1952, still a Leiden University student of physics. Dijkstra having built up the experience and influenced by Gerrit Blaauw, working on the second ARRA and installing the FERTA at Fokker, definitely had developed a vision for himself on the construction of computers. To him the accord on the construction of a computer was to serve like a contract between constructor and programmer, binding both parties.[27] Accordingly Dijkstra was leaving his mark on the consecutive machines of the Mathematical Center, not starting with programming when the machine was finished but from the very first scratch of the design. For example, in the case of X1 it seemed only natural to choose the length of words and the basic instruction set in line with the earlier machines; but things took a turn.

Two crucial events deeply influenced the outcome. Anton Dek had been reading on UNIVAC computers being equipped with an interrupt system. Input and output were the notoriously slow portions of processing, often causing delay. An interrupt system might help to run the whole process more smoothly, so "would that not be a desirable feature in the design of our machine"?[28] Dijkstra jumped on to Dek's suggestion and came back with a solution that was both thorough and elegant. His idea not only showed the way towards improving the communication between a computer and its peripherals; it allowed a more abstract view on the functioning of an information processing machine.

The solution of Dijkstra was about interfering in processes, on interrupting, and it showed that under certain conditions multiple processes can run simultaneously. In particular, it showed ways to avoid the waiting of the whole computer system for the relatively slow processes of input and output. On the one hand, the interrupt idea marked the design of the X1 and indeed "online interrupt" was promoted as a key innovative feature of the system. On the other hand, Dijkstra took it on as his dissertation topic, "Communication with an automatic computer."[29] Electrolog-

[27] Dijkstra, Edsger W. 1980. A programmer's early memories. In *A history of computing in the twentieth century*, edited Metropolis, N., J. Howlett en G. Rota. New York: Academic Press.

[28] Interview Dek (cf. note 16); Note to the NILLMIJ board in Djakarta, 1953: Nota dd. 27 Juli 1953 aan de Directie te Djakarta, 2. AEGON company archives: folder 251, X.046.1:658.564; Dijkstra, E.W. 1959. Verslag van de voordracht door Dr. E.W. Dijkstra, gehouden op 11 december 1959. De faciliteit tot interruptie in de X1. *Mededelingen van het Rekenmachinegenootschap* 2(1):3–8, cf. page 6; Electrologica. 1958. Korte algemene beschrijving van de elektronische rekenmachine X1 (EL-3) [Brief description of the electronic computer X1], Technical Report EL-3. Electrologica, 's-Gravenhage, cf. page 27; Loopstra, B.J. 1959a. Input and output in the X-1 system. In *Information Processing: Proceedings of the International Conference on Information Processing, Unesco, Paris 15–20 June 1959*, 342–344. München: Oldenbourg Verlag.

[29] Dijkstra, Edsger W. 1959a. *Communication with an automatic computer*. [PhD Thesis. October 28, 1959. Universiteit van Amsterdam]. Excelsior, Rijswijk.

ica compensated him for the programming work and purchased 250 copies of his dissertation. For Dijkstra writing the interrupt programs was a formative experience.

The other crucial event was Mathematical Center Computation Department's participation in international developments in the field of programming. Working with computers was more than inserting a list of coded instructions into a machine, more than feeding a coded sequence, more than transferring the reckoning to the machine. More than preparing the calculation for transfer, it comprised coding the sequence, and increasingly, letting a machine do the preparation. That third step came to be called auto-coding or automatic programming.

Around 1955 the debate on the design of auto-coding systems shifted towards the design of easy systems of notation of programs, if could be, universal systems of notation, and preferably, mathematical notations of programs. At that point coding systems came to be considered not just as notation systems, but rather as languages. This was the transition from coding systems to programming languages.[30] Both for Europe and the USA the transition to language was the agenda of a field in the making, the transition towards a universal programming language, ideally a language fit for notation of code for any machine, yes, independent of machines. If there were great differences between the USA and Europe in the availability and sophistication of machinery, the language agenda united the two.

The shared agenda and the international cooperation towards the composition of an "algorithmic language" unfolded during those very years, 1957 to 1960, the years of building up Electrologica. In 1958 Van Wijngaarden and Dijkstra jumped in. By January 1960, they were part of the community represented by the international committee gathering in Paris for the final decisions on the design of ALGOL.[31]

In the first place, the agenda pushed the concept of programming to a higher level of abstraction. Concepts like subroutine and program library were current from 1950. By 1955 a superprogram was something, i.e., a program that ties together subroutines. Such conceptual enrichments, like the concept of auto-coding, deeply influenced programming and in doing so changed the design of automatic calculators. Gradually automatic calculators came to be called "automatic computers" or just "computers." Not in Dutch, though; in the 1950s "automatische rekenmachine" would be the most current expression; Van Wijngaarden's favorite expression was "rekentuig." In programming, the field of auto-coding came to be sown with concepts like operating systems, compiler, and programming language. The field itself was rebaptized "software."

Dijkstra and Van Wijngaarden, though late entrants, engaged vigorously in the design of ALGOL. They reconceptualized a programming language as a mathematical object, an item with mathematical design and elegance. After what had seemed a

[30] Nofre, D., M. Priestley, and G. Alberts. 2014. When technology became language: the origins of the linguistic conception of computer programming, 1950–1960. *Technology and Culture* 55(1):40–75.

[31] Alberts, G. 2014a. Algol culture and programming styles; guest editor's introduction, algol culture and programming styles. *IEEE Annals for the History of Computing* 36(4):2–5, special issue; Alberts, G., and E. Daylight. 2014c. Universality versus locality: the Amsterdam style of ALGOL implementation. *IEEE Annals for the History of Computing* 36(4): 52–63.

final decision in Paris, they boldly interfered with the definition process of ALGOL
to the effect of it allowing recursive procedures as legitimate expressions.

Back home in Amsterdam, the two strings of events entangled, when Aad van
Wijngaarden commissioned Edsger Dijkstra and his colleague Jaap Zonneveld to
make this new language, ALGOL, run on the Electrologica X1 computer. It implied
writing a program to translate expressions in ALGOL into sequences of instructions
on the machine, in other words: writing an ALGOL compiler for the X1. They
fulfilled their task at a pace that surprised everyone, starting February 16, delivering
it working on the X1 on August 16 of 1960. They surprised the programming
specialists even more with their novel approach, opening new vistas for compiler
writing.

The Electrologica X1 came into existence in a setting where it was natural to think
of programming in terms of program libraries and subroutines and superprograms,
where it went without saying to think about programming and design in the most
abstract concepts, and where an out of the ordinary superprogram was written, the
ALGOL compiler for the X1. Of course, not every aspect of the X1 was touched by
the context of this most progressive thinking about programming and computers, but
in itself the context created an image that made the machine a most attractive option
for those on the mathematical side of the computing community. It came as no sur-
prise that university computing centers, scientific and industrial laboratories would
favor a machine with such pedigree. Werkspoor, Fokker Aircraft, Reactor Centrum
Nederland, a center for nuclear research, and National Aeronautical Laboratory, all
signaled their preference for the Electrologica machine even before a single program
had run on it, as did MBP, the Mathematical Consultancy and Programming Service
in the Ruhr area, as well as the coal and steel corporation consulting it.

NILLMIJ, both the company through its investments and its managers in person,
Engelfriet and Dek, had for over a decade cultivated the ties with the culture of
abstractions speeding into the future. The engagement did not necessarily appropriate
the machine for the kind of data processing that would have priority in the office of
an insurance company, but it certainly explains their appetite.[32]

Though the challenge of connecting the computer to a multitude of input-, output-,
and storage facilities would hardly solve itself automatically, it was readily phrased
in the abstract terms of peripherals, buffers, and timing. Dijkstra and his fellow
programmers at the Mathematical Center had accumulated a library of programs
apt for scientific computation at the Computation Department, at the Aeronautical
Laboratory, or at the Nautical Towing Tank. The experience in cooperatively building a library did allow Electrologica to phrase the needs on the side of insurance
companies, and the Central Bureau of Statistics in terms of a programming library
for office applications, and to suggest hiring programmers for the job and sending
them in secondment to the Mathematical Center to get a taste of programming. But
the detour of abstraction did not meet the practical demands nor did it remedy the
inaptitude of the X1 for large scale data processing.

---

[32] Interview Dek (cf. note 16).

2.7 Electrologica's Company Strategy

With the order book well filled Electrologica was prospering. Managers and board happily speculated on upgrades of the X1 or cheaper versions for the office automation market. They thought of an X0 to serve smaller business; X2 to present a much faster and bigger machine, hundredfold. But the design of an X0 proceeded so slowly that it would not even be cheap anymore, let alone meet a market demand. In as far as there was a market for machines of modest capacity, it was largely served by IBM, carrying the IBM 1401, and other manufacturers. It took Electrologica long to part with the idea of a cheaper machine and stop investing in developments to that end.[33]

The company proffered new versions of X1 to prospective clients, versions that never saw the light of day. Came the day when even Van Wijngaarden felt obliged to notify his fellow board members that the X1 had lost its attraction in the very field of scientific computing—that, indeed, it was facing obsolescence.[34]

It was Bram van der Sluis, head of the Utrecht University Computing Center, who in November 1962 served Electrologica a thorough shake-up. Utrecht had received an attractive and immediate offer from the part of the English computer manufacturer Elliot: a much larger machine, Elliot 503, in two years, and to bridge the gap an Elliot 803 to be delivered in one year. Back on the alert Electrologica countered that if Utrecht would agree to order an X1', a machine eight time faster than the X1, to be delivered in two years, it would come with a discount and a free X1 for the meantime. The indication X1' was an improvisation on the spot and was soon replaced by X8. The X2 concept was dismissed to the empire of dreams.[35]

Electrologica X8 was deployed to a full concept and prioritized. The Utrecht order was placed early 1963. The Mathematical Center ordered an X8 as well. The Center was to receive the prototype, as it would easily deal with a machine without the software finished and, after all, it would not care too much about the exterior look of an experimental contraption. Desperate moves these were. After the profitable years 1959 and 1960 Electrologica was now incurring losses.

Fed with the experience of its poor performance to the office automation branch, Electrologica again explicitly chose for a design primarily dedicated to the market of scientific use, but with the option of connecting any number of peripherals. For this purpose X8 was equipped with a central controlling device for input and output, called CHARON, Centraal Hulporgaan Autonome Regeling Overdracht Nevenapparatuur,

[33] Minutes of Electrologica board meetings: Notulen E.L.-vergadering d.d. 22 december 1961, 2; . . . d.d. 3 april 1962, 1; . . . d.d. 3 mei 1962; . . . d.d. 19 oktober 1962; . . . d.d. 29 oktober 1962, 1; Enkele conclusies en overwegingen besproken door Prof. Engelfriet, Hr. Dek en Hr. Schmidt op 27 oktober 1962, AEGON company archives: folder 171, X.008.13.053.7 G.

[34] Minutes of Electrologica board meetings: Notulen E.L.-vergadering d.d. 26-7-1960, 2. AEGON company archives: folder 171, X.008.13.053.7 G.

[35] A note on the Utrecht University Computing Center: Electronisch Rekencentrum der Rijksuniversiteit Utrecht (1 november 1962), 1. AEGON company archives: folder171, X.008.13.053.7 G; Minutes of an Electrologica board meeting: Notulen EL-vergadering gehouden op donderdag 29 november 1962 ten kantore van de Nillmij te 's-Gravenhage, 2; . . . d.d. 10 december 1962, 1. AEGON company archives: folder 171, X.008.13.053.7 G.

which stands for Central Aid for Autonomous Control of Peripherals. Charon, of course deriving its name from the mythological ferryman to the underworld, was one of the most characteristic features of the X8, housed in the largest cabinet centrally placed in the room-filling system. The exterior, even stronger than the X1, had a strikingly minimalist design that was sustained in every part and detail of the installation.

Sixteen copies of the Electrologica X8 were delivered. The company never returned to the level of making profits. By 1963 IBM announced its family of IBM System/360 computers, delivering the first in 1964. Speaking of a family, IBM meant to present a range of interchangeable computers; all operating by a notion of Fred Brooks and Gerrit Blaauw, under the same "architecture." Electrologica promoted in its leaflets the same idea of a family of compatible computers, X2-X4-X8 and X3-X5-X8; in vain. It was not so much that Electrologica came late to the party. Rather, there was no party. A player like Electrologica had little chance to compete with a company that was able to single-handedly define and market "third generation computers."

2.8 Knowledge and Propriety at Philips

All the while Philips was quite well informed, including the latest on the state of Electrologica's business. It made rational policy decisions, and a few machines. Philips' Physics Lab presented the machine it had started in 1953 in 1956 as PETER, for Philips Elementair Tweetallig Electronisch Rekenapparaat. Remaining within the experimental setting of the laboratory Wim Nijenhuis and his team continued by constructing two identical machines.

Since the late 1940s the corporation had directed its comportment after a tacitly assumed sharing of the market with IBM. A formal agreement implying that IBM would purchase electronic parts from Philips, which in turn was to withhold from entering the market of computers, was signed only in 1956. Coordination with IBM would not stop Philips from constructing the twin computers at Physics Lab, PASCAL and STEVIN. By the time these were completed in 1960 the laboratory was about to move away from the Eindhoven town center to the suburb of Waalre. The two computers moved in a different direction, to be installed in the newly established company computing center. Philips had not failed to notice that IBM upon expiration of the agreement had not silently continued the same pattern, as Philips itself would have done in accordance with its Loupart doctrine, but instead purchased parts from other suppliers as well. Even if in the Philips boardroom one felt taken in, and even if at the corporate level a committee had been looking into the possibilities of starting the manufacturing of computers, the management felt obliged to IBM to keep up appearances. At the establishment of the company computing center next to installing its own two computers, it leased two IBM 650 machines.

Other than these sustained proprieties suggested, the corporate management had as early as 1958 assigned a working committee NIT. NIT was company slang for the broad specter of digital computing and digital control technology: "Numerieke

InformatieTechniek." Numerical control was one of Philips' strongholds, cultivated within its division PIT—Products for Industrial Applications.[36] PIT had simultaneously been assigned the construction of an electronic, semiconductor version of PASCAL and STEVIN. The resulting P3, with transistors instead of vacuum tubes, was finalized at the Physics Lab and found a home at MBLE, the Brussels branch of Philips.

Similar double standards governed its comportment towards Electrologica. In 1960 Engelfriet called on Philips once more, asking for participation in the enterprise.[37] Philips and NILLMIJ, sat together but played "hard to get." NILLMIJ was surprised to see Philips, in spite of its motivation for earlier refusals, develop computers of its own. Bram Loopstra expressed Electrologica's feeling by advising Engelfriet to take a tough stance. Philips apparently negotiated on the topic of the name a possible future cooperation should carry. In fact it was leaning back because internally it was well aware that Electrologica's financial situation was far worse than Engelfriet knew—or cared to admit.

Inside Philips meanwhile Numerical Information Technology figured prominently on the agenda of corporate management and in February 1961 the working committee morphed into a Steering Committee,[38] meaning business. By the end of June 1961 a two-day retreat was held at "Huize Voorbeek," a corporate villa, resulting in the Steering Committee requesting a "statute" of its own, implying the liberty to take real world initiatives. The week after, July 6, Philips terminated the talks with Electrologica and put CDC on hold—CDC was the US based Control Data Corporation, manufacturer of supercomputers, with which it was quietly negotiating in the perspective of purchasing the company.

Thus the road was cleared for decision making. Computer manufacturing was to be undertaken, but not within any of the existing divisions. A new division, a "Hoofdindustriegroep," was called into existence at a new location. In 1962 Philips Computer Industry started in the city of Apeldoorn: PCI.

Jorna, coming in from the military industry of Philips subsidiary Hollandse Signaal, was called to be its manager. Adri Duijvestijn, who earlier moved from Van Wijngaarden's team at the Mathematical Center to Nijnhuis' team at Philips PhysicsLab to develop programming at the PETER, was hired as a consultant and Jan Berghuis, who after his years at Mathematical Center and with Engelfriet via the Mathematical Service, Wiskundige Dienst, of the Delft Technical University had landed with Bull in France, was called upon to build up and lead PCI's software group.

---

[36] Lugt, Ch. 1958. Toepassing van numerieke informatietechniek in industriële processen [A note on Numerical Information Technology in Industrial Processes to the Philips division Product for Industrial Applications], Notitie Philips PIT, 3 januari 1958; PCA folder 814.9 'Numerieke besturing'.

[37] Wit, D. de. 1992. Wat niet te verzekeren valt: Electrologica als casus uit de opbouw van een Nederlandse computerindustrie (1956–1967). *Jaarboek voor de Geschiedenis van Bedrijf en Techniek* 9:261–291, specifically pages 275–276.

[38] Lopes Cardozo, M. 1958. Verslag van de Quo Vadis Numerieke Informatietechniek 8/1/'58, 18 Jan. 1958. Philips Company Archives folder 814.8 Map 1; Philips Company Archives folder 81 Map 2, 'Mechanisatie/Automatisering (Numerieke Informatietechnique) 1960–1961'.

Vis à vis Electrologica, Philips quietly waited until it would fall into its lap. In 1964 Electrologica was for sale, that is NILLMIJ withdrew. In 1965 Philips, much to Engelfriet's dismay, did not purchase a majority share but only 40% and only in 1967 did Philips take over the whole company including the debts and obligations. Doing so it inducted a large group of highly qualified computer specialists. In 1968 Philips-Electrologica was inaugurated—by the same Prince consort Bernhard. Both in the name and in the corporate culture the influence of the Mathematical Center lived on in Apeldoorn.

2.9 European Perspective

Following suit of the United States, a majority of European governments around 1950 supported the construction of computers. Subvention would be organized mainly through national research agencies.

ZWO, the Dutch organization for Pure Scientific Research, the channel to fund the Mathematical Center, showed the same pattern of history as the National Science Foundation in Washington. Prepared and de facto functioning from 1945 onwards, their respective legislations would only pass in 1950. European government money reaching computer initiatives would flow on one occasion to research at universities, like in Manchester or Cambridge, on another occasion to new research institutes like the Mathematical Center.

Academies were mainly absent with the exception of a few countries that reformed their traditional academies for new research purposes. In Denmark, for example, Regnecentralen was an academy institute. Several European countries saw their PTT's play an active role in new laboratories, incidentally joining in computer construction efforts, like the ZEBRA.

Nowhere was the financing of research through various government departments as massive as in the USA. The Department of Defence and the Department of Energy led the way both in funding research and in commissioning industry with contracts for machinery, for software and for consultancy. Indeed, from the mid-1930s the US government held the adage "Research—a national resource." It is a characteristic of the Cold War era that the dominant state kept supporting the industry in full continuity, while the governments of other nations took their hands off.[39]

Other than in the USA, in Europe state support for computer related research and development was discontinued from the mid 1950s. Everywhere, except for the USA where the various departments remained dominant commissioners and continued supporting research institutes, ideology had it and policy made it that the market should take up the initiative.[40] Privatizing seemed the natural way to go. At the

---

[39] Krige, J. 2006. *American hegemony and the postwar reconstruction of science in Europe.* Cambridge, MA: The MIT Press; Alberts, G. 2010 Appropriating America: Americanization in the history of European computing. *IEEE Annals of the History of Computing* 32(2):4–7.

[40] Ellwood, D.W. 2018. The force of american modernity: World war II and the birth of a soft power superpower. *International Journal For History, Culture And Modernity* 6(11):1–17.

Dutch Organization for Pure Scientific Research a sigh of relief could be heard, when the Mathematical Center did not turn into an assembly line for computers. Manufacturing, production in series, was not proper for a research institute.[41] What for academically oriented researchers and their managers was only natural, the ethos of pure scientific research for the common cause and free from private interests, had a flip side during the Cold War. The market was invoked and the market did its work,. . . for a while, until a market of completely different proportions switched off the lights.

Philips inhabited that second market of the larger scale, with IBM, AT&T and Siemens as neighbors.[42] Philips did not perceive it as an obligation to pick up and nurture the initiatives left by the roadside by the governments. The expectations of the entrepreneurial academics represented no business reality for Philips or IBM.

The paradox of this history shines through most clearly in the immaterial side of automatic computers, i.e. in the field of software. Engineer Woldringh of TPD, the scientists at Mathematical Center and even the employees of state enterprise PTT, considered themselves to be servants of the common cause. Be it through a university, through a research institute, or through a state enterprise, they were all directly or indirectly civil servants and felt serving to be their primordial obligation, a civil duty. Their design of an automatic computer, their software, and their expertise had already been paid for and was there in the public interest. They demanded no reward—they were rewarded anyway; Electrologica was no exception in paying its consultants. The appeal which the executive of the state enterprise PTT, Reinoud, and the entrepreneur for higher goals like Engelfriet, explicitly made to Philips, viz. to act for the common cause of a national industry, presupposed the same natural inclination to serve the common cause as the seemingly natural ethos guiding the scientists. The reality of Philips' playing field was a different one.

The incompatibility of realities contributes to an understanding of the fate of Electrologica, not as a national industry or a national champion, but by being subsumed in a division of "a light bulb manufacturer in the south."

Acknowledgements To Bas van Vlijmen, Huub de Beer and Jos Peeters I would like to express my deep gratitude for the cooperation in the research supporting the present chapter. Thanks to the foundation PAOi, Stichting Fonds Post Academisch Onderwijs in de Informatica, for subventioning parts of the research by Van Vlijmen and De Beer. I am most grateful to Marc Rensen of Philips Company Archives and Pierre Don, company archivist with AEGON, for their most forthcoming support in making the sources accessible. The collegial comments by Danny Beckers and pertinent remarks by anonymous reviewers have contributed to the quality of the text.

---

[41] Alberts, G., and P.C. Baayen. 1987b. De hoeder van de stichtingen. Interview met J.H. Bannier. In *Zij mogen uiteraard daarbij de zuivere wiskunde niet verwaarloozen*, eds. Alberts G., F. van der Blij, and J. Nuis, 101–114. Amsterdam: CWI.

[42] For the period after 1960 this policy is investigated further. Coopey, Richard, ed 2004a. *Information technology policy. An international history*. Oxford: Oxford University Press. In this bundle, in particular: Coopey, Richard. 2004b. Empire and technology: Information technology policy in postwar Britain and France. In Coopey (2004a), *Information technology*, 144–168; Ende, J. van den, N. Weinberg, and A. Meijer. 2004. The influence of Dutch and EU government policies on Philips' information technology product strategy. In Coopey (2004a), *Information technology*, 187–208.

Chapter 3
From the X1 to the X8

A Brief History of the First Dutch Computer Industry, Electrologica

Huub de Beer
Faculty of Mathematics and Computer Science, Eindhoven University
of Technology, Eindhoven, The Netherlands

Abstract Key to the history of Electrologica was the internal struggle to unite two cultures of computing in one company. The successful manufacturing of the X1 did not suffice to gain a stable foothold in the market for administrative computers. Still, the very struggle to make a machine for scientific computing suitable for office applications did result in a remarkably innovative computer, the X1.

The founding of Electrologica appeared as a logical step for both Nillmij and the Mathematical Center. While it was only natural to conceive of a computer as a calculation device, the requirements of administrative use deeply influenced the design of the X1. Moreover, efforts were made to develop proprietary peripherals as a point of attraction for customers in the administrative field. Even so, the X1 came with a Bull card reader and an IBM typewriter. High ambitions and diverging aims for the successor to the X1 caused considerable postponement. However, once forced to deliver, Electrologica quickly decided for the X8.

By the time of manufacturing the X8, system programs were called "software." In a cooperative effort university costumers and Electrologica installed a committee Z8, in Dutch pronounced "zacht," meaning "soft" as in software. The user-led initiative produced compilers for ALGOL and FORTRAN, an assembly language ELAN, and the famous THE-multiprogramming system.

Electrologica's story ended dramatically in the eventual acquisition by Philips.

3.1 Introduction

In 1956, two cultures of early computing in the Netherlands came together towards a common goal, to develop an advanced computer. Life insurance company Nillmij founded Electrologica to acquire a computer and realize its ambition of automating its office operations and life insurance calculations. The Mathematical Center joined in Electrologica for the continuity of its computer construction group. The research center kept its dream alive of a very large computer but could not afford the construction group solely for that purpose.[1]

Despite moderate expectations, Electrologica's first computer, the X1, was a success. During the first two years, while the total number of computers in the Netherlands grew from five to eleven (cf. Table 3.2), Electrologica received no less than ten orders for an X1.[2] Eventually, Electrologica built and delivered 34 X1 computers.

Once beyond the star-tup phase, Electrologica planned the development of a successor to the X1. Or rather, it explored the development of two successors, one computer aiming at administrative applications, the X0, and another dedicated to scientific computing, the X2. In both directions the design took more time than anticipated. However, when customers for the X2 lost their patience and started looking for a computer elsewhere, Electrologica did react and moved swiftly. Within one month, Electrologica announced an improved version of the X1, eight times faster, hence named X8. Even though the X8 had more options for connecting peripherals than the X1, it was primarily appreciated in circles of scientific computing. Commercially, the X8 was unable to match the success of the X1.

In 1960, on a total number of 34 computers in the Netherlands, Electrologica's market share was over 10% (cf. Table 3.2). By 1963, while the number of computers had increased more than sixfold, its market share had dropped below 7.5%. By contrast, IBM's market share had grown from 32% to 60%. Electrologica was unable to compete, in particular, in the field of administrative computers. When IBM introduced their System/360 "family of computers" in 1964, Electrologica made a desperate attempt to enter the same market and announced a family. To no avail. The company's losses continued to mount. In the same year, Nillmij incorporated Electrologica. In 1965 Philips did take a share in Electrologica, but only 40%. A year on, Electrologica turned out to be in such bad shape that Philips was forced to take over the entire company. It may be considered a mark of honor that Philips Computer Industry renamed itself Philips Electrologica.

3.2 Towards Electrologica's Founding

The history of Electrologica's founding in 1956 revolves around two early enthusiasts for computers in their fields, Johannes J. (Jojo) Engelfriet, director of the life insurance company "Nillmij van 1859" in The Hague, and Adriaan (Aad) van Wijngaarden, head of the computation department of the Mathematical Center in Amsterdam. It was Nillmij's quest to automate the life insurance administration. The

---

[1] Alberts, Gerard, and Huub T. de Beer. 2008a. De AERA. Gedroomde machines en de praktijk van het rekenwerk aan het Mathematisch Centrum te Amsterdam, *Studium* 2, 101–127. Amsterdam: Amsterdam University Press.

[2] N.V. Electrologica, Jaarverslag 1957 in: "Nota aan H.H. Gedelegeerde Commissarissen van "Ned. Nillmij" en "Arnhem," 13 november 1958," p. 1. Oud Archief AEGON. Afd. Documentatie nr. 165, X.003.3:657.372.

Mathematical Center constructed a series of computers in support of its computing work. Founding Electrologica was the outcome of the encounter of the two men and brought both organizations together in their efforts to be at the forefront of computers in their fields.

Modernizing Nillmij. In 1952, life insurance companies "Nillmij van 1859" and "Arnhem" had merged into a single company, Nillmij. Upon the merger, Engelfriet became one of its directors. He seized the opportunity of the merger to integrate and modernize the separate administrations.[3] In the 1950s, setting up a modern administration implied reaching beyond a system of mechanical punched card machines towards an electronic calculator. Engelfriet was particularly interested in performing large-scale insurance-related calculations on an electronic computer. In order to determine how best to do this, he addressed three manufacturers of office machinery, IBM, Remington Rand, and Bull, with a request to run a test job for Nillmij.[4] Writing to Van Wijngaarden as well, he asked the Mathematical Center for advice and suggested the possibility of building for Nillmij an automatic calculator with a magnetic memory of two to four thousand digital numbers.[5]

Responses were disappointing. IBM did not respond at all. Remington's reply was unsatisfactory: they would be able to perform the test job, but it would take too long. Better news came from the third manufacturer, Bull. Using the Bull GAMMA 3 calculator, they could run the test job.[6] Nillmij decided to order a Bull GAMMA 3 and, simultaneously, migrated its administration to Bull punched card machinery.[7] By the choice for Bull, Nillmij seemed to have dropped its interest in having a computer built at the Mathematical Center, but Engelfriet advised his company otherwise. Fascinated by the idea of a memory drum and desiring "to have a hand in any further developments in this special electronic field (...). We have placed a preliminary order with the [Mathematical] Center to build a machine capable of performing automatic correspondence and all kinds of typing work."[8]

Nillmij canceled the preliminary order, but did maintain an interest. In 1954, it organized talks between Nillmij, Bull, Philips, the Mathematical Center, and "Nederlandse Handelsmaatschappij." Although nothing tangible came out of these talks, the Nillmij board observed "that people now realize what value [collaborating] holds for them. So much knowledge in this field is available in the Netherlands, that it may

---

[3] Wit, D. de. 1992. Wat niet te verzekeren valt: Electrologica als casus uit de opbouw van een Nederlandse computerindustrie (1956–1967). *Jaarboek voor de Geschiedenis van Bedrijf en Techniek* 9:261–291, pp. 267–268.

[4] "Rapport Directie te Djakarta betreffende Mechanisatie ('s-Gravenhage, 20 juli 1953)." Oud Archief AEGON. Afd. Documentatie nr. 251, X.046.1:658.564.

[5] "Brief van J. Engelfriet aan de directie van het Mathematisch Centrum van 25 Maart 1953." Oud Archief AEGON. Afd. Documentatie nr. 172, X.009.02.

[6] "Rapport Directie te Djakarta betreffende Mechanisatie ('s-Gravenhage, 20 juli 1953)." AEGON:251, X.046.1:658.564.

[7] "Nota dd. 27 Juli 1953 aan de Directie te Djakarta." AEGON:251, X.046.1:658.564.

[8] "Nota dd. 27 Juli 1953 aan de Directie te Djakarta." AEGON:251, X.046.1:658.564.

be expected that Dutch parties will find common ground."[9] And so it happened. In 1955, two of these parties did find each other. Talks between Nillmij and the Mathematical Center evolved into serious negotiations on the establishment of a Dutch computer industry, Electrologica.

Building Computers at the Mathematical Center. From its founding in 1946, the Mathematical Center held ambitions in the realm of the so-called "automatic calculating machines." When a plan to build such computing machines in collaboration with partners from Belgium and France[10] fell through, the Mathematical Center decided to continue on its own. In August 1947 two physics students, Bram Loopstra and Carel Scholten, were hired to build a modern computing machine.[11] Van Wijngaarden traveled the UK and the US to explore the various efforts to construct computing machinery. Upon return he set up the Computation Department at the Mathematical Center, hired a team of young women to actually perform numerical calculations and appointed Loopstra and Scholten to head the computer construction group. Their machine under construction was dubbed ARRA, "Automatische Relais Rekenmachine Amsterdam." By 1950 a first prototype was able to spit out a table of inverse squares. Midsummer 1952, a completed ARRA was ready to play a part in the inauguration of the Mathematical Center's new building. In front of the official invitees, the ARRA produced a list of random numbers. That first public appearance was also ARRA's last contribution to the calculations of the Mathematical Center.[12]

Little later, in the fall of 1952, Gerrit Blaauw joined the computer construction group. Blaauw had taken his PhD under the supervision of Howard Aiken at Harvard in Cambridge, Massachusetts. The subject of his dissertation was the design of a part of the Harvard Mark IV computer. Upon return from the US he brought electronic parts, and much more importantly, engineering expertise. The computer construction group now including Blaauw built a reliable computer, again called ARRA.[13] From early 1954 the Mathematical Center had a working ARRA at its disposition.

Besides Nillmij another Dutch industry, aircraft manufacturer Fokker, showed an interest in having a computer built by the Mathematical Center. In May 1954, Fokker and the Mathematical Center agreed that a copy of the ARRA was to be built for Fokker. In under a year, the computer construction group built an improved version of the second ARRA. Upon delivery on April 1st, 1955, Fokker renamed the machine FERTA.[14]

---

[9] "Extract uit brief van de directie te 's-Gravenhage (w.g. J. Engelfriet) aan Hr. Dek d.d. 24 Maart 1954," p. 1. AEGON:251, X.046.1:658.564.

[10] "Vierde Curatorenvergadering van het Mathematisch Centrum te Amsterdam op Maandag 7 Juli 1947 te 10.00 u. op de kamer van den Wethouder van Onderwijs, Mr. A. de Roos ten stadhuize." Rijksarchief in Noord-Holland, Archief van de Stichting Mathematisch Centrum (RAHN, SMC), 1946-1980, inv. nr. 4.

[11] JMC46. *Jaarverslag Stichting Mathematisch Centrum* [Annual Report Foundation Mathematical Center] (1946), p. 10.

[12] Alberts and de Beer (2008a), AERA, p. 108.

[13] Only in later publications the two ARRA's were distinct and called ARRA I and ARRA II, respectively. Alberts and de Beer (2008a), AERA, pp. 109–111.

[14] Alberts and de Beer (2008a), AERA, p. 114.

By that time, in April 1955, the working ARRA had become outdated and on top of that the Mathematical Center expected a further growth in service calculation work. Although Van Wijngaarden dreamt of building a truly large computer for the Mathematical Center, the AERA, research and development for that ambitious computer would take too long. Instead, Mathematical Center decided to build an intermediate machine, the ARMAC.[15] It took a year for the computer construction group to finish the ARMAC. The new computer was so much faster and more reliable than the ARRA that it allowed the Mathematical Center to decommission the old computer as well as its IBM punched card machines. From mid-1953, the latter had been in use to perform a good portion of the actual calculations in service of third parties.[16]

With the ARMAC completed the computer construction group was at a crossroad. It embodied expertise built up over a decade, but the Mathematical Center could not afford to keep it working. When different members from the group received offers from other institutes and manufacturers, from the Netherlands and abroad, it seemed that the breakup of the group was imminent.[17] In a confidential memorandum, the board of directors of the Mathematical Center stated that such a course of events would "imply a major loss of scientific and technical potential for the Mathematical Center in particular, and for our country in general." While, being a research center, not envisaging the commercial production of computers, the Mathematical Center was looking for ways to prevent such loss.[18] Throughout 1955, they worked on a solution together with Nillmij: Establishing a Dutch computer industry, Electrologica.[19]

Founding Electrologica. Before Nillmij officially founded Electrologica on June 21st, 1956, the Mathematical Center and Nillmij had engaged in firm negotiations on the terms of cooperation.

On behalf of Electrologica, i.e., Nillmij, the computer construction group at the Mathematical Center would be commissioned to "design and construct electronic computers of high value, which might also be of interest to third parties."[20] In

---

[15] Alberts and de Beer (2008a), AERA; "ARRA, FERTA, ARMAC, AERA. Verslag van machines met het oog op de curatorenvergadering van 15 April 1955." RAHN, SMC, inv. nr. 91.

[16] Alberts and de Beer (2008a), AERA, p. 111.

[17] "Vertrouwelijk memorandum d.d. 18 september 1956, inzake de werkgroep voor de constructie van electronische rekenmachines van het Mathematisch Centrum," p. 1. RAHN, SMC, inv. nr. 52; "Notulen der 16e Curatorenvergadering van het Mathematisch Centrum op Dinsdag 7 Februari 1956 in het gebouw van het M.C., 2de Boerhaavestr. 49," p. 5. RAHN, SMC, inv. nr. 4.

[18] "Vertrouwelijk memorandum d.d. 18 september 1956, inzake de werkgroep voor de constructie van electronische rekenmachines van het Mathematisch Centrum," p. 1. RAHN, SMC, inv. nr. 52.

[19] "Notulen der 16e Curatorenvergadering van het Mathematisch Centrum op Dinsdag 7 Februari 1956 in het gebouw van het M.C., 2de Boerhaavestr. 49," p. 6. RAHN, SMC, inv. nr. 4.

[20] "Vertrouwelijk memorandum d.d. 18 september 1956, inzake de werkgroep voor de constructie van electronische rekenmachines van het Mathematisch Centrum," p. 1. RAHN, SMC, inv. nr. 52; "Notulen der 16e Curatorenvergadering van het Mathematisch Centrum op Dinsdag 7 Februari 1956 in het gebouw van het M.C., 2de Boerhaavestr. 49," p. 5. RAHN, SMC, inv. nr. 4.

return, Nillmij guaranteed to safeguard the Mathematical Center from any financial risk issuing from its participation.[21]

A start-up period was agreed of two years, during which the construction group remained part of the Mathematical Center and was to build all computers. For their work Electrologica was to pay fl 150,000 spread over two years, plus 4% of Electrologica's annual turnover with a minimum of fl 50,000 up to fl 100,000 a year. Furthermore, the Mathematical Center was to receive 4% of the first fl 12,500,000 turnover, 3% of the next fl 12,500,000, and 2% over the rest. Finally, the Mathematical Center would be allowed to purchase computers from Electrologica at cost.[22]

After the agreed two years of start-up, the computer construction group was to be transferred to Electrologica and the Mathematical Center would cease building computers. The research center could continue fundamental research in this field, but it was not allowed to disseminate its computer construction knowledge and experience to third parties unless Electrologica agreed. Finally, all patents relating to computers developed by the center would be owned by Electrologica.[23] It remained unclear what the agreement meant for developments in the area of software.

Although Nillmij and the Mathematical Center signed the agreements on June 25th, 1956, Nillmij agreed to make them retroactive from April 1st, 1956.[24] From that date, Loopstra was appointed technical director of Electrologica. Meanwhile, Scholten stayed at the Mathematical Center to head the computer construction group. He immediately set his team to work developing the prototype of Electrologica's computer, X1.[25]

3.3 Electrologica X1

The history of the X1 started with the development of the prototype for Nillmij. Unsurprisingly, the first designs were similar to those of the computer finished a year before, the ARMAC. Yet, in order to accommodate Nillmij's need for a computer to run its administration, the computer construction group transformed from a small in-house research and development team for scientific computers into a much larger computer manufacturing team with a focus on administrative computing.

From the founding of the company, Electrologica had trouble to keep up with the unexpected success of the X1 and its ambition to cater the field of administrative

---

[21] "Garantie-overeenkomst" (Amsterdam, 25 juni 1956). RAHN, SMC, inv. nr. 52.

[22] "Overeenkomst tussen Electrologica en Stichting Mathematisch Centrum, 25 juni 1956." RAHN, SMC, inv. nr. 52.

[23] "Overeenkomst tussen Electrologica en Stichting Mathematisch Centrum, 25 juni 1956," p. 2. RAHN, SMC, inv. nr. 52.

[24] "Vertrouwelijk memorandum d.d. 18 september 1956, inzake de werkgroep voor de constructie van electronische rekenmachines van het Mathematisch Centrum," p. 2. RAHN, SMC, inv. nr. 52.

[25] "Notulen van de 19e Curatorenvergadering van het Mathematisch Centrum op Dinsdag 16 October 1956 te 14.45 uur in het gebouw van het Mathematisch Centrum, 2de Boerhaavestraat 49 te Amsterdam," p. 6. RAHN, SMC, inv. nr. 4.

computing. The company set out to build all kinds of peripherals, promising its customers peripherals outperforming the competition. None of these was completed, certainly not in time. And what was finally delivered, was often a single prototype built by Electrologica. The exception was the fast punched tape reader, the EL 1000.

Reliable hardware was no longer the sole selling point for a computer. Customers wanted to know what software came with it. In the absence of a software department Electrologica could lean on the Mathematical Center for the scientific computing part of software development. On the administrative side of things, Electrologica struggled.

3.3.1 Developing the Prototype for Nillmij

In January 1957, the computer construction group at the Mathematical Center reported that "the design for the new machine, the X1, is completed."[26] Six months on, part of the machine was developed and built. In the meantime, other parties were showing an interest in the X1, even foreign research institutes.[27] Another six months later, in early 1958, most of the X1 prototype was ready to be tested. The extension of the fast memory to 4069 words was not finished. And the connection to the punched card machines at Nillmij had yet to be settled. Still, Electrologica emphatically claimed the design of the X1 to be finished.[28]

An Electrologica brochure read: "In its basic set-up the machine comprises the arithmetic unit, various internal registers, the control unit, etc. The physical appearance is close to a regular writing desk on top of which various control switches and indicator lights have been added. The circuits in all electronic parts are completely transistorized, resulting in a very low power demand for a machine of this size (a few hundreds of Watts.)."[29] The X1 was the first computer built at the Mathematical Center that did not use any vacuum tubes. Using transistors, the machine produced less heat and was much more reliable than the ARMAC computer, completed two years before. Compared to an addition at the ARMAC taking $417\,\mu s$ plus an average waiting time on the drum memory of 7 ms, the X1 would add two numbers in $64\,\mu s$ with negligible waiting time for the ferrite core memory.[30]

---

[26] "Notulen van de 20ste Curatorenvergadering van het Mathematisch Centrum op Donderdag 10 Januari 1957 te 10.00 uur v.m. in het gebouw van het Mathematisch Centrum, 2de Boerhaavestraat 49 te Amsterdam," p. 4. RAHN, SMC, inv. nr. 4.

[27] "Notulen van de 21ste Curatorenvergadering van het Mathematisch Centrum op dinsdag 11 juni 1957 te 10.00 v.m. in het gebouw van het Mathematisch Centrum, 2e Boerhaavestraat 49 te Amsterdam," p. 9. RAHN, SMC, inv. nr. 4.

[28] "Notulen van de 22e Curatorenvergadering van het Mathematisch Centrum op donderdag 13 maart 1958 te 14.30 uur in het gebouw van het Mathematisch Centrum, 2e Boerhaavestraat 49 te Amsterdam," p. 13. RAHN, SMC, inv. nr. 4.

[29] Electrologica. 1957. Electrologica, Korte algemene beschrijving van de X-1, Technical report EL-1-N, p. 1.

[30] Donselaar, P.J. van. 1967. De ontwikkeling van elektronische rekenmachines in Nederland (Een historisch overzicht van Nederlandse computers), Technical report (Amsterdam: Stichting Het Ned-

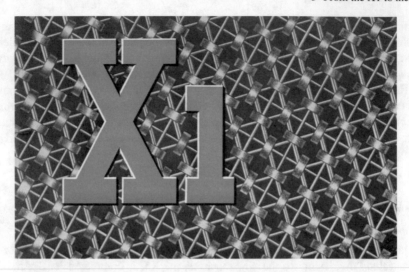

Fig. 3.1 Cover of an Electrologica X1 brochure from the early 1960s. The X1 logo is laid out on a background with a stylized ferrite core memory

The X1's memory consisted completely of magnetic ferrite core memory[31] and was divided in a small "dead" part and a large "living" part[32]. The read-only "dead" memory contained the system software of the X1, such as the communication programs, some standard programs, and also some standard subroutines. Electrologica could produce this "dead" memory much cheaper than the random-access "living" memory. To some extent, customers could customize the contents and size of the "dead" memory when they ordered an X1. The minimal amount of "living" memory customers could order was one memory cabinet. Each cabinet fit eight memory units of 512 words of 27 bits, or 4096 words. The "dead" memory was divided in units of 64 words. Customers could upgrade the total memory in their X1, "dead" and "living" memory combined, to 32,768 words spread over eight memory cabinets (Fig. 3.2).[33]

The X1 contained two 27 bit registers, A and S, both of which could be used for arithmetic and logical operations. Furthermore, there was a smaller modification register B of 16 bits that could also perform some addition operations. Finally, there were four jump operations: the additive jump, the normal jump, the counting

---

erlands Studiecentrum voor Administratieve Automatisering en Bestuurlijke Informatieverwerking), pp. 19–24.

[31] See Fig. 3.1 for a stylized look of a ferrite core memory. This memory consisted of magnetic rings of ferrite, knitted together with copper wire.

[32] In Dutch they called it "dood" (dead) and "levend" (living) memory. In Loopstra, B.J. 1959b. The X-1 computer. *The Computer Journal* 2(1):39–43, p. 39, Loopstra called them "passive" and "active" memories, respectively. In modern terms, the "dead" memory is ROM, Read-Only Memory, and the "living" memory RAM, Random-Access memory.

[33] Loopstra (1959b).

Fig. 3.2 Setup of the X1 installation at the *Centraal Bureau voor de Statistiek* in The Hague in an Electrologica X1 brochure from the early 1960s

jump, and the subroutine jump. The counting jump was used in combination with a counter in a dedicated memory location, allowing for simple iterations of a constant number of steps. With the additive jump, the contents of an address was added to the instruction counter. This construction allowed the user to jump over a given number of addresses in memory.

An instruction of 27 bits was divided into five parts: an address on the first 15 bits (hence the maximum memory of 32,768 words), followed by six bits to specify the operation, and three groups of two bits each to configure that operation. For example, one possibility was to specify an operation to use the address part not as an address but instead as a number. Another possibility was to increase the address of an operation with the contents of modification register B. This change could also be written back into memory. Other possibilities were setting all sorts of conditions, like sign changes, zero tests, and so on. Furthermore, the conditional jump or conditional operation could be specified. The last six bits, those configuring the operation, made the instruction set of the X1 significantly different from the earlier machines of the Mathematical Center.[34]

Next to the arithmetical and logical instructions, 48 in all, the X1 had the so-called "communication instructions," including shift operations, normalization operations, register transport operations, quick multiplication by ten, stop operations, and operations to control all input and output peripherals.[35] For the "communication oper-

---

[34] Electrologica (1957).

[35] Electrologica (1957).

ations," the address part of the operation was always interpreted as some code that would influence how the operation worked exactly and did not refer to an address.

The developers of the X1 in the computer construction group were familiar with connecting a tape puncher, a tape reader, and the electric typewriter. Thus, just like with previous machines, input to the X1 was done through a punched tape reader. The output went via a tape puncher and an electric typewriter. The operations to control these peripherals were similar to those of earlier machines. What was different this time was that Nillmij wanted to use the X1 to automate its administration, which just a couple of years back had been standardized to Bull punched card office machinery. By consequence the computer construction group faced the task of connecting the X1 prototype to a Bull punched card reproducing machine.

Connecting a computer to mechanical peripherals would always create issues of synchronization. Peripherals, like punched card readers, work at their own speed, in no way matching the clock speed of the X1. For example, when reading and processing data from punched cards, the X1 might be ready to process more data, while the punched card machines were still reading. Or conversely, the X1 might need more time to process the already read data, causing the punched card reader to wait before it could read the next card. The issue was partly resolved by using a buffer memory. However, the developers "aimed to limit such extra buffers to a practical minimum while designing the X1."[36]

Unfortunately, for administrative applications, involving huge amounts of input and output of data, buffers would not suffice to solve the synchronization issue. In 1957, Anton Dek, one of the directors at Nillmij, tried to design a program for the X1 to read and process 12 punched cards per second. He discovered that it was impossible, unless the computer construction group would introduce an interrupt mechanism to the X1.[37] Once a punched card reader was finished reading the next card into a buffer, it should generate an interrupt signal to the X1. The X1, then, would pause the program it was running. Instead, it would write the data from the buffer into the X1's "living" memory. Subsequently, once the reader-generated interrupt routine was finished, the X1 would restore its prior state and resume running the program it had paused to handle the interrupt.[38] "In other words, once there is work of higher priority, the X1 is automatically "lent out" to the interrupt program, which would immediately run the "rush job." Compared to solutions without an interrupt, the actual productivity of the X1 was increased enormously, not in the least because

[36] Dijkstra, E.W. 1959. Verslag van de voordracht door Dr. E.W. Dijkstra, gehouden op 11 december 1959. De faciliteit tot interruptie in de X1. *Mededelingen van het Rekenmachinegenootschap* 2(1):3–8, p. 6; Electrologica. 1958. Korte algemene beschrijving van de elektronische rekenmachine X1 (EL-3) [Brief description of the electronic computer X1], Technical Report EL-3. Electrologica, 's-Gravenhage, p. 27; Loopstra, B.J. 1959a. Input and output in the X-1 system. In *Information Processing: Proceedings of the International Conference on Information Processing, Unesco, Paris 15–20 June 1959*, 342–344. München: Oldenbourg Verlag.

[37] Dijkstra, Edsger W. 1980. A programmer's early memories. In *A history of computing in the twentieth century*, edited Metropolis, N., J. Howlett en G. Rota. New York: Academic Press, p. 10; Alberts, Gerard, and Huub T. de Beer. 2008b. Interview met A.W. Dek, directeur van de Nillmij en commissaris van Electrologica, gehouden op 8 januari 2008, unpublished.

[38] Electrologica (1958), p. 27; Loopstra (1959b), p. 43.

it was by then possible to have the X1 cooperate with several mutually synchronized peripherals."[39]

The X1 could control multiple different peripherals via dedicated machine code instructions. Each peripheral required a separate interrupt program. The interrupt programs were divided into seven categories of increasing levels of priority. Interrupt programs with higher priority could not be interrupted by interrupt programs of lower priority. The seventh and highest category belonged to the X1 itself, to its console (see Fig. 3.3). This category of interrupt programs could not be interrupted by any other interrupt signal, except for signals from other programs of the seventh category.[40] Using this interrupt mechanism, Electrologica could make the X1 more suitable for administrative applications. It even allowed running two programs at the same time.[41]

Interrupt programs, as well as subroutines to handle the interrupt mechanism, and all sorts of input and output programs and subroutines were wired into the X1's "dead" memory. These programs were included with the computer. At the Mathematical Center, the conglomerate of programs and subroutines was called the "communication program." Edsger Dijkstra wrote the communication program for the X1, like he had been doing for the computers built by the computer construction group before the X1. He worked as a programmer at the Mathematical Center since 1952 and had gained experience writing such programs for the internals of the machine.[42]

The introduction of the interrupt drastically changed the situation for Dijkstra. Because the communication program was wired into the "dead" memory, possible errors could only be resolved by replacing whole physical units of dead memory. To make matters worse, Dijkstra could not test his communication program in advance.[43] The apparent non-deterministic nature of the interrupt program, as suggested by Dek, added to the concern. Upon closer inspection Dijkstra even proved that the interrupt as it had been presented to him, could not work. But after thorough revision of the interrupt design, Dijkstra did trust the interrupt mechanism without test based on theoretical considerations. He now did start the implementation of his communication program and finished it early 1958.[44] The very same work on the communication program conveyed major theoretical insights. It was elaborated to build the core of his PhD thesis, *Communication with an automatic computer*, defended at the University of Amsterdam in 1959.[45]

---

[39] Electrologica (1958), p. 27.

[40] Electrologica (1958), pp. 27–29.

[41] Loopstra (1959b), p. 43.

[42] The later term "system software" is avoided here in an effort to stick to the terminology of the day. In retrospect Dijkstra characterized his working relation to the computer construction group as "feeling like a contract."Dijkstra (1980), p. 10.

[43] Dijkstra (1980), p. 10.

[44] Dijkstra (1980), p. 10.

[45] Dijkstra, Edsger W. 1959a. *Communication with an automatic computer.* [PhD Thesis. October 28, 1959. Universiteit van Amsterdam]. Excelsior, Rijswijk.

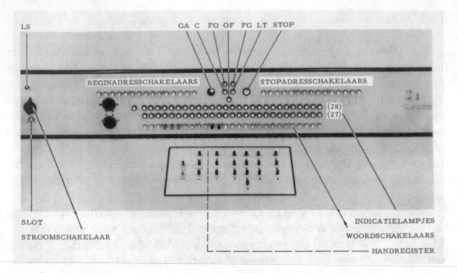

Fig. 3.3 Overview of the X1 console

Using the communication program, users could call on various input and output programs running independently. Each of these programs was started pressing the so-called "auto start buttons" on the console (see Fig. 3.3). The X1 had eleven such auto start buttons. Each started a different program, for example, to either read from punched tape, to type the contents of an address on the electric typewriter, to put a sequence of addresses in memory, or to start a program. Parameters to these auto started programs could be entered using switches on the console. The console itself, in turn, was controlled by the communication program.

Most of the functionality available through the auto start buttons was also available via subroutines. For example, a programmer could call the typewriting subroutine to lay out a page with numbers and then print those numbers. Alternatively, a programmer could control punching the tape. Finally, there were some facilities to control the interrupt mechanism itself.[46]

Next to Dijkstra's communication program, further interrupt programs for punched card equipment and other administrative peripherals were written by programmers from Electrologica, employed by Nillmij. By the end of 1958, the status of these supplementary programs was still unclear. Would they be given away for free with an X1 installation? Or should customers order and pay for them? Scholten even suggested writing some simple interrupt programs to give away for free, and then tell customers they could pay for an extended version. His proposal was rejected.[47] Software was included with the X1.

---

[46] Dijkstra (1959a), pp. 62–121.

[47] "Notulen van de vergadering gehouden op woensdag 1 oktober 1958 ten kantore van de Nillmij te 's-Gravenhage," p. 1. Oud Archief AEGON. Afd. Documentatie nr. 171, X.008.13.053.7 G.

3.3.2 Electrologica Takes off

While the construction team worked hard to realize the X1 prototype, Nillmij culti-vated Electrologica's commercial activities. When Engelfriet and Van Wijngaarden founded Electrologica, they expected to build an X1 for Nillmij, and likely another one for the Mathematical Center. Nillmij sought potential customers among other life insurance companies, but they were reluctant. They hesitated to make themselves dependent on their competitor by ordering an X1.[48]

Despite moderate expectations, Electrologica had caught public attention. Even before the X1 prototype was completed for testing in early 1958, no less than nine orders for the X1 were brought in[49] (see Table 3.1). Furthermore, as anticipated, the Mathematical Center also ordered their X1 computer[50], bringing the total number of pre-orders to ten. The first X1, the prototype, was installed at Nillmij later in 1958.

A Dortmund connection led to an entry on the German market. Six out of the nine early orders came in from Germany. Hans Konrad Schuff of the Dortmund consul-tancy firm, Mathematische Beratungs- und Programmierungsdienst in Dortmund, a subsidiary of Hoesch, showed more than an incidental interest. His programming services would easily follow the sales of Electrologica's computers and he even suggested to position himself as the Dutch firm's sales representative.[51] Electro-logica recognized the importance of the German market. Schuff's order of an X1 was not taken lightly. Failure or delay might jeopardize the opportunity to reach German customers. The second copy of the X1, built immediately following the Nillmij prototype, was swiftly completed and delivered in 1959 to Schuff's Math-ematische Beratungs- und Programmierungsdienst. Electrologica did not even take the time to fully test the machine.[52] At the same time, rather than relying on a sales representative, Electrologica opened a branch in Dortmund to serve the German market.[53]

Putting the bets on the German market was successful and at the same time absorbed all energy. The result was a backlog of orders. In the spring of 1958 Electrologica installed a freeze of orders until 1960 to deal with this unexpected situation. Electrologica sought to focus on scaling up production and building the already ordered X1 computers.[54]

---

[48] Alberts (2008b).

[49] N.V. Electrologica, "Jaarverslag 1957" in: "Nota aan H.H. Gedelegeerde Commissarissen van "Ned. Nillmij" en "Arnhem," 13 november 1958," p. 1. AEGON:165, X.003.3:657.372.

[50] "Notulen van de 22e Curatorenvergadering van het Mathematisch Centrum op donderdag 13 maart 1958 te 14.30 uur in het gebouw van het Mathematisch Centrum, 2e Boerhaavestraat 49 te Amsterdam," p. 16. RAHN, SMC, inv. nr. 4.

[51] Alberts (2008b).

[52] "Notulen van de vergadering gehouden op Donderdag 16 April 1959 ten kantore van de Nillmij te 's-Gravenhage," p. 1. AEGON:171, X.008.13.053.7 G.

[53] Wit, de (1992), p. 274; N.V. Electrologica, "Jaarverslag 1960" ('s-Gravenhage), p. 5. AE-GON:165, X.003.055.5.

[54] "Notulen van de 22e Curatorenvergadering van het Mathematisch Centrum op donderdag 13 maart 1958 te 14.30 uur in het gebouw van het Mathematisch Centrum, 2e Boerhaavestraat 49

When Electrologica was founded, the Mathematical Center had agreed to construct all computers for Electrologica as long as Electrologica's turnover was under fl 2,500,000.[55] To fulfill this agreement given the demand for the X1, the Mathematical Center doubled the size of the computer construction group to a 60 employees in 1958.[56]. The rapid growth of the computer construction group caused problems for the Mathematical Center. Not only did it lack the physical space to shelter such a large group, producing computers at an industrial scale did not align with the goals of a mathematical research institute. At the same time, because of its success, Electrologica wanted to present itself to the outside world more independently from the Mathematical Center.[57] Electrologica and the Mathematical Center decided to advance the transfer of the computer construction activities to Electrologica. Through intervention of the municipality of Amsterdam, Electrologica was able to rent a factory space in the suburb of Duivendrecht. On November 1st, 1958, the first 22 employees, and with them most of the actual computer construction activities moved from the Mathematical Center to the new location. Research related to computer construction stayed at the Mathematical Center until January 1st, 1959, when the other 38 employees moved out to the Electrologica factory.[58]

All in all, Electrologica received orders to build 36 X1 computers (Table 3.1), including the prototype for Nillmij and a test machine for use in the factory. Of those 34 external orders, 18 came from 12 German customers. Out of the other 16 orders, two computers went to Electrologica's own computer service center. Fokker and Utrecht University did not actually order an X1, but temporarily got one in 1963 until Electrologica could deliver the X8 computers they did order. The success of the X1 in Germany was even more pronounced than already appeared at first sight.

In the Netherlands, a varied set of customers purchased an X1. Next to Nillmij, two other insurance companies chose Electrologica, and used the X1 for administrative applications in the insurance field. The Centraal Bureau voor de Statistiek (National Statistics Agency) used its X1 for data-intensive statistical calculations.

te Amsterdam." RAHN, SMC, inv. nr. 4; "Notulen van de 23e Curatorenvergadering van het Mathematisch Centrum op donderdag 26 juni 1958 te 10.00 uur in het gebouw van het Mathematisch Centrum, 2e Boerhaavestraat 49 te Amsterdam.' RAHN, SMC, inv. nr. 4.

[55] "Overeenkomst tussen Electrologica en Stichting Mathematisch Centrum, 25 juni 1956." RAHN, SMC, inv. nr. 52.

[56] JMC56. *Jaarverslag Stichting Mathematisch Centrum* [Annual Report Foundation Mathematical Center] (1956), pp. 4-7; JMC57. *Jaarverslag Stichting Mathematisch Centrum* [Annual Report Foundation Mathematical Center] (1957), pp. 5-6; JMC58. *Jaarverslag Stichting Mathematisch Centrum* [Annual Report Foundation Mathematical Center] (1958), pp. 43–45.

[57] "Notulen van de 23e Curatorenvergadering van het Mathematisch Centrum op donderdag 26 juni 1958 te 10.00 uur in het gebouw van het Mathematisch Centrum, 2e Boerhaavestraat 49 te Amsterdam," 8. RAHN, SMC, inv. nr. 4.

[58] "Notulen van de 22e Curatorenvergadering van het Mathematisch Centrum op donderdag 13 maart 1958 te 14.30 uur in het gebouw van het Mathematisch Centrum, 2e Boerhaavestraat 49 te Amsterdam." RAHN, SMC, inv. nr. 4; "Notulen van de 23e Curatorenvergadering van het Mathematisch Centrum op donderdag 26 juni 1958 te 10.00 uur in het gebouw van het Mathematisch Centrum, 2e Boerhaavestraat 49 te Amsterdam," 8. RAHN, SMC, inv. nr. 4, JMC58 (1958), pp. 43–45.

# Customer	O-year	CC	I	A	I-year	R
X1-1 Nillmij	1956	NL	N	A	1958	
X1-2 Mathematische Beratungs- und Programmierungsdienst	1957	DE	S	S	1959	X, lease
X1-3 (Nieuwe) Eerste Nederlandse	1957	NL	N	A	1960	
X1-4 CBS	1957	NL	M	A	1960	X, bought in 1961
X1-5 Hoesch AG (1)	1957	DE	I	A	1960	X
X1-6 Mathematisch Centrum	1958	NL	C	S	1960	
X1-7 Mannesman AG (1)	1957	DE	I	B	1960	X
X1-8 Hoesch AG (2)	1957	DE	I	A	1960	X
X1-9 Ruhrkohle Treuhand GmbH (1)	1957	DE	I	?	1960	
X1-10 Interatom AG	1957	DE	I	S	1960	X
X1-11 Nederlands Scheepsbouwkundig Proefstation	1960	NL	R	S	1961	
X1-12 Universiteit Kiel	1960	DE	U	S	1961	
X1-13 Rijksuniversiteit Leiden	1960	NL	U	S	1962	X
X1-14 Algemene Kunstzijde Unie NV	1960	NL	I	S	1962	X
X1-15 Rheinelbe Bergbau	1960	DE	I	S	1961	X
X1-16 Hoesch AG (3)	1960	DE	I	A	1963	X
X1-17 TH Braunschweig	1960	DE	U	S	1962	
X1-18 Nationaal Luchtvaartlaboratorium	1960	NL	R	S	1962	
X1-19 Amstleven/Hollandsche Sociëteit	1961	NL	N	A	1963	
X1-20 Reactor Centrum Nederland	1961	NL	R	S	1962	X
X1-21 Rekencentrum Electrologica (1)	1961	NL	C	B	1963	
X1-22 Algemeen Rekencentrum Amsterdam NV	1962	NL	C	A	1964	X
X1-23 Margarine Union GmbH (1)	1962	DE	I	A	1963	X
X1-24 Werkspoor NV	1962	NL	I	?	1963	X
X1-25 Hoesch AG (4)	1962	DE	I	A	—[3]	
X1-26 Universiteit Saarbrücken	1962	DE	U	S	1964	
X1-27 Ruhrkohle Treuhand GmbH (2)	1962	DE	I	?	—[3]	
X1-28 Tchibo	1963	DE	I	A	1965	X
X1-29 Rijksuniversiteit Utrecht [1]	—	NL	U	S	1963	
X1-30 Fokker [1]	—	NL	I	S	1963	
X1-31 Coöperatieve vereniging U.A.	1963	NL	I	?	1965	X
X1-32 Margarine Union GmbH (2)	1963	DE	I	A	1964	X
X1-33 Industrie Companie Kleinewefers GmbH	1963	DE	I	S	1964	X
X1-34 Rekencentrum Electrologica (2)	1964	NL	C	B	1965	
X1-35 Mannesman AG (2)	1964	DE	I	B	1965	X
Electrologica[2]		NL	I	T		

: Serial number of the X1 computer
O-year : Order year
CC : Customer country code
  I : Main industry in which the customer operated: I(ndustry), N (insurance company), R(esearch), C(omputer service center), U(niversity), S(oftware consultancy) of M(iscellaneous).
  A : Main application type: A(dministration), S(cientific computing) or B(oth). The computer for the Electrologica factory was used for T(esting) purposes.
I-year : Installation year
  R : Rental. Unclear where lease constructions fit in

[1] : Until their X8 was delivered
[2] : Only for testing purposes in their factory
[3] : Order withdrawn in 1963

sources : Annual reports Electrologica 1956, 1960, 1961, 1962, 1963, 1964, 1965, "Periodieke rapportering 5 April 1966"

Table 3.1 Electrologica X1 computers

Electrologica also provided computing services to customers. In 1961, it still ran service jobs on the X1 at Nillmij. Due to the success of the service, the situation became untenable, and Electrologica decided to order a separate X1 for the service.[59] A year later, Electrologica both founded its own computing service center, Electrologica Rekencentrum, and took a 40% share in a further computing center, the Algemeen Rekencentrum Amsterdam.[60] The first, Electrologica Rekencentrum, was so successful that it installed another X1 in 1964 to meet the demand.[61] Overall, about half of Electrologica's Dutch customers ordered the X1 for administrative applications. The other customers, including universities, research institutes, and some industries, used their X1 for scientific computing.

Year	Number	Bull	EL	IBM	STC	S	M
1952							
1953	1					1	
1954	3					2	1
1955	4					2	2
1956	5					3	2
1957	7			2		3	2
1958	11		1	2	4	2	2
1959	25	5	2	10	5	1	2
1960	34	7	4	11	8	1	3
1960	76	7	8	45	8	2	6
1961	117	19	11	64	8	2	13
1963	227	25	17	130	9	2	44

The top of this table lists the number of installed and working computers in the Netherlands between 1952 and 1960 per year, divided by manufacturer: Bull, Electrologica (EL), IBM, Standard Telephones and Cables (STC), self-built (S) en miscellaneous (M).

At the bottom this table lists the number of installed and ordered computers between 1960 and 1963. The data about the number of orders in 1960 is an estimate.[62]

Table 3.2 The number of installed computers in the Netherlands (1950–1960) and the number of installed and ordered computers (1960–1963)

Electrologica viewed in isolation may have appeared a flourishing enterprise, but seen in the context of the Dutch market for computers its situation was precarious. At the end of the 1950s, the Electrologica X1 was a medium-sized computer at a reasonable price. In 1960, out of 34 computers in the Netherlands (Table 3.2), 21 were used

---

[59] N.V. Electrologica, "Jaarverslag 1961" ('s-Gravenhage), p. 2. AEGON:165, X.003.055.5.

[60] N.V. Electrologica, "Jaarverslag 1962" ('s-Gravenhage), p. 2. AEGON:165, X.003.055.5.

[61] N.V. Electrologica, "Jaarverslag 1964" ('s-Gravenhage), p. 2. AEGON:165, X.003.055.5.

[62] Informatie. 1959a. Enkele gegevens met betrekking tot geplaatste en bestelde machines. *Informatie* 2:7–8; Informatie. 1959b. Enkele gegevens met betrekking tot geplaatste en bestelde machines. *Informatie* 3:11; Informatie. 1959c. Enkele gegevens met betrekking tot geplaatste en bestelde machines. *Informatie* 5:8–9; Informatie. 1960. Enkele gegevens met betrekking tot geplaatste en bestelde machines. *Informatie* 8:16; Informatie. 1961. Overzicht van in Nederland per 1 oktober 1961 geplaatste en in bestelling zijnde computers. *Informatie* 17:16; Bruijn, W.K. de. 1964. Computers in de Benelux. *Informatie* 30:2–3.

for administrative applications. Electrologica came in third with three computers, after IBM (11) and Bull (7). IBM and Bull were large, well-known manufacturers of office machinery. Larger companies seeking to automate their already mechanized administrations would first look at these trusted suppliers of office machines for their first computer. Even when the X1 was a modern computer compared to the supply IBM and Bull had on offer, Electrologica had trouble entering that market. When IBM offered its own medium-sized second generation computer, in late 1959, it soon dominated the administrative market in the Netherlands. Electrologica had to up its game.

3.3.3 Electrologica's Connection to Peripherals

Electrologica's default punched tape reader, tape puncher, and typewriter, or the optional Bull punched card machines would not suffice to convince costumers in the administrative field to choose Electrologica. Customers asked for other peripherals, like a fast line printer, magnetic tape units, drum memory, and disc memory. Electrologica was eager to serve its customers. Most requests to connect new peripherals would come in after the X1 had already been ordered. But even if requests had been done in advance, usually the X1 installation was delivered and installed before the connections to the extra peripherals were prepared and made available.

Electrologica was keen to develop peripherals in-house rather than purchase them from other manufacturers. Not unusual was the situation that Electrologica actually delivered a peripheral built on purpose, delivering the single prototype to the customer. Development took years, delivery was late, and after installation, the connection between the X1 and the peripheral was not without issues.

Four developments of peripherals characterized Electrologica's efforts in this direction.

Punched Card Machinery. Developed for Nillmij, the X1 could work together with the Bull reproducing punched card machine, type P.R.D. To cement the relationship between Electrologica and Bull, the two companies entered serious negotiations about selling and servicing each other's products. However, Electrologica feared that close cooperation with Bull would hamper ambitions to build a successor to the X1.[63] While slowing down talks with Bull, Electrologica also looked into starting negotiations with other manufacturers and even considered developing punched card machines in-house themselves.[64] In July 1959, Bull and Electrologica agreed that Bull would deliver punched card machines to Electrologica without any further obli-

---

[63] "Notulen van de vergadering gehouden op donderdag 17 juli 1958 ten kantore van de Nillmij te 's-Gravenhage." AEGON:171, X.008.13.053.7 G; "Notulen van de vergadering gehouden op donderdag 10 juli 1958 op het Mathematisch Centrum te Amsterdam." AEGON:171, X.008.13.053.7 G.

[64] "Notulen van de vergadering gehouden op vrijdag 4 april 1958 ten huize van drs. B.J. Loopstra." AEGON:171, X.008.13.053.7 G; "Notulen van de vergadering gehouden op dinsdag 9 september 1958 ten kantore van de Nillmij te 's-Gravenhage," 1. AEGON:171, X.008.13.053.7 G.

gations. More so, Bull retained the right to refuse to deliver its machines might it harm its commercial interests. Electrologica on its part could connect punched card machines from other manufacturers to the X1 as well in regions and markets where Bull was not active. Although Electrologica continued talks with other manufacturers, the agreement, however noncommittal, did put an end to Electrologica's interest in other punched card equipment than Bull's.[65]

Paradoxically, Electrologica did hang on to the prospect of developing a card puncher and a fast punched card reader in-house. When other research and development activities took precedence in 1959, plans for the card puncher were shelved. Work on the fast punched card reader was continued for two more years, until the looming obsolescence of punched card technology forced to stop this as well.[66]

High-Speed Printer. In 1957, funded by Nillmij, the computer construction group had started developing a high-speed printer. A year on, the development seemed to be going well.[67] Unfortunately, in 1959, the printer was far from ready, but the demand for it from X1 customers had increased. Electrologica had to choose between speeding up the development of the printer, or purchasing one from another manufacturer and connect that to the X1 instead.[68] Electrologica's technical director looked into it, and the Xeronic high-speed printer was added to the Electrologica assortment. All the same, the in-house development was continued as well, because the high-speed printer was subject of Electrologica's negotiations with the potential customer Atlas.[69]

It hoped to finish its own high-speed printer by May 1960 and offer that to clients at fl 301,000.[70] May 1960 came too early. Scaling down ambitions, Electrologica decided to focus on developing an offline version only. "Offline" implied that the printer no longer would be connected to the X1. Instead, the printer was to be controlled through an external medium, such as a punched tape or magnetic tape. The latter option was the more modern and for that reason preferred.[71] In late 1962, Electrologica delivered its first high-speed printer, its prototype, to a customer. The

---

[65] "Notulen van de vergadering gehouden op Maandag 6 Juli 1959 ten kantore van de Nillmij te 's-Gravenhage." AEGON:171, X.008.13.053.7 G.

[66] "Notulen van de vergadering gehouden op 1 december 1959 bij de Nillmij," 1. AEGON:171, X.008.13.053.7 G; "Notulen E.L.-vergadering d.d. 18 oktober 1961," p. 1. AEGON:171, X.008.13.053.7 G.

[67] N.V. Electrologica, "Jaarverslag 1957" in: "Nota aan H.H. Gedelegeerde Commissarissen van "Ned. Nillmij" en "Arnhem" 13 november 1958" ('s-Gravenhage). AEGON:165, X.003.3:657.372; "Notulen van de vergadering gehouden op Vrijdag 28 maart 1958 ten huize van Prof. Dr. Ir. A. van Wijngaarden," p. 1. AEGON:171, X.008.13.053.7 G.

[68] "Notulen van de vergadering gehouden op Maandag 9 maart 1959 ten kantore van de Nillmij te 's-Gravenhage," p. 1. AEGON:171, X.008.13.053.7 G.

[69] "Notulen van de vergadering gehouden op 19 juni 1959 ten kantore van de Nillmij te 's-Gravenhage," p. 1. AEGON:171, X.008.13.053.7 G.

[70] "Notulen van de vergadering gehouden op dinsdag 22 oktober 1959 ten kantore van de Nillmij te 's-Gravenhage," p. 1. AEGON:171, X.008.13.053.7 G.

[71] "Notulen E.L.-vergadering d.d. 26-7-1960," p. 1. AEGON:171, X.008.13.053.7 G.

delivery signaled the immediate end to the development of high-speed printers at Electrologica.[72]

Magnetic Tape Units. Developing magnetic tape units was a painful affair for Electrologica. The most severe problems occurred when connecting magnetic tape units to the X1 at the biggest customer, Hoesch AG in Germany. In 1960, it was forced to postpone the planned delivery date to March 1962.[73] The magnetic tape unit project got a bad reputation in Electrologica circles, and served as a warning of how not to develop the successor to the X1.[74] Eventually, it took over three years to deliver the first two tape units. Even then, performance was unsatisfactory.[75] The next year, in 1964, Electrologica continued to struggle with the tape units. It failed to fulfill some of the further orders for tape units. The lack of new orders for the X1 was attributed to the failure to connect tape units in time.[76]

Fast Punched Tape Reader. Amidst all these stories of struggle and failure, one story of triumph stood out, the EL 1000 high-speed punched tape reader. The EL 1000 could read 1000 symbols per second.[77] Starting in 1961, Electrologica delivered the EL 1000 as part of the basic machine instead of the Creed tape reader it had used before.[78] Given the success of the EL 1000, Electrologica's board of directors considered marketing the EL 1000 to third parties.[79] Interest in distributing the EL 1000 abroad came from various parties, including parties from the USA, Canada, and Australia.[80]

Electrologica was unable to carry out the multitude of research and development projects on connecting peripherals and in-house design of machinery. Increasingly, the development of a successor to the X1 was urgent. The limited capacity for research and development was under growing stress. In spite of ambitions, Electrologica simply could not keep up with other manufacturers. It lacked the expertise, the experience, and the financial means to compete.

---

[72] "Notulen E.L.-vergadering d.d. 18 oktober 1961," p. 1. AEGON:171, X.008.13.053.7 G; N.V. Electrologica, "Jaarverslag 1962" ('s-Gravenhage), p. 2. AEGON:165, X.003.055.5.

[73] "Notulen van de vergadering gehouden op maandag 28 maart 1960 ten kantore van de Nillmij te 's-Gravenhage." AEGON:171, X.008.13.053.7 G.

[74] "Verdere toekomstige mogelijkheden" (23 mei 1961), p. 2. AEGON:171, X.008.13.053.7 G.

[75] N.V. Electrologica, "Jaarverslag 1963" ('s-Gravenhage), p. 3. AEGON:165, X.003.055.5.

[76] N.V. Electrologica, "Jaarverslag 1964" ('s-Gravenhage), p. 3. AEGON:165, X.003.055.5.

[77] Electrologica. 1966. *Programmering EL X8*. Den Haag: N.V. Electrologica, par. 9.3.

[78] N.V. Electrologica, "Jaarverslag 1961" ('s-Gravenhage), p. 2. AEGON:165, X.003.055.5.

[79] "Notulen E.L.-vergadering d.d. 3 april 1962," p. 1. AEGON:171, X.008.13.053.7 G.

[80] "Verkoop/vertegenwoordiging voor de EL 1000 in de V.S. en Canada" ('s-Gravenhage, 7 juni 1963). AEGON:171, X.008.13.053.7 G; "Notulen EL-vergadering d.d. 9.7.1963." AEGON:171, X.008.13.053.7 G.

3.3.4 Delivering Software

Alongside a growing concern for peripherals, software became a serious issue in Electrologica's business. As described in Sect. 3.3.1, the X1 came with basic programs installed in its "dead" memory: Dijkstra's communication program, some input and output subroutines and programs, and programs controlling the interrupt mechanism. However, to effectively use the X1, users needed more code. Most administrative applications were unique projects, whereas in scientific computing many similar problems were solved using a set of standard numerical algorithms.

Software for Scientific Computing. Halfway 1958, the Mathematical Center agreed with Electrologica to offer an extensive subroutine library for the X1. It would write such programs for its own use anyway, and did not mind sharing it with other X1 customers on a basis of reciprocity.[81] The Center did not expect great gain from this reciprocity. In 1959, it started programming the library and published it as the series MCP.[82]

As a service to its customers with scientific computing problems, Electrologica hired a number of programmers and seconded them to the Mathematical Center to work under leadership of Dijkstra.[83] Not all customers were satisfied with this programming service. According to Fokker, the Mathematical Center limited the assistance to providing the subroutine library.[84]

In the late 1950s, programming languages became a vibrant area of research in which the Mathematical Center aspired to assume an active role. The Computation Department joined the international effort to define an algorithmic language, ALGOL.[85] Upon publication of the ALGOL 60 report[86] in early 1960, Edsger Dijkstra and Jaap Zonneveld took up the task to write a compiler for ALGOL 60 on the X1. In just six months, from their visit to Copenhagen where they invited Algol-report editor Peter Naur and his team to come to Amsterdam and see the results in half a year, they finished the compiler. They were the first in the world to develop an almost complete ALGOL 60 compiler. Electrologica, proudly announced: "The Algol compiler has arrived, and programmed for the X1."[87] In under two years, the share of

---

[81] "Notulen van de vergadering gehouden op donderdag 18 september 1958 op het Mathematisch Centrum te Amsterdam," p. 2. AEGON:171, X.008.13.053.7 G.

[82] JMC59. *Jaarverslag Stichting Mathematisch Centrum* [Annual Report Foundation Mathematical Center] (1959), pp. 38, 45.

[83] "Notulen van de vergadering gehouden op donderdag 18 september 1958 op het Mathematisch Centrum te Amsterdam," p. 2. AEGON:171, X.008.13.053.7 G; "Notulen van de vergadering gehouden op dinsdag 10 juni ten kantore van de Nillmij te 's-Gravenhage," p. 1. AEGON:171, X.008.13.053.7 G.

[84] "Notulen E.L.-vergadering d.d. 22 september 1961," p. 2. AEGON:171, X.008.13.053.7 G.

[85] For more information about this ALGOL effort, see Beer, H.T. de. 2006. The history of the ALGOL effort, Master's thesis, Technische Universiteit Eindhoven.

[86] Naur, Peter, ed. 1960. J.W. Backus, F.L. Bauer, J. Green, C. Katz, J. McCarthy, A.J. Perlis, H. Rutishauser, K. Samelson, B. Vauquois, J.H. Wegstein, A. van Wijngaarden, M. Woodger, Report on the algorithmic language ALGOL 60. *Num. Mathematik* 2:106–136.

[87] "Notulen van Electrologica-vergadering dd. 10-9-1960," p. 2. AEGON:171, X.008.13.053.7 G.

ALGOL 60 programs that ran on the X1 of Mathematical Center grew from 20% to 70%.[88] Alongside the subroutine library written in machine code, the Mathematical Center also published a program library in ALGOL 60.

Unsurprisingly, other scientific computing customers were also interested in the ALGOL 60 compiler for the X1.[89] The Mathematical Center was happy to share the work, but porting the compiler was far from straightforward. Different X1 systems were not one-to-one compatible. The first X1 to which it was tried to convey the ALGOL 60 compiler was the computer of the Scheepsbouwkundig Proefstation in Wageningen. Once this transfer succeeded, porting to other X1 installations would become easier.[90] Soon, early 1961, the Mathematical Center announced that its ALGOL 60 compiler was available for the X1; Electrologica would bear the costs of porting the compiler for their customers.[91]

As was wont in the field of scientific computing, customers and users of the X1 shared their knowledge, experience, and programs. More so, some of the customers founded user associations dedicated to the Electrologica X1 in the Netherlands, Düsseldorf, and Braunschweig.[92]

Software for Administrative Applications. While the Mathematical Center's numerical subroutine library would serve Electrologica's scientific computing customers, Nillmij knew that this library would not be very useful for the administrative customers.[93] Nillmij created an administrative programming group, which it placed as a subdivision under Electrologica's sales department at Nillmij. If there was a starting point for a software department of Electrologica it was this subdivision stationed in The Hague. Except, the work was not called software. The first task for this new programming group was to develop interrupt programs for the Bull reproducing punched card machine for the prototype of Nillmij. In late 1959, it was decided that the group write a library of subroutines and programs for administrative applications. This library would be set up similar to the MCP series with numerical subroutines developed at the Mathematical Center.[94] Furthermore, this programming group would be available for consultancy to help Electrologica's customers with their automation projects.

Electrologica realized that software was becoming more and more important for the customers. Customers wanted more ready-made programs, such as programs to support their programmers in writing programs and control peripherals. It was such

---

[88] JMC62. *Jaarverslag Stichting Mathematisch Centrum* [Annual Report Foundation Mathematical Center] (1962), p. 64.

[89] "Notulen van Electrologica-vergadering dd. 10-9-1960," p. 2. AEGON:171, X.008.13.053.7 G.

[90] "Notulen E.L. vergadering d.d. 14 maart 1961," p. 2. AEGON:171, X.008.13.053.7 G.

[91] "Notulen E.L.-vergadering d.d. 29 maart 1961-," p. 1. AEGON:171, X.008.13.053.7 G.

[92] "Notulen E.L.-vergadering dd. 21 oktober 1960," p. 1. AEGON:171, X.008.13.053.7 G.

[93] "Notulen van de vergadering gehouden op dinsdag 10 juni ten kantore van de Nillmij te 's-Gravenhage," p. 1. AEGON:171, X.008.13.053.7 G; "Notulen van de vergadering gehouden op donderdag 18 september 1958 op het Mathematisch Centrum te Amsterdam," p. 2. AEGON:171, X.008.13.053.7 G.

[94] "Subroutine-bibliotheek van de X 1 gebruiken," *Programmeermededeling* 12 (1 december 1959). Oud Archief AEGON. Afd. Documentatie nr. 254, X.046.1:658.564.

programs for programming that first came to be called software. For example, when in 1962 the Centraal Bureau voor de Statistiek eyed for the installation of magnetic tape units, it wanted to know whether Electrologica would include with the hardware the service of delivering or help to compose programs for sorting, aggregating, and conversion.[95] From 1960 on, also in the field of administrative applications, the demand grew for programming languages. And indeed in the USA higher level programming languages such as COBOL were designed for the administrative domain. Electrologica, on this side of the ocean, needed more time than anticipated to fulfill the promises for administrative software. On top of that, at the start of the 1960s the board of Electrologica realized they needed to develop a successor to the X1, which also would entail a growing need for software.

3.4 Seeking a Successor: X0 and X2, or the X8

3.4.1 Ambitious Successors to the X1

From the outset, Electrologica knew it had to build a successor to the X1. By the end of 1959, the company was not sure what machine to build. Would it envisage a large computer, or, like the X1, go for a medium-sized system at about fl 1,500,000? And Engelfriet wished to preserve the option of building smaller machines dedicated to administrative applications. One year before, in 1958, the board had even discussed building a decimal machine with lots of peripherals for the purpose.[96] But later, in 1960, Van Wijngaarden issued a warning that the X1 was about to lose its attraction even for scientific computing.[97] Decisions about a successor to the X1, an X2, would bear no further delay.

Soon, the technical director of Electrologica reported that it would be impossible to sufficiently speed up the memory of the X1, say by 20 times. Elementary arithmetical operations in under 10 µs should be feasible. The board lamented that, particularly for administrative applications, Electrologica still did not know exactly what was wanted.[98] During 1961, two concepts were presented, a large and fast computer for scientific applications, the X2, and a smaller administrative machine, the X0:

- For the X2, the research and development department reported that by using newer and faster transistors, the speed of the X2 could be increased 30-fold compared to

[95] "Brief van Prof. Dr. Ph. J. Idenburg, directeur-generaal van de statistiek, aan Prof. Dr. J. Engelfriet, directeur Nillmij, over X1-installatie, 27 juni 1962." AEGON:171, X.008.13.053.7 G.

[96] "Notulen van de vergadering gehouden op woensdag 1 oktober 1958 ten kantore van de Nillmij te 's-Gravenhage," p. 2. AEGON:171, X.008.13.053.7 G.

[97] "Notulen E.L.-vergadering d.d. 26-7-1960," p. 2. AEGON:171, X.008.13.053.7 G.

[98] "Notulen E.L. vergadering d.d. 29 november 1960, gehouden in de fabriek," p. 2. AEGON:171, X.008.13.053.7 G.

the X1. Using even faster transistors made little sense, since increasing the speed of the memory access accordingly was beyond their powers.

The advent of programming languages had an impact on the design of the X2. Designers contemplated the idea of adding special machine instructions to facilitate ALGOL 60 compilers. On the downside, they noted that such dedicated instructions might not be very useful for other programming languages. And the X2 should certainly be capable to run many different programming languages, so they thought. To resolve this issue, they looked into introducing some sort of microprogramming. That would allow them to create a variable instruction set.

Besides the peripherals for which connections had already been construed to the X1, they would like to add a large random-access memory, like a drum or disk memory. Magnetic tape units, punched card machines, and printers appeared on their wish list as well. Finally, the designers dreamt of time-sharing features.[99]

- The X0 was envisaged as a totally different machine. Not a successor of the X1, as such, but an improved version of the X1 dedicated to administrative applications. By using functional bits in the instruction set, this X0 was thought to be easy to program. Floating-point arithmetic should be a built-in feature. Customers should be given the option to connect the X0 to very large memory units. For the ease of input and output, the designers had in mind to offer a choice of character-reading devices, telecommunication devices, punched card machines, and magnetic tape units.[100]

Aiming at computer speeds as envisioned for the X2, implied speculations on the use of new and unfamiliar components. The result was a high degree of uncertainty whether the X2 project was achievable in the short term. Therefore, halfway 1961, Electrologica decided to first focus on developing the X0. The board was convinced that in six months, enough progress would have been made to officially announce an X0. An initial price was estimated just below that of the X1, assuming that margins on the X0 would be large enough to lower the price later.[101]

By the end of 1961, the concept of the X0 was taking shape. It would consist of a basic machine, with punched card I/O, and two magnetic tape units, extendable to four units. A fast printer and a large random-access memory were optional. For programming the X0, Electrologica wanted a fully interpretative system. The use of functional bits allowed microprogramming the instructions, i.e., before delivery in the "dead" memory. The instruction set was thus easily adaptable to various programming languages, and could, in particular, be set to facilitate the construction of a COBOL compiler, by that time the typical choice for administrative applications. Although the memory and logic of the machine would be much faster than that of the X1, the interpretative nature of the X0 system would result in a machine of similar speed as the X1.[102]

---

[99] "Beschouwingen betreffende toekomstige machines" (19 mei 1961). AEGON:171, X.008.13.053.7 G.

[100] "Verdere toekomstige mogelijkheden" (23 mei 1961). AEGON:171, X.008.13.053.7 G.

[101] "Notulen E.L.-vergadering d.d. 26 juni 1961," p. 2. AEGON:171, X.008.13.053.7 G.

[102] "Notulen E.L.-vergadering d.d. 22 december 1961," p. 2. AEGON:171, X.008.13.053.7 G.

Meanwhile, research and development for the X1 in a number of projects and dreams, was ongoing. Too little experience and expertise was available to turn the advanced ideas for an X0 into a practical design.[103] While six months before, Electrologica had moved its focus to the X0, in early 1962, it turned its sails again and decided to continue the work on the X2 as well, and tried to accommodate the customers for a scientific computer. The board held that developing an X2 might go a lot faster than creating a completely new design for the X0. The X2 was intended to be similar to the X1, be it equipped with floating-point arithmetic in hardware rather than in software.[104]

Delays pushed the prospected price of an X0 system. To be profitable annual sales had to reach 25 machines per year, which in turn demanded a considerable expansion of the company's sales team. A cheaper X0 would compromise the design. By consequence the introduction of the X0 had to be postponed. Electrologica had been working on the X0 for too long, particularly in the face of what was happening outside.[105] If the X0 was to target the market for smaller customers, IBM's 1400 series presented an insurmountable competition. The X0 might even turn out to be more expensive. It was time for Electrologica to rethink, but the board of directors had no idea how. Loopstra, the technical director, exclaimed "it would be better if the commercial department would formulate what exactly should be built."[106]

Facing the decision to put the development of the X0 on hold, Engelfriet, Dek and Schmidt returned to the idea of upgrading the X1. They would extend the X1 with more peripherals, like a drum memory, a disc memory, fast magnetic tape units, and a fast tape puncher.[107] But the X1 was not suitable to connect so many extra peripherals. What could be done was to speed up the X1 by about 8 times, and to connect a limited number of peripherals. Varying versions of the X1 could be sold, each version with a different, but limited set of peripherals. Electrologica's board liked this idea because it could be realized at relatively low cost.[108]

The X0 on hold and the X2 stalled put Electrologica in an untenable position in the market. It had to shelve its dreams of an administrative machine and to appease its customers in the field of scientific computing, and act swiftly at that.

3.4.2 A Realistic Successor to the X1, the X8

Utrecht University was the first to lose its patience. Waiting for an X2, it had received a very good offer from Electrologica's English competitor Elliot. Elliot was to deliver an Elliot 503 computer with 8000 words of memory at a price below fl 800,000. It

---

[103] "Notulen E.L.-vergadering d.d. 22 december 1961," p. 2. AEGON:171, X.008.13.053.7 G.

[104] "Notulen E.L.-vergadering d.d. 3 april 1962," p. 1. AEGON:171, X.008.13.053.7 G.

[105] "Notulen E.L.-vergadering d.d. 3 mei 1962." AEGON:171, X.008.13.053.7 G.

[106] "Notulen E.L.-vergadering d.d. 19 oktober 1962." AEGON:171, X.008.13.053.7 G.

[107] "Enkele conclusies en overwegingen besproken door Prof. Engelfriet, Hr. Dek en Hr. Schmidt op 27 oktober 1962." AEGON:171, X.008.13.053.7 G.

[108] "Notulen E.L.-vergadering d.d. 29 oktober 1962," p. 1. AEGON:171, X.008.13.053.7 G.

Fig. 3.4 Cover of an Electrologica X8 brochure from the mid-1960s. The text reads: "Electronic calculation and administration machine"

promised that, in case of delay, Utrecht University would get an Elliot 803 computer free-of-charge, until the moment of delivery.

For fear of losing its first customer for the X2, Electrologica immediately made Utrecht University a counter-offer: "*Our proposal*: To build for Utrecht a computer with exactly the same code as the X1 (hereafter called X1-prime), with a speed-up of 1:8, both with respect to the memory and operations. Not included [in this speed-up], of course, input and output devices. The machine will contain 16,000 words [of memory] and have floating-point arithmetic built-in. Furthermore: punched tape reader, typewriter, and tape puncher."[109] The offer came with a discount, and an X1 for rent until the completion of the X1-prime.[110] Within a month, Electrologica renamed "X1-prime" to "X8" (Fig. 3.4).

Utrecht University was the first customer to order an X8. The Mathematical Center followed soon after. To keep Utrecht University happy with the choice for the X8, Electrologica sped up production by building the X8 prototype and the first copy of

---

[109] "Electronisch Rekencentrum der Rijksuniversiteit Utrecht" (1 november 1962), p. 1. AE-GON:171, X.008.13.053.7 G.

[110] "Electronisch Rekencentrum der Rijksuniversiteit Utrecht" (1 november 1962), p. 1. AE-GON:171, X.008.13.053.7 G.

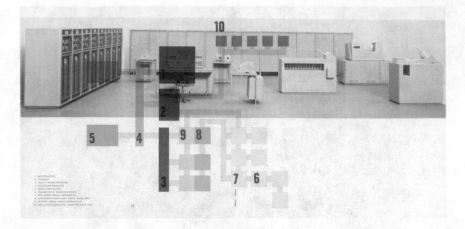

Fig. 3.5 Schematic overview of the X8 computer overlaid on a photo of a trade show maquette of the X8 from an Electrologica X8 brochure from the mid-1960s

the series production. The prototype was to be installed at the Mathematical Center given its experience in working with computers of unfinished appearance.[111]

Electrologica intended to accommodate customers for whom the X1 was getting outdated, and who could not wait for an X2 either. Development and delivery of the X8 got priority over the lingering desire for an X2 and an X0. The X8 clearly aimed at scientific computation. Even so, Electrologica would not give up the wish to build an administrative machine, and envisioned that the X8 would be an attractive option for administrative work by connecting all sorts of peripherals to it (Fig. 3.5).[112]

The X8 system consisted of a central unit: the basic machine with memory. The minimal configuration had a core memory of 16,384 words that could be upgraded to 262,144 words of 27 bits plus a parity bit. For the X1, Electrologica had built the core memory in-house. Now, for the X8, memory was purchased from an external manufacturer. A novelty in the X8 setup was the central device to control input and output, called CHARON, "Centraal Hulporgaan Autonome Regeling Overdracht Nevenapparatuur." Per type of I/O device, multiple peripherals could be connected and use the memory of the X8 independently from the central processing unit.[113]

The peripherals available at the outset were a teleprinter, a clock, an EL 1000 fast punched tape reader, a tape puncher, a printer, a drum memory, magnetic tape units, and also a magnetic disc storage. At a later stage, customers could connect a period clock, telecommunication devices, punched card machines, an optical reader, a magnetic character reader, a multi-channel selector, a photo-printer, Plessy memory,

[111] "Notulen E.L.-vergadering d.d. 10 december 1962." AEGON:171, X.008.13.053.7 G.

[112] "Notulen EL-vergadering gehouden op donderdag 29 november 1962 ten kantore van de Nillmij te 's-Gravenhage," p. 2. AEGON:171, X.008.13.053.7 G.

[113] Electrologica. 196xc. Electrologica ELX-series. General Description. Rijswijk. https://web.archive.org/web/20070719094844/http://kmt.hku.nl/~hans/pdf_files/electrologica-engl.pdf. Accessed 10 February 2022, p. 6.

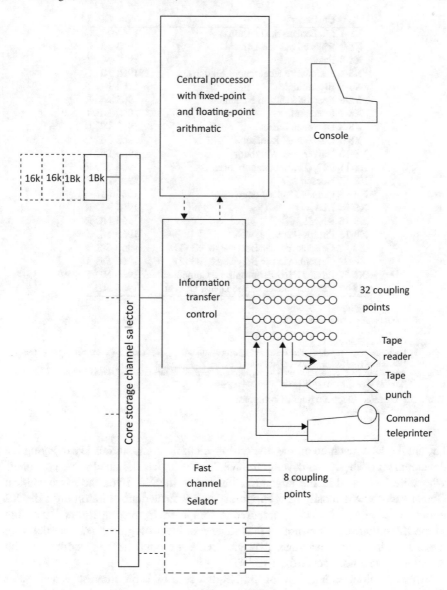

Fig. 3.6 Schema of the Electrologica X8 computer system

and even an X1 computer.[114] Thus, at stage two, Electrologica meant to satisfy administrative customers as well (Fig. 3.6).

Despite efforts to make the X8 suitable for administrative applications, the listing of X8 computers in operation leaves little doubt (cf. Table 3.3). The Electrologica X8 found its customers in the field of scientific computation exclusively. The X8 was, by

---

[114] "Verslag EL-vergadering d.d. 30 mei 1963." AEGON:171, X.008.13.053.7 G.

# Customer	Year	CC	I
X8-1 Mathematisch Centrum	1963	NL	C
X8-2 Rijksuniversiteit Utrecht	1963	NL	U
X8-3 Fokker	1963	NL	I
X8-4 Technische Hogeschool Eindhoven	1963	NL	U
X8-5 Electrologica	1963	NL	I
X8-6 Reactor Centrum Nederland	1963	NL	R
X8-7 Interatom	1963	DE	I
X8-8 Universiteit Kiel	1963	DE	U
X8-9 Universiteit Karlsruhe	1963	DE	U
X8-10 Universiteit Würzburg	1963	DE	U
X8-11 PTT (Dr. Neherlaboratorium)	1964	NL	R
X8-12 Hoesch AG	1964	DE	I
X8-13 Grande Dixence (stuwdam)	1964	CH	H
X8-14 IKO	1965	NL	R
X8-15 KNMI	1965	NL	R
X8-16 Philips (NatLab)	1965	NL	I
X8-?? Gelsenkirchener Bergwerke AG (1)	1966	DE	I
X8-?? Gelsenkirchener Bergwerke AG (2)	1966	DE	I
X8-?? Philips (HIG Electronische Componenten)	1966	NL	I
X8-?? Centrale Melkcontrole Dienst Utrecht	1966	NL	I

     # : Serial number of the X8 computer
Year : Order year
   CC : Customer country code
    I : Main industry in which the customer operated: I(ndustry), R(esearch), C(omputer service center),
        U(niversity) or H(ydroelectric power station)
Sources : Annual reports Electrologica 1963, 1964, 1965 and "periodieke rapportering," 2 maart 1966. Also: Philips,
        "Philips Data Systems 1959–1969" (year unknown).

Table 3.3 Ordered Electrologica X8 computers

far, not the best machine on the market for scientific computation. By delaying the development of the X2 to develop the X8, Electrologica alienated some customers who were interested in the larger X2, but not in the X8. Even the Mathematical Center saw the X8 mostly as a temporary and intermediate solution until the X2 could be delivered.[115] Worse, compared to computers from competitors, the design of the X2 at that stage was not all that advanced. Electrologica hoped that delaying the X2 could be an advantage. It might create the opportunity to come up with something even more powerful later.[116]

After an initial enthusiasm for the X8, ten sold in 1963, interest waned. Sales dropped quickly, to three orders in 1964 and 1965, and another four in 1966. Electrologica blamed the lack of X8's success to the growing competition from abroad,[117] in particular, IBM. On April 7th, 1964, IBM announced the "third generation" of computers, the IBM System/360. Announced as a family of computers, the IBM System/360 offered a range of machines of increasing power, supposedly compatible, software for one machine in the range was to be portable to any of the other models.

---

[115] "Notulen E.L.-vergadering d.d. 10 december 1962," p. 1. AEGON:171, X.008.13.053.7 G.

[116] "Notulen E.L.-vergadering d.d. 10 december 1962," p. 1. AEGON:171, X.008.13.053.7 G.

[117] N.V. Electrologica "Jaarverslag 1964" ('s-Gravenhage). AEGON:171, X.008.13.053.7 G.

IBM had the position in the market to authoritatively define a new, "third," generation of computers. Electrologica did not compare. The X1 was no longer interesting for the market and the X8 had been introduced too late.

3.4.3 Users Get Involved: The Z8 Software Committee

A failure from a commercial point of view, the X8 did satisfy the small circle of its customers. These involved themselves as an active user group, turning the use of the X8 into a better experience. In particular, they stepped up to write software for scientific computing for the X8. Their contributions allowed Electrologica's programmers to focus on system software and administrative software.

In the summer of 1963, Professor Weise from the University of Kiel asked Electrologica if his department could be commissioned to write a Fortran compiler for the X8. He expected to order an X8 later that year.[118] In June of that year, Electrologica held a meeting with a team at Utrecht University, to discuss their ambition to develop a simple assembler, or auto-code, for the X1 they had on rent. During the meeting, parties came to the conclusion that it would be more prudent for the Utrecht University team to write an assembler for the X8 instead.[119] Electrologica called this assembly language for the X8, "ELAN," short for "Electrologica LANguage."[120] Other customers also expressed interest to develop such an auto-code,[121] and Electrologica expected that various customers would develop compilers and other software for the X8 anyway. To coordinate these efforts, and to avoid duplication, Electrologica created the committee "Z8" and sought the participation of the best and brightest of Dutch computer science. Z8 would pronounce "zacht," which is Dutch for soft, as in software. Electrologica intended Aad van Wijngaarden to chair the committee, and wanted Willem van der Poel on board, known for his Stantec ZEBRA computer and for "functional bits" in defining instructions, as well as Edsger Dijkstra, who had been called to a chair at the Eindhoven University of Technology in 1962.[122]

Most Dutch research institutes and universities that ordered an X8 participated in the Z8 committee. If considered a user group, the committee gathered the very elite users. Each of the institutes took on a specific task:

- The Mathematical Center wrote an ALGOL 60 compiler, just as it had done for the X1.
- Dr. Neher laboratory of the Dutch PTT wrote a tracer program and ELAN assembler.
- Utrecht University also wrote an ELAN assembler.

---

[118] "Notulen EL-vergadering d.d. 14-6-1963," p. 2. AEGON:171, X.008.13.053.7 G.

[119] "Verslag bespreking "Autocode" X1 dd. 20 juni 1963." AEGON:171, X.008.13.053.7 G.

[120] For more information about ELAN, see Electrologica (1966).

[121] "Notulen EL-vergadering d.d. 9.7.1963." AEGON:171, X.008.13.053.7 G.

[122] "Notulen EL-vergadering d.d. 3-9-1963." AEGON:171, X.008.13.053.7 G.

- Eindhoven University of Technology, under leadership of Dijkstra, wrote the famous THE-multiprogramming operating system[123] with its own ALGOL 60 compiler.
- University of Kiel wrote a FORTRAN compiler.

The Z8 committee and its members covered the software for the X8 for scientific computing. That left Electrologica with much software to write. In particular, the company had to develop the basic software controlling the input and output. Electrologica greatly improved the connectivity to the X8 compared to the X1. Instead of controlling all peripherals by the main computer, it used the separate component, CHARON. The Electrologica programming department wrote the software to control the interaction between CHARON and the X8. The same group was responsible for all software for administrative applications, and would write some of the software for scientific computing.

The task was gigantic. Electrologica estimated that its programming department would need to write about 130,000 lines of code for the X8, taking about 130 man-year.[124] The department grew, both in terms of number of programmers and budget, but Electrologica was not up for the task. It failed to complete a COBOL compiler, which was estimated to take tens of thousands of instructions and many man-years of effort.[125] More so, the programmers found that they would have to extend the X8 instruction set to write a correct implementation of COBOL.[126] As an alternative, they tried to write a COBOL compiler in ALGOL 60. That project failed as well. Without the software, the X8 was just not a suitable computer for administrative applications. And none of the customers tried to use it in that field.

3.5 The ELX Series Marked the End

After making a profit in the early 1960s, Electrologica suffered major losses in 1963 and 1964. A reversal of that trend seemed unlikely.[127] In an almost desperate attempt to compete with IBM's System/360 in the Dutch market, Electrologica countered with its own "family" of increasingly more powerful but compatible computers. In 1964, Electrologica announced two different ranges of computers, the X2, X4, and X8 series, and the X3, X5, and X8 series.[128] The ELX series computers targeted small and medium-sized companies. The X2 and X3 were the starter machines of both series. Customers wanting more power or more capacity, could upgrade to

---

[123] Dijkstra, Edsger W. 1968. The structure of the THE-multiprogramming system. *Communications of the ACM* 11(5):341–346. https://www.cs.utexas.edu/users/EWD/ewd01xx/EWD196.PDF.

[124] "Notulen EL-vergadering 20-4-1966," p. 2. AEGON:171, X.008.13.053.7 G.

[125] "Communicatiebijeenkomst medewerkers HA Verkoop en Bedrijfadviezen en HA Programma Research" (28-5-1965). AEGON:171, X.008.13.053.7 G.

[126] "Notulen EL-vergadering 19-8-1965," p. 1. AEGON:171, X.008.13.053.7 G.

[127] Wit, de (1992), p. 277.

[128] N.V. Electrologica, "Jaarverslag 1964" ('s-Gravenhage). AEGON:171, X.008.13.053.7 G.

Fig. 3.7 Cover of an Electrologica brochure for the even ELX series with subtitle "Electronic administration machines," from the mid-1960s

the next machine in the series, the X4 or X5. The top of both series was the X8. Electrologica explained: "These EL systems can grow as the company grows, since their flexibility is practically unlimited. With the smallest model one may lay the foundations for the largest installation (Fig. 3.7)."[129]

With the even ELX series, Electrologica tried to revive the dream of developing computers for administrative applications. For scientific computing, it recommended the odd-numbered series because these computers had built-in floating-point arithmetic. As a result, the odd series consisted of more expansive machines with respect to registers, machine code operations, and index registers. Other than that, the two series were the same.[130] Because the X8 also had built-in floating-point arithmetic, the computers in the odd series resembled the X8 more than those computers in the even-numbered series. By implication computers in the odd series were more compatible with the X8. Thus programs written for the X3 could be run on the X5 and X8, or vice versa, provided there was enough memory in the smaller computers.[131]

The only difference between the starter computers and the middle computers in the series was the number of possible connected peripherals. The smallest machines could not work together with a magnetic drum, magnetic disc, or fast magnetic tape units because the system lacked the fast channel selector. Each system in the series

[129] Electrologica. 1965a. Electrologica EL elektronische informatieverwerkende systemen ELX3, ELX5. Den Haag: N.V. Electrologica 1966. Rijksarchief in Noord-Holland, Archief van de Stichting Mathematisch Centrum, 1946–1980, inv. nr. 52, p. 5, RAHN, SMC.

[130] Electrologica. 1965b. Electrologica EL elektronische informatieverwerkende systemen ELX2, ELX3, ELX4, ELX5. Den Haag: N.V. Electrologica 1966. Rijksarchief in Noord-Holland, Archief van de Stichting Mathematisch Centrum, 1946–1980, inv. nr. 52, pp. 1, 2, RAHN, SMC.

[131] Electrologica (1965a), p. 9.

# Customer	Year	CC	I
X2-1 Willem Smit Transformatoren[1]	1964	NL	I
X2-2 Verenigde Touwfabrieken	1965	NL	I
X2-3 Intromart	1965	NL	R
X2-4 Belgische Spoorwegen	1965	BE	T
X4-1 C.M.C.D.	1965	??	I
X4-?[2] Willem Smit Transformatoren	1966	NL	I
X4-?[2] Steenkolenhandelsvereniging NV	1966	NL	I

: Serial number of the X2/4 system
Year : Order year
CC : Customer country code
 I : Main industry in which the customer operated: I(ndustry), R(esearch), T(ransport).

[1] : Unclear if this was an X2 or an X3. The annual report of 1964 notes that Willem Smit Transformatoren ordered an X3. However, in all other sources it is put under X2.
[2] : Unclear if these two computers were actually ordered. And if they were, it is unclear if they were X2 or X4 machines.

Sources : Annual reports Electrologica 1964, 1965, "Periodieke rapportering 2 maart 1966," and Philips, "Philips Data Systems 1959–1969" (year unknown).

Table 3.4 Orders for the Electrologica X2, X3, X4 en X5 computers

could connect to a fast punched tape reader, a tape puncher, line printer, teleprinter, magnetic tape units, punched card machines, plotter, telecommunication devices, measuring devices, and a clock.[132]

The minimum configuration of an ELX series computer system consisted of a basic machine with a core memory of 4069 words of 28 bits including a parity bit. Customers could extend that memory to 32,768 words. All computers could be programmed with ELAN; an ELAN assembler was part of the standard software. Furthermore, Electrologica would deliver testing programs, sorting programs, tabulating programs, communication programs, a programming library, and more. For the X3 and X5, customers could also run FORTRAN and ALGOL compilers. Finally, the X4 and X5 would support multiprogramming.[133]

As early as August 1965, Electrologica decided to give up the even-numbered series, and focus on the X3 and X5 series. Cutting one of the two series, the company hoped to gain enough time to develop software and documentation. The X3 would be on offer for the price of an X2.[134] Although, no X3 or X5 machines were ordered, Electrologica did receive four orders for an X2 computer, and a single order for the X4 (Table 3.4). It is unclear if these X2 and X4 computers were actually X2 and X4 machines, or if these customers got a rebranded X3 or an X5 machine instead.

---

[132] Electrologica (1965b), pp. 1, 2; Electrologica (1965a), p. 9.

[133] Electrologica (1965b), p. 5.

[134] "Notulen EL-vergadering 19-8-1965," p. 2. AEGON:171, X.008.13.053.7 G; "Notulen EL-vergadering 26-8-1965," p. 1. AEGON:171, X.008.13.053.7 G.

Time failed Electrologica to turn the ELX series into a success. Two years after the announcement of the two ELX series, Electrologica was sold to Philips Computer Industry. Almost invisibly, the first Dutch computer industry came to an end.

Acknowledgements I thank *Stichting PAOi* for enabling me to investigate the history of Dutch computer science in the 1950s and early 1960s. During my investigations of Electrologica's history, I was greatly helped by P. Don, archivist at AEGON, to dig up sources about Nillmij and Electrologica from this era.

Chapter 4
Software Without Memory

Paul Klint
Centrum Wiskunde & Informatica, SWAT.engineering, Amsterdam,
The Netherlands

Abstract A personal view of the history of computer science in the Netherlands with some key figures and institutes that dominated the field in the early years is provided. The key figures are Frielink, van Wijngaarden, Blaauw, van der Poel, Dijkstra, and Kruseman Aretz. The institutes are the Mathematisch Centrum, the Dr Neherlab, the Natlab, the three technical universities, and the University of Amsterdam. It is remarkable that this recent history seems to be largely forgotten.

4.1 Introduction

Software and memory form a complex marriage: some even claim that software should not have any memory at all and have mostly eliminated the concept of a global state from their favorite language. I will not address *that* controversy.

There are, however, other aspects of memory that affect software. First and foremost, the lack of historical awareness of software researchers and practitioners alike. Such negligence has a negative impact on our field: old concepts and ideas are reinvented and recycled on a regular basis. They get new names and are presented as the next breakthrough. Forgetfulness not only deprives the original inventors of their deserved credits, it also robs us of the original motivation for and experience with the concepts, thus hampering real progress. Passing on experiences is part of the growth of a discipline. Standing on the shoulders of one's predecessors is better than standing on the floor. In this paper, I will try to contribute to the historical awareness of computer science by presenting a personal view on some key figures that dominated the field.

A tangential aspect of memory that affects software is the *lack* of memory. I will briefly touch upon early day solutions for that problem.

This paper focusses on the developments in the Netherlands exclusively and refrains from any attempt to position them in an international context.

Fig. 4.1 Early computer science research in the Netherlands

4.2 Early Computer Science in the Netherlands

Locations. My personal selection of crucial locations for the development of Computer Science in the Netherlands[1] is shown on the map in Fig. 4.1. These represent the main research and development locations in the period 1945–1970. In Delft the **Technische Hogeschool** (TH,[2] today: TUD, Delft University of Technology), was founded in 1842 aiming at the education of civil engineers. Its departments of Mechanical Engineering, of Electrical Engineering and of Physics together and in competition constituted a most fruitful breeding ground for advanced computing. In fact Aad van Wijngaarden, Willem van der Poel, and Gerrit Blaauw all had their initial education in this institute. Computer Science, as a study course avant la lettre, gradually grew in the 1960s as a specialization inside the newly established course of Mathematical Engineering. Around the corner from Delft, in The Hague, Dutch postal service PTT in 1946 established its Central Laboratory, after a decade re-

---

[1] Alberts, Gerard, and Bas van Vlijmen. 2017. *Computerpioniers: het begin van het computertijdperk in Nederland*. Amsterdam: Amsterdam University Press.

[2] Kamp, A.F., ed. 1955. *De Technische Hogeschool te Delft 1905–1955*. 's-Gravenhage: SDU. Baudet, H. 1992. *De lange weg naar de Technische Universiteit Delft*. Den Haag: SDU.

named **Dr Neherlaboratorium** (NeherLab)[3] and now part of TNO research. This very laboratory had a Mathematics Department offering a home to Willem van der Poel during his computer construction years in the 1950s.

Eindhoven housed the same combination of a university and an industrial laboratory. **Philips Natuurkundig Laboratorium** (NatLab)[4] was founded in 1914 as the research department of Dutch electronics company Philips. While the company as such was slow in entering computer production—the computer division PCI was established only in 1962—the NatLab created space for experiments in computer construction and even software. **Technische Hogeschool Eindhoven** (THE, today: TU/e, Eindhoven University of Technology)[5] was the second polytechnic of the Netherlands, founded in 1956. Like in Delft, the Mathematics study course saw a specialization in Computer Science. Eindhoven became the home for Edsger Dijkstra, when he was appointed to a chair in Computer Science, and for Frans Kruseman Aretz for the second part of his career.

Amsterdam cherishes a long academic tradition. The Athenaeum Illustre of 1632 turned **Universiteit van Amsterdam** (UvA, the University of Amsterdam)[6] in the 19th Century. After WW II its strong mathematics department offered a special professorship to Aad van Wijngaarden in 1952 and saw both Van der Poel and Dijkstra defend their doctoral dissertations with him. Among the immediate postwar research institutes, the **Mathematisch Centrum** (MC) (today: Centrum voor Wiskunde & Informatica)[7] was the first, founded February 11th 1946, with a goal to promote the systematic study of pure and applied mathematics as well as their applications. One of its four sections was the Computation Department, headed by Van Wijngaarden. This is the spot where, next to commissioned Numerical Analysis, computers were constructed and thoughts on software were developed in a systematic way.

Computer construction grew too big and met with commercial demand, occasioning the spin-off of computer construction into the private enterprise Electrologica. Electrologica was the manufacturer of the X8. The systematics of thinking about programming started by hiring Edsger Dijkstra in the spring of 1952 "for the programming of the ARRA," the ARRA then still existing as an automatic computer under construction. In the autumn of that year Gerrit Blaauw returned from the USA and joined the Mathematisch Centrum team.

---

[3] Nieuwe Giessen, D. van de. 1996. *Onderzoek en ontwikkeling bij KPN. Een geschiedenis van de eerste honderd jaar*. Leidschendam: KPN Research.

[4] Vries, Marc de., and Kees Boersma. 2005. *80 Years of Research at the Philips Natuurkundig Laboratorium (1914–1994); the Role of the Nat.Lab. at Philips*. Amsterdam: Pallas Publications.

[5] Bakker, M.S.C., and W.H.P.M. van Hooff. 1991. *Gedenkboek Technische Universiteit Eindhoven, 1956–1991*. Eindhoven: Technische Universiteit Eindhoven; Rem, Martin, and Hans Schippers. 2006. Operating Systems; Edsger W. Dijkstra en zijn THE systeem. In *Gedreven door nieuwsgierigheid; een selectie uit 50 jaar TU/e onderzoek*, edited Lintsen, Harry, and Hans Schippers, 225–231. Stichting Historie der Techniek en Technische Universiteit Eindhoven, Eindhoven.

[6] Miert, Dirk van. 2005. *Illuster onderwijs: het Amsterdamse Athenaeum in de Gouden Eeuw 1632–1704*. Amsterdam: Bakker; Knegtmans, P.J. 1998. *Een kwetsbaar centrum van de geest: de Universiteit van Amsterdam tussen 1935 en 1950*. Amsterdam: Amsterdam University Press.

[7] Alberts, Gerard. 1998a. *Jaren van berekening. Toepassingsgerichte initiatieven in de Nederlandse wiskunde-beoefening 1945–1960*. Amsterdam: Amsterdam University Press.

Fig. 4.2 Key historical figures of Dutch computing: Frielink, van Wijngaarden, Blaauw, van der Poel, Dijkstra, and Kruseman Aretz

The third polytechnic in the Netherlands was **Technische Hogeschool Twente** (THT, today: UT, University of Twente)[8] Enschede, founded in 1961. After a further career in the USA with IBM, Gerrit Blaauw returned to the Netherlands again to join THT (Fig. 4.2).

People. Dutch computer science has been fragmented from the start, or even before its start. One way of analyzing this fragmentation is by tracing the work and influence of a number of key figures[9] whom I will call the "builders." We will encounter builders of research schools, of schools in accountancy and in computer science. We will also encounter builders of computers and builders of software.

Building Research Schools. Abraham Barend Frielink[10] (1917–1998) was accountant by education and was appointed professor in administrative organization in 1957 at the Faculty of Economic Sciences of the Universiteit van Amsterdam. Frielink was the junior one among the team of professors in accountancy who followed in 1958 a course in Amsterdam organized by John Diebold as an instigation to promote office automation. He took up the position of director of SSAA, the Stichting Studiecentrum Administratieve Automatisering resulting from that first initiative. SSAA, organizing conferences, publishing case-studies of computers installed in Dutch business and developing a program of research and education, was a natural partner in the debate on higher education in computing and automation. Frielink successfully chaired the committee on vocational education.

The debate on university education, by contrast, took 12 years without reaching a conclusion. The major point of controversy was the relation between the study

---

[8] Sorgdrager, Winnie. 1981. *Een experiment in het bos. De eerste jaren van de Technische Hogeschool Twente 1961–1972*. Alphen aan de Rijn: Samsom; Groenman, Bert, ed. 2001. *Van landgoed tot kenniscampus. Lustrumboek ter gelegenheid van het veertigjarig bestaan van de Universiteit Twente in Enschede*. Universiteit Twente, Enschede.

[9] By focusing on a small group of persons I will unfortunately be unable to mention and honor the many other pioneers that have contributed to Dutch computer science.

[10] Zutphen, Luc van. 1998. Ter nagedachtenis aan Abraham Barend Frielink Registeraccountant. *De Accountant* 1998(7):430; Bindenga, A.J., and H.H.J. Nordemann. 1984. *Hoor en wederhoor: artikelen aangeboden aan prof. dr. A. B. Frielink bij zijn afscheid als buitengewoon hoogleraar*. Amsterdam: Vakgroep Bedrijfsinformatica en Accountancy van de Faculteit der Economische Wetenschappen van de Universiteit van Amsterdam; Hartman, W. 1983. De betekenis van Frielink voor de informatica. In Bindenga (1984), 21–31.

of machines, software, and the study of fields where computers were used. Where was "Informatica," as the field of computer science was named in Dutch, to be located and what were to be the relations between the branches? Frielink had the depth of vision to not see these relations in terms of theory and applications, but to embrace the consequences of computerization of all fields of science and society. The consequence is that Informatica is everywhere. He suggested to approach the field as "paninformatica."

In 1980, Frielink received an honorary doctorate from the Vrije Universiteit Amsterdam. He wrote a standard treatise on accountancy (*Leerboek Accountantscontrole*[11]) that first appeared in 1985 and is still available. It has been studied by many generations of Dutch accountants. Since banks and insurance companies were early adopters of computers, Frielink clearly saw the societal impact of computers and viewed computer science as a pan disciplinary field of study.

Aad van Wijngaarden[12] (1916–1987) took his PhD in mechanical engineering at the Delft TH in December 1945. Soon afterwards he was hired to set up the Computing Department of the Mathematisch Centrum starting January 1st 1947. Later he served the Center as its director, from 1961 to 1981. Overseeing the construction of automatic calculators, hiring Gerrit Blaauw, teaching how to program the modern computing machines, hiring Edsger Dijkstra to do so, supervising Willem van der Poel in 1956 and Edsger Dijkstra in 1959 in what were arguably the first dissertations in computer science in the Netherlands, Van Wijngaarden prepared the ground for a strong research tradition in software.

He is known for his work on the programming languages Algol 60 and Algol 68. The road towards Algol 68 was paved with Van Wijngaarden's groundbreaking concepts of orthogonal design and the so-called two level grammars, also known as Van Wijngaarden grammars[13] or just W grammars. Identifying as a mathematician, Van Wijngaarden held a strong mathematical view on computer science. If the European discipline "Informatics" generally stands for a more theoretical orientation than computer science, Van Wijngaarden would steer towards the mathematical side of Informatics, in particular, in the struggle for a proper definition and institutionalization of an academic study course.

[11] Frielink, Abraham Barend, and J.C.E. van Kollenburg, eds. 2000. *Leerboek accountantscontrole*. Vols 1–8. Groningen: Noordhoff Uitgevers; Schoonderbeek, J.W. 1980. A.B. Frielink Eredoctor. *De Accountant* 1980(3):140–142. Hen, P.E. de (1995) Aartsvaders van het Nederlandse accountantsberoep. In: Hen, P.E. de (1995) *Hoofdstukken uit de geschiedenis van het Nederlandse accountantsberoep na 1935*. NIVRA, Amsterdam, pp. 247–262.

[12] Baayen, P.C., and J. Nuis. 1988. In memoriam A van Wijngaarden 1916–1987. *Nieuw Archief voor Wiskunde* 6(3):269–282; Alberts, G., and P.C. Baayen. 1987a. Ingenieur van taal. Interview met A. van Wijngaarden. In *Zij mogen uiteraard daarbij de zuivere wiskunde niet verwaarloozen*, eds. Alberts G., F. van der Blij, and J. Nuis, 276–288. Amsterdam: CWI; Bakker, J.W. de, and J.C. van Vliet, eds. 1981. *Algorithmic languages. Proceedings of the International Symposium on Algorithmic Languages*. Amsterdam: North-Holland.

[13] Wijngaarden, Adriaan van. 1965. Orthogonal Design and Description of a Formal Language. *Reports Stichting Mathematisch Centrum* MR 76. Mathematisch Centrum, Amsterdam. [https://ir.cwi.nl/pub/9208] cf. https://en.wikipedia.org/wiki/Van_Wijngaarden_grammar.

Both Frielink and Van Wijngaarden have had a large impact on Dutch computer science although they had diametrically opposing views. Frielink saw computer science as a crosscutting discipline and strongly valued applications, while Van Wijngaarden saw computer science primarily as a mathematical discipline. In the 1970s the mathematical view prevailed.

Van Wijngaarden's contributions have enriched various domains, including numerical analysis, programming languages, and formalization, but his mathematical vision has also hampered the further development of Dutch computer science with a (too) strong focus on formalization. Frielink's much broader view was only accepted much later by the majority of Dutch computer scientists.[14]

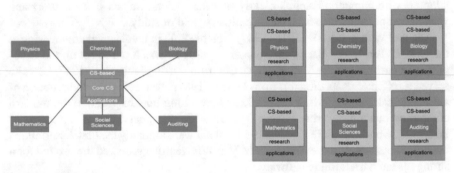

Fig. 4.3 1980s view on computer science (left) and today's view (right)

The classical self-image of Dutch computer science in 1980 is shown in Fig. 4.3 at the left. It consists of core computer science ("real" or "pure" computer science) and is surrounded by applications that directly use computer science results. There is a large distance to other research or application domains.

Today's view is shown in Fig. 4.3 at the right: computer science is used in each and every research or application domain. Software for modeling, simulation, and data analysis is becoming the key research tool in many disciplines. The proliferation of computer science in many domains and the lack of historical awareness leads to re-invention of the same idea over and over again. The role of mathematics is relatively diminishing in computer science itself but it is becoming more important for modeling aspects of computerization in many other domains. Clearly, Frielink's view was closer to today's reality than that of Van Wijngaarden. It is also obvious that computer science will face major challenges to avert the unavoidable reproduction crisis in research and to avoid societal accidents that will occur when the quality of software and data is not sufficiently guaranteed.

---

[14] The debate between these two schools of thought has been extensively documented in Dael, Ruud van. 2001. *'Iets met computers': over beroepsvorming van de informaticus*. Delft: Eburon.

Building Computers. Gerrit Blaauw[15] (1924–2018) graduated in Delft in Electrical Engineering, then left for the USA, where he renewed his engineering degree and continued to acquire his PhD in 1952 at Harvard under supervision of Howard Aiken for work on the Mark III and Mark IV computers.[16] Returning to the Netherlands he was the designer of the ARRA II at Mathematisch Centrum in Amsterdam. Parting for the USA a second time, he did leave his mark on the Amsterdam computer design which was to spin off from Mathematisch Centrum and became Electrologica. Blaauw joined IBM and is widely known as designer, next to Fred Brooks and Gene Amdahl, of IBM System/360, where they introduced concepts such as time sharing and virtual memory. Together with Fred Brooks he published the influential book *Computer Architecture: concepts and evolution*.[17] He joined Technische Hogeschool Twente in 1965 on the chair on Digitale Techniek, and from that position he helped shape the discipline of Informatica in the Netherlands.

Willem van der Poel[18] (1926), Delft Physics Engineer, got his PhD in 1956 at the Universiteit van Amsterdam under supervision of Van Wijngaarden. He worked for the Dr Neher Laboratory of Dutch PTT and is known for his work on early Dutch computers including PTERA, ZERO, and ZEBRA. The subject of his dissertation was the design of the latter machine.[19] The E in all these designs is for "Eenvoudig," ZE for "Zeer Eenvoudig," simple, very simple, reflecting the motto of simplicity that governed Van der Poel's career in "Informatica," the usual Dutch denominator for Computer Science. In 1962 he joined Technische Hogeschool Delft, establishing his very own research tradition in hardware but even more in software. When Electrologica announced its X8 computer, it gathered from its academic clients a committee for the software for this machine, Z8—in Dutch "zacht," or soft. Van der Poel was an influential member of Z8.

Willem van der Poel chaired the IFIP working group WG2.1 which designed Algol 68. He has built several implementations of Lisp and combinatory logic and he is a prolific designer of mechanical puzzles. He has also contributed to documenting the early history of computers in the Netherlands.[20]

Both Blaauw and Van der Poel are real engineers and Dutch computer pioneers. Blaauw was more focused on hardware, but he also used APL to describe the mean-

---

[15] Poel, Willem L. van der. 2019. Gerrit Anne Blaauw 17 juli 1924–21 maart 2018, *Levensberichten en herdenkingen 2019*, Koninklijke Nederlandse Akademie van Wetenschappen, Amsterdam, 22–25. https://www.knaw.nl/nl/actueel/publicaties/levensberichten-en-herdenkingen-2019/.

[16] Blaauw, Gerrit A. 1952. *The application of selenium rectifiers as switching devices in the Mark IV calculator*. Dissertation, Harvard University (Mass.).

[17] Amdahl, Gene, Gerrit Blaauw, and Fred Brooks. 1964. Architecture of the IBM system. *IBM Journal of Research and Development* 8(2):87–101; Blaauw, Gerrit A., and Frederick P. Brooks. 1997. *Computer architecture: Concepts and evolution*. Boston: Addison-Wesley Pub.

[18] Bogaard, Adriënne van den. 2008a. Styles of programming 1952–1972. *Studium* (Rotterdam, Netherlands) 1(2):128–144; cf. Alberts and Van Vlijmen (2017), Computerpioniers, Chapter 3; cf. https://en.wikipedia.org/ wiki/Willem_van_der_Poel.

[19] Poel, Willem L. van der. 1956. *The logical principles of some simple computers*. Dissertation, Gemeente Universiteit Amsterdam.

[20] Poel, Willem L. van der. 1989. De ontwikkeling van de computer in Nederland. *Histechnicon* 15(1):2–9

ing of machine instructions. Van der Poel also had a strong interest in programming languages. Both have had successors in Dutch academia but as a whole one may say that later attempts in designing and building computers never matched their early successes.

Building Software. Edsger Dijkstra[21] (1930–2002) joined Mathematisch Centrum in the spring of 1952 employed "for programming the ARRA," the first automatic computer which was then still under construction. Graduating in physics at the University of Leiden, he proceeded to take a PhD in 1959 at the Universiteit van Amsterdam under supervision of Van Wijngaarden, on *Communication with an automatic computer*.[22] The automatic computer under consideration was in fact Electrologica X1; his work a was case study in the design of input-output routines. Edsger Dijkstra, in cooperation with Jaap Zonneveld, wrote the first Algol 60 compiler for the Dutch Electrologica X1 computer. He revolutionized compiler design. Dijkstra was called to a professorship at the Technische Hogeschool Eindhoven, where he led a team designing the operating system for the university's Electrologica X8 computer, the THE operating system.

Dijkstra started his career at Mathematisch Centrum and later moved to Technische Hogeschool Eindhoven, Burroughs Corporation, and finally University of Texas. He was honored with the Turing award in 1972. Dijkstra evolved from a practicing programmer to a logician and was a strong proponent of a mathematical approach to software. His slogan "goto considered harmful" and his pleas for "structured programming" are well-known.

Frans Kruseman Aretz[23] (1933) got his PhD in physics[24] in 1962 at the Universiteit van Amsterdam under supervision of De Boer before succeeding Edsger Dijkstra at Mathematisch Centrum in 1962. He implemented the Milli operating system and a new Algol 60 compiler both for the Dutch Electrologica X8 computer. In 1966 he was appointed as professor at the Universiteit van Amsterdam on the chair of Programming methods for Numerical Mathematics. In 1969 he joined Philips NatLab, Physics Lab, and in 1971 he moved to THE, Technische Hogeschool Eindhoven. Kruseman Aretz has remained a prolific programmer while keeping a keen eye for the mathematical aspects of programming. He has also contributed to documenting the history of computing, for instance, by describing the Dijkstra-Zonneveld Algol 60 compiler for the Electrologica X1[25] that I have already mentioned above.

---

[21] Apt, K.R. 2002. Edsger Wybe Dijkstra (1930–2002): A portrait of a genius. *Formal Aspects of Computing* 14(2):92–98.

[22] Dijkstra, Edsger W. 1959a. *Communication with an automatic computer*. [PhD Thesis. October 28, 1959. Universiteit van Amsterdam]. Excelsior, Rijswijk

[23] Kruseman Aretz, Frans E.J. 1995. *33 jaar beoefening van de informatica*. Valedictory lecture. Technische Universiteit Eindhoven; cf. https://research.tue.nl/nl/persons/frans-ej-kruseman-aretz

[24] Kruseman Aretz, Frans E.J. 1962. *Moment expansions in the theory of cooperative phenomena, Dissertation*. Amsterdam: Gemeente Universiteit Amsterdam.

[25] Kruseman Aretz, Frans E.J. 2003. *The Dijkstra-Zonneveld ALGOL 60 compiler for the Electrologica X1*. CWI Report SEN-N301. Centrum voor Wiskunde en Informatica. Amsterdam, The

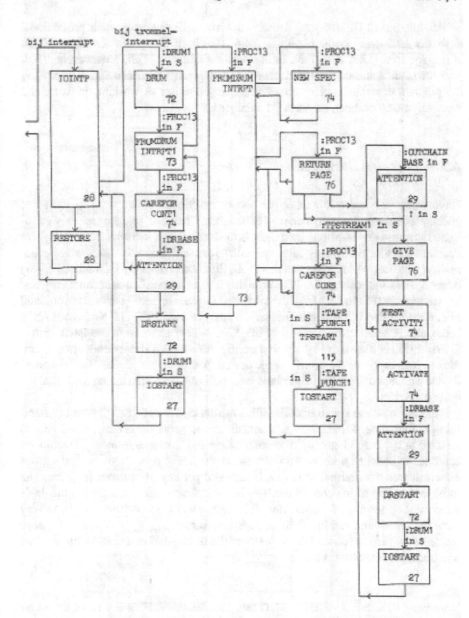

Fig. 4.4 Flow chart of the drum interrupt

A detailed reconstruction of this same compiler has recently been made by Van den Hove.[26]

As different as Dijkstra and Kruseman Aretz were as person, their professional activities had many commonalities. Both have built compilers for Algol 60 on X1, respectively, X8. Both have built operating systems: Milli, respectively, THE. Dijkstra made a mid-career switch from practicing programmer to logician focusing on program correctness. Kruseman Aretz stayed closer to working software and worked, amongst others, on parsing techniques.

4.3 A Personal Perspective

Having been a witness to part of the history described above I want to add some anecdotal evidence from my personal experience. Computer science was only established as a study course in its own right in the Netherlands in 1981. Before, de facto curricula in Informatica existed as specializations within mathematics, a.o. mathematical engineering in Delft (Van der Poel), Eindhoven (Dijkstra), Twente (Blaauw) or mathematics in Amsterdam (Van Wijngaarden), or as a variant of accountancy, e.g. in Amsterdam (Frielink). My personal "pre-computer science" education consisted of courses by Van Wijngaarden (numerical analysis, Algol 68) and Kruseman Aretz (computer programming[27] aimed at the X8). A flow chart from the latter course (1970–1971) is shown in Fig. 4.4. It describes how the Milli operating system handles an interrupt[28] of the drum storage device. A drum is a cylinder-shaped storage device with an outer magnetic surface. Information was written to and read from the outer surface.

"Limitations" are key to understanding the basic idea and discipline of programming at that time. Limitations in available memory (as further discussed below) resulted in the careful staging of computations and storing intermediate results on external media when necessary. Limited access to actual computer time had various effects. It was not unusual to have one time slot per day to run your program. The most trivial typo in job control cards or in the software itself could spoil the day's window of opportunity for a test run. This regime would force programmers to very carefully check and rethink their code before submitting it for a test run. Labor intensive indeed, but potentially superior to the testing-before-thinking attitude that one frequently encounters today.

Netherlands; Kruseman Aretz, Frans E.J. (2020). The Mathematical Center, ALGOL 60 and the Electrologica X8, Chap. 5, this volume.

[26] Hove, G. van den. 2019. *New insights form old programs, the structure of the first ALGOL 60 system*. PhD thesis. University of Amsterdam.

[27] The Dutch title was Programmeren van rekenautomaten; computers were called "rekenautomaat" (computing automaton).

[28] Drum (Dutch: "trommel") and interrupt (Dutch: "ingreep") lead to the unforgettable Dutch word "trommelingreep."

Fig. 4.5 The X8 paper punch

Although despised by a person like Dijkstra, testing is one of the pillars of programming. Many of the test techniques in use today have their origin in the early history of programming. One example is what is today called a "mock object," and, at the time a "stub" or "place holder." The idea was to design a system in a top-down fashion and to test it before all parts of the system had been programmed in full detail. For testing purposes, not yet finished program parts were replaced by a place holder that mimicked the behavior of the unfinished part for some fixed test values.

One of the external devices I alluded to above is the, now obsolete, tape punch device (Fig. 4.5) that produced paper tapes with punched holes to represent information. This device had to be controlled by the X8 operating system Milli and a device driver was needed for that purpose.[29] The ELAN code (the assembly language of the X8) for the punch driver is shown in Fig. 4.6 and originates from Kruseman Aretz' course notes.

Two aspects of software and memory (or the lack thereof) cannot remain unmentioned here. First, compilers use multiple phases to process their input and produce output and that is not a problem with today's ample main memory and file systems. What to do when those are missing? Answer: produce intermediate results on paper tape. Each phase reads the results from the previous phase, does the required processing, and produces a new tape to be consumed by the succeeding phase.

Second, when memory is scarce, programmers have to resort to tricks to reduce memory usage. One of these tricks is self-modifying code that is possible in computer architectures where storage for executable code and for data are not distinguished or protected.

Consider two solutions to code a statement like

```
IF FLAG THEN A ELSE B END.
```

---

[29] Watch https://www.youtube.com/watch?v=0WpVQidHfag if you want to see a tape punch in action.

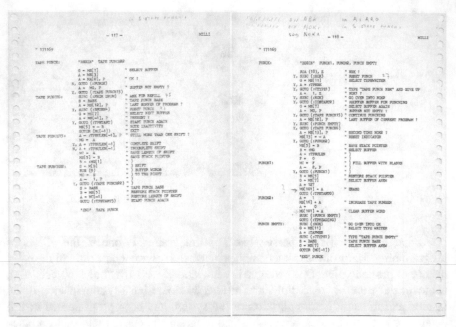

Fig. 4.6 Tape punch driver (part 1 at the left and part 2 at the right)

The first solution uses a data location to store the flag and stores 0 or 1 in that location to set the flag to false (MOVE #0, FLAG) or true (MOVE #1, FLAG).

```
FLAG: 0        // storage for FLAG
...
LOAD FLAG      // IF statement starts here
JZERO L        // jump to else part when FLAG is false (0)
A              // fall through and execute then part A
JMP M          // jump over else part
L: B           // execute else part B, fall through to
               // end of IF statement
M:             // IF statement ends here
```

A self-modifying version uses the code itself to store the value of the flag. In this case a JMP or NOOP instruction has to be placed in the FLAG field, e.g., set the flag true (MOVE "NOOP", FLAG) or false (MOVE "JMP", FLAG).[30] Here is the self-modifying version:

---

[30] We use here "NOOP" and "JMP" to represent the numeric value of the corresponding instructions.

```
FLAG: JMP L   // IF statement starts here, contains
              // either JMP L or NOOP
A             // fall through and execute then part A,
              // then jump over else part
JMP M         // jump over else part
L: B          // execute else part, fall through to end
              // of IF statement
M:            // IF statement ends here
```

Depending on the precise architecture the latter version will be several memory words shorter than the former one.

4.4 Two Suggestions for History Research

Although I am not a historian myself, I take the liberty to suggest two topics for further history study in computer science.

History of Hardware and Software Concepts. Computers have a rich history and it is important to develop a genealogy of their underlying concepts. Having a software background I propose, as examples, the following software concepts for historical study: subroutine, calling mechanisms, parameter mechanisms, recursion, self-modifying code, data versus control, libraries and modules, assembler, compiler, linker, loader, testing, and configuration management. Some of these concepts have already been studied from a historical perspective, but only in isolation and not in a systematic framework. I take inspiration from Carl Linnaeus' *Species Plantarum*[31] that lists every known plant. Why not develop *The Species of Hardware* and/or *The Species of Software*?

History of Jargon. Although English has become the *lingua franca* for computer science, there is merit in preserving the Dutch words that were used in the early development of computers. Here are some examples: rekenaar (human computer), ingreep (interrupt), doofheid (disabled interrupts), trommel (drum), sprong (jump), schuif (shift), bedieningslessenaar (console), invoer (input), uitvoer (output), regeldrukker (printer), toekenning (assignment). Why not develop a dictionary of historical Dutch terminology in computer science?

---

[31] Linneaus, Carl. 1753. *Species plantarum*. Sweden: Laurentius Salvius.

Chapter 5
The Mathematical Center, ALGOL 60, and the Electrologica X8

Text Written at the Occasion of the Placing of an Electrologica X8 in Rijksmuseum Boerhaave

Frans Kruseman Aretz
Waalre, The Netherlands

Abstract This chapter provides a personal account of the development of an ALGOL 60 compiler for the Electrologica X8 in the period 1963–1965, placed in the context of the development of computers and the design of compilers at the Mathematical Center in Amsterdam.

5.1 Introduction

This paper is devoted to the Electrologica X8, a mainframe brought to market by the Dutch computer factory Electrologica in 1965. A large part of it describes the work, done at the Mathematical Center in Amsterdam from 1963 up to 1965, for the development of an ALGOL 60 implementation for the EL X8. For a better understanding, some historical context is provided.

Soon after the foundation of the Mathematical Center in 1946 an activity was started to construct an automatic calculator, as it was called in that time. For this purpose Bram Loopstra and Carel Scholten had been appointed for the hardware in 1947 and Edsger Dijkstra for the software in 1952. This led to the development of a series of successive computers: the ARRA (1952), the ARRA II (1953, with a large contribution of Gerrit Blaauw), the ARMAC (1956), and the X1.[1] Each new machine built clearly on the experiences learned at the previous one. Alas, those lessons are nowhere described well.

In order to facilitate the construction of a number of X1's, a company was founded 1956, Electrologica,[2] with the money and the commercial experience of the Nillmij (a Dutch insurance company) and the know-how of the Mathematical Center. The machine was fully transistorized and had as main innovations a core store, an index

---

[1] Dijkstra, Edsger W. 1959a. *Communication with an automatic computer.* [PhD Thesis. October 28, 1959. Universiteit van Amsterdam]. Excelsior, Rijswijk.

[2] Beer, H. de (2008) Electrologica, Nederlands eerste computerindustrie. *Informatie* Informatie 50(10):30–37.

© The Author(s), under exclusive license to Springer Nature Switzerland AG 2022   87
G. Alberts, J. F. Groote (eds.), *Tales of Electrologica*, History of Computing,
https://doi.org/10.1007/978-3-031-13033-5_5

register and an interrupt mechanism for in- and output. Its speed was about 20 000 instructions per second, the core store was in units of 4096 words with a cycle time of 32 microseconds. The first EL X1 was installed at the Nillmij in 1958, the sixth one at the Mathematical Center in 1960.

One of the great successes of the EL X1 and of the Mathematical Center was the completion of the first ALGOL 60 implementation in the world, written by Edsger Dijkstra and Jaap Zonneveld.[3] ALGOL 60 was a programming language for numeric calculations that abstracted strongly from all existing hardware. It was the first imperative programming language with a clear block structure and recursive procedures, and the first one with a grammar in Backus-Naur form. Soon a large part of the calculation programs at the Mathematical Center were written in ALGOL 60, notwithstanding the fact that their execution cost a multiple of machine time compared with equivalent programs written in machine code.

In 1965 Electrologica launched the EL X8 as a successor of the EL X1.

At an early stage Electrologica made an appeal to a number of institutions that ordered an EL X8, to assist in the development of the basic software. The construction of an ALGOL 60 implementation was assigned to the Mathematical Center. That brings together the central theme of my contribution to the Electrologica Symposium, *"The Mathematical Center, ALGOL 60, and the Electrologica X8."*

5.2 My Years at the Mathematical Center

When I, as freshly graduated theoretical physicist, entered my employment at the Mathematical Center it had four departments: pure mathematics, applied mathematics, statistics, and the Computation Department (Fig. 5.1). The latter stood under the leadership of Adriaan van Wijngaarden and counted a scientific staff of eight collaborators: Jaap Zonneveld, Dirk Dekker, Freek Barning, and Martin Potters for numerical mathematics, Jan Nederkoorn and Piet van de Laarschot were constructing a second ALGOL 60 implementation for the EL X1, and Jaap van Berckel used the EL X1 to investigate word frequencies in Dutch newspapers. Technician Joop van Loenen did the maintenance of the X1. Edsger Dijkstra was appointed full professor at the Technical University Eindhoven and had just left the Mathematical Center. My task would be the development of programs for large-scale physical computations such as the analysis of bubble-chamber photos of CERN-Geneva. But things worked out differently.

In earlier years, I had taken a course "Programming for the ARMAC" and during a couple of years I enjoyed the lectures Numerical Mathematics of Van Wijngaarden at the University of Amsterdam. Besides the numerical mathematics itself also

---

[3] Kruseman Aretz, Frans E.J. 2003. *The Dijkstra-Zonneveld ALGOL 60 compiler for the Electrologica X1*. CWI Report SEN-N301. Centrum voor Wiskunde en Informatica. Amsterdam, The Netherlands; Dijkstra, Edsger W. 1961. An ALGOL 60 Translator for the X1. *ALGOL Bulletin Supplement* 10:3–22. Mathematical Centre, Amsterdam; Dijkstra, Edsger W. 1961. Making a translator for ALGOL 60. *Algol Bulletin Supplement* 10:23–33. Mathematical Centre, Amsterdam.

Fig. 5.1 The Mathematical Center, 2de Boerhaavestraat 49, Amsterdam

programming of calculation problems was a theme of these lectures, first for the ARMAC, next for the EL X1, and finally in ALGOL 60. On the basis of all this I decided to leave physics after my doctorate and to become a numerator.

The Computation Department, and probably the whole Mathematical Center, was characterized by great freedom in the way of working. And how hard we worked! One had an assignment and one should find out how to attack the problem oneself. Besides my work for the analysis of bubble-chamber photos, I wanted to test an ALGOL 60 program that I wrote as preliminary examination for numerical mathematics (for which Van Wijngaarden rewarded me the highest grade, a 10, as mark). But it did not function as it should, and ultimately, thanks to an execution of the program step by step together with Nederkoorn it became clear that it was not my ALGOL 60 program that contained a bug but the ALGOL 60 implementation of Dijkstra and Zonneveld. That was the motivation to dive into that implementation so deeply that we could correct the bug. That was the start of my career in system software. It was not long before I was asked to try to implement other improvements to the system, especially to enhance the manageability of the ALGOL 60 system for the EL X1.

The ALGOL 60 system was a unique achievement: a compiler of 2000 instructions and the so-called "complex," a piece of software supporting the execution of compiled programs, of about 2000 instructions, too. All that software could work on a machine of 4096 words store. By consequence, for the compilation and execution of the average ALGOL 60 program, no less than 8 paper-tape rolls had to be read (and rolled up again). By 1962 the size of the store had increased to 12144 words, and I could, in several steps, reduce the start of an execution of an ALGOL 60 program to the reading of 3 paper-tape rolls.

Moreover, the routines by which these paper-tape rolls were read originally used the interrupt system of the EL X1. That was a relevant gain in efficiency for a tape reader that could read 50 punchings per second. But the input device had in the meantime been replaced by an EL 1000 paper-tape reader that could read 1000 punchings per second. However, while reading a binary paper-tape roll, the interrupt system demanded already the execution of on average 51.8 instructions and 2566 milliseconds for each punching read. This reduced the reading speed to less than 390 punchings per second. By reading paper-tape rolls directly, and thus getting around the interrupt system, the EL X8 could operate the paper-tape reader at top speed. The so-called "load-and-go" system became operational in 1963, and the speeding up of paper-tape reading in 1964.

I learned quite a lot through all this work in basic software. Where I started as programmer apprentice in 1962, I felt that I fully mastered the programming discipline, both in ALGOL 60 and in machine code after two years. Moreover, I paid much attention to user comfort and impediments to efficiency at places where it really did matter. Also, I always wanted to be able to convince myself that my software was correct, something requiring a clear structure.

When in 1963 the Mathematical Center took on the task of making an ALGOL 60 implementation for the Electrologica X8, the successor of the EL X1, it was obvious that I should participate in the working group charged with that task. The working group was headed by Zonneveld and further consisted of Nederkoorn, Van de Laarschot, Barning, and me. Nederkoorn and Van de Laarschot had acquired their knowledge when building a second ALGOL 60 implementation for the EL X1. This implementation was slower than the one made by Dijkstra and Zonneveld but could execute much larger programs. It was, however, used for that purpose only rarely. Its main use was checking the syntactic correctness of programs, a feature almost completely lacking in the Dijkstra-Zonneveld system. Barning got the specific task to build an EL X1 program by which the EL X8 could be emulated, so that EL X8 programs could be tested on the EL X1 even before the delivery of the EL X8.

5.3 The Electrologica X1 and X8

The Electrologica X1 (see Fig. 5.2) was a nice and compact machine that fitted amply in a (former) class room at the Mathematical Center.

The central machine of the EL X1 was housed in the side-walls of a large writing-desk. The horizontal plane held a number of switches. The vertical back plane showed a large number of signaling lights. Spread over the room stood a table with a typewriter, a paper-tape punch and a paper-tape reader, and 3 further cabinets with 4096 words core store each. A fast paper-tape punch and a plotter were added later.

The address part of an EL X1 instruction consisted of 15 bits, on paper denoted as 3 × 5 bits. We all knew the 32 possible decimal values of 5 bits by heart, such as 27 for 11011. So one would work for addresses in the 32-ary scale. Programs on paper in assembly language were noted on pages of 32 instructions. Such programs had to be punched on 5-hole paper tape on a primitive Telex punch device: again a 32-ary code for that matter.

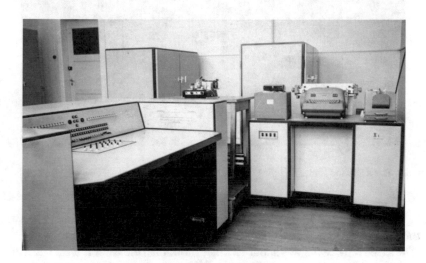

Fig. 5.2 The Electrologica X1 at the Mathematisch Centrum

For ALGOL 60 programs a Flexowriter was chosen (Fig. 5.5), a kind of typewriter that during typing could produce both a print on paper and a 7-hole paper tape: a tremendous progress!

The EL X1 of the Mathematical Center was operated in "open shop." Users made reservations for a certain amount of time. They brought with them their own programs on paper tape and operated the machine themselves.

The Electrologica X8, brought to market 7 years later, was much larger and filled half of a (gymnasium) hall (see Fig. 5.3). The central machine was housed in three high cabinets, the separate input/output processor in a fourth cabinet. Also two (and later on three) core-store cabinets with 16384 words each, a cabinet with a magnetic drum store of 512 K words, a punched card reader, a card punch, a line printer, small tables with a paper-tape reader, a paper-tape punch, a plotter, and a Teleprinter (the latter for the operators) had their place in the room. Finally, a desk with switches and lights was in the room, in this case not meant for operation by the operators, but for the technicians.

The EL X8 was operated in "closed shop." Exclusively ALGOL 60 programs could be offered for service. Envelopes, the size of a line-printer sheet, containing the paper-tape rolls with a program and the data to be processed by the program,

Fig. 5.3 The X8 at the NatLab, Philips Physics Laboratory, 1972

could be handed in at the service counter. The results could be collected afterwards in the same envelopes. The EL X8 was operated by operators exclusively.

The Electrologica X8 was about 12 times faster than the EL X1. It executed about 240 000 instructions per second. The core store, in units of 16384 words, had a cycle time of 2.5 microsecond. The EL X8 was more or less upwards compatible with the EL X1, so that EL X1 programs could be executed on the EL X8 without too drastic modifications (I do not know whether or not this ever happened). But the EL X8 had a number of important extensions directed especially to the execution of ALGOL 60 programs. Very remarkable: while early programming languages had been strongly inspired by the hardware, in this case the design of the hardware was influenced by a programming language! As a consequence such programs were executed circa 60 times faster on the EL X8 than on the EL X1. An ALGOL 60 program of which the execution on the EL X1 took a whole hour, was executed on the EL X8 in one minute.[4]

An important general extension was the addition of a floating-point register with the corresponding operations of addition, subtraction, multiplication, and division.[5] The floating-point numbers had a mantissa of 40 bits and a binary exponent of 12 bits. With a mantissa m (with $0 \leq m \leq 2^{40} - 1$) and an exponent e ($-2047 \leq e \leq +2047$) its value was $m \times 2^e$. The numbers ranged from circa 10^{-616} to 10^{+628} with a precision

---

[4] Kruseman Aretz, Frans E.J. 2008. *A comparison between the ALGOL 60 implementations on the Electrologica X1 and the Electrologica X8*. CWI report SEN-E0801, Centrum Wiskunde & Informatica, Amsterdam.

[5] Dijkstra, Edsger W. 1965c. *Globale beschrijving van de drijvende arithmetiek van de EL X8* [EWD145] Available at https://www.cs.utexas.edu/users/EWD/transcriptions/EWD01xx/EWD145.html.

upwards to 12 decimals. The Grau representation used had the advantage that the whole numbers were a true subset of the floating-point numbers (with $e = 0$) and that the EL X8 could evaluate expressions containing both whole numbers and fractions without any number conversion. The implementation was quite nice: the four arithmetical operations mentioned above all resulted in the best value possible: the floating-point value nearest to the mathematically exact result of the operation.

The EL X1 did not have such a register with the corresponding operations. In the EL X1 such computations had to be carried out completely by means of software. By consequence, division of 10.3 by 3.14, together with the fetch of the divisor, took the execution of 49 instructions and 4066 microsecond, whereas the EL X8 could do it by 1 instruction of 62.5 microsecond. That is a factor of 65.1 faster.

A second general extension was that all registers, even the instruction counter, could be used as index register.

A language-oriented extension was the fact that most instructions fetching a value from store or writing a value to store had a (un-)stacking variant. This variant used register B as stack pointer that was decremented (in fetching a value from the stack) or incremented (in writing a value to the stack) appropriately. Especially the stacking subroutine call, writing the return link data to the stack, was a major new feat.

Another language-oriented extension was the so-called dynamic, or two-phase addressing variant. In this variant the operand $Mp[q]$ of an instruction was interpreted by the hardware as operand $M[[M[63] + p] + q]$.[6]

Also, an execute instruction was introduced, by which the word in store that was pointed to by the address part of the instruction was executed as an instruction. This feature was very useful for the implementation of the parameter mechanism of (ALGOL 60) procedures.

5.4 ALGOL 60

ALGOL 60, developed by an international committee, was a programming language for numeric computations. This ALGOrithmic Language abstracted completely of all hardware and introduced a number of new concepts. By doing so, ALGOL 60 set the tone for the whole further development of programming languages. The final definition of the language, edited by Peter Naur, was the first to make use of a formal grammar as devised by John Backus. The variant of the grammar used here came to be known as the "Backus-Naur Form." The defining report was named "Report on the Algorithmic Language ALGOL 60."[7] In 1964 a slightly revised version was published (Fig. 5.4).

---

[6] $M[63]$ was the display pointer, $M[M[63] + p]$ the address of a block cell for a block with p embracing blocks and q the relative address of the operand in that block cell.

[7] Naur, Peter, ed. 1960. J.W. Backus, F.L. Bauer, J. Green, C. Katz, J. McCarthy, A.J. Perlis, H. Rutishauser, K. Samelson, B. Vauquois, J.H. Wegstein, A. van Wijngaarden, M. Woodger, Report on the algorithmic language ALGOL 60. *Num. Mathematik* 2:106–136.

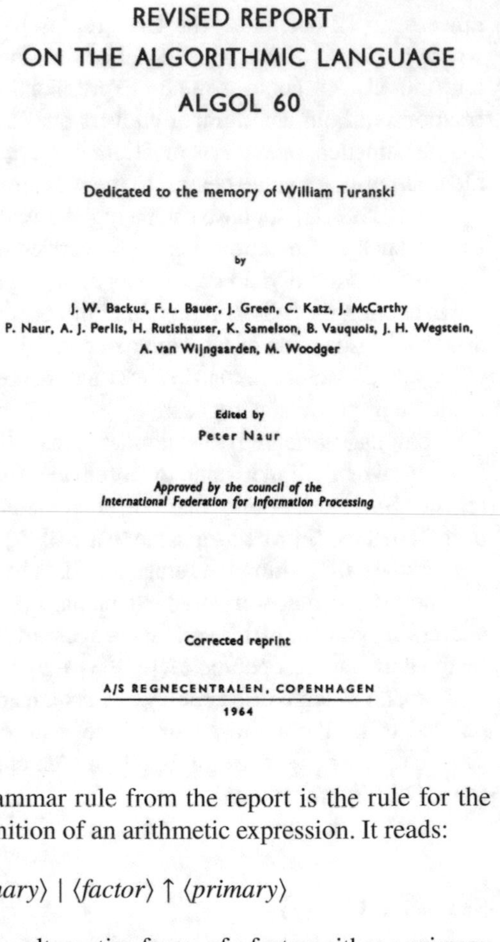

Fig. 5.4 The front matter page
of the (revised) defining report
for Algol 60

REVISED REPORT
ON THE ALGORITHMIC LANGUAGE
ALGOL 60

Dedicated to the memory of William Turanski

by

J. W. Backus, F. L. Bauer, J. Green, C. Katz, J. McCarthy
P. Naur, A. J. Perlis, H. Rutishauser, K. Samelson, B. Vauquois, J. H. Wegstein,
A. van Wijngaarden, M. Woodger

Edited by
Peter Naur

Approved by the council of the
International Federation for Information Processing

Corrected reprint

A/S REGNECENTRALEN, COPENHAGEN
1964

An example of such a formal grammar rule from the report is the rule for the definition of a factor, part of the definition of an arithmetic expression. It reads:

$$\langle factor \rangle ::= \langle primary \rangle \mid \langle factor \rangle \uparrow \langle primary \rangle$$

The rule expresses that there are two alternative forms of a factor: either a primary or a factor followed by the symbol $\uparrow$ followed by a primary.[8] Given that "2," "3," and "4" are examples of a primary, "2" is therefore also a factor. Using the grammar "2 $\uparrow$ 3", meaning 2^3, is a factor, too, and, recursively, so is "2 $\uparrow$ 3 $\uparrow$ 4," meaning $(2^3)^4$.

A major novelty in the language was the introduction of a nested block structure. A block is a section of a program with a number of variables and procedures of its own. These variables and procedures only live and take up storage space as long as the execution of this section lasts. The procedure body of a procedure was a substantive block. ALGOL 60 allowed that among the statements of a procedure a call of the procedure itself could occur, a so-called recursive use of the procedure. All this required a completely new form of store management, using a stack. A number of the hardware innovations of the EL X8 were directed towards the efficient use of a stack and towards the addressing of variables in a nested block structure.

---

[8] Words between $\langle$ and $\rangle$, like $\langle primary \rangle$ and $\langle factor \rangle$, denote grammatical notions.

5.5 The MC Implementation of ALGOL 60 for the Electrologica X8

In 1963 a team was formed within the Computation Department of the Mathematical Center with the assignment of constructing an ALGOL 60 implementation for the EL X8. The team was headed by Zonneveld and further consisted of Nederkoorn, Van de Laarschot, Barning, and myself. The implementation of a programming language builds up out of four strongly interdependent parts:

- to decide what variant of the language will be implemented,
- to determine a mapping from the source language to the object language,[9]
- to develop a compiler for that mapping, and
- to determine the user interface.

The first three of these will be detailed below.

5.5.1 Language Choice and Language Interpretation

To start with the first item. It was our ambition to implement ALGOL 60 as defined in the Revised Report as faithfully as possible. So, including the possibility of not specifying so-called name parameters, an arbitrary order of declarations in a block, integer labels of statements, and a labeled block as procedure body[10]. The only aspects of the language that we did not want to implement were own arrays and the interpretation of a switch designator as a dummy statement if the index value was outside the bounds.

We also did not want to extend the language by complex numbers, as Dijkstra would do later in his THE system. The only extension that we added was a type "string," complete with simple variables, array variables, and functions of that type.

Still, that did not solve everything. At some points, the *Revised Report* had not provided full clarity, and we had to decide for our own interpretations.

Of course, our ambition to check programs went without saying. Our compiler was to check every ALGOL 60 program exhaustively against syntactical errors preceding to its execution, and against semantic errors, during its execution.

5.5.2 The Mapping from Source Language to Object Language

The second part of our project was started in 1963 and completed in 1964. Soon Van de Laarschot uncoupled, and the work was continued in daily meetings by

---

[9] Kruseman Aretz, Frans E.J. 1971a. *Het objectprogramma, gegenereerd door de X8-ALGOL-vertaler van het M.C.*. Mathematical Centre report MR 121/71. Mathematical Centre. Amsterdam; Dijkstra, Edsger W. 1963c. *Objectprogramma, gegenereerd door de M.C. vertaler*. Mathematical Centre report MR 55. Amsterdam: Mathematical Centre.

[10] In the MC implementation for the EL X1 the latter led to a disaster as the compiler did not generate the code to declare arrays which led to incomprehensible behavior of the compiled program.

Nederkoorn and me. Nederkoorn faithfully wrote a review of our discussions of which a few copies were printed with document number R915, but which was never formalized into a published report.

An early decision was to reserve a number of registers each for a specific type of value:

register	reserved for
F	arithmetic values
A	addresses
C	logical values (**true** of **false**)
B	the stack pointer

As a consequence of these choices the stack use was reduced: the content of a register was saved in the stack only if that register contained a value that was still relevant and was required for another activity.

That can be nicely illustrated by the translation of a term "$a[i, j]$" in an arithmetic expression, with "a" an array with elements of type real. In the code of the translation the value of the first index is written to the stack in order to make place in register F for the second index. Routine "IND" of the "complex" rounds all index values to an integer value if necessary, checks whether they fall inside the bounds, and delivers in register A the address of the array element. In the final instruction of the translation register A is used as index register: operand "MA," abbreviation for "MA[0]," means "M[A+0]." By "$@i$" is meant the address that the compiler assigns to variable i.

For the EL X8 the translation was:

```
G = M[@i]    value of i in F                         5.0 microsecond
MC = F       save F in the stack                     7.5
G = M[@j]    value of j in F                         5.0
A = M[@a]    address storage function of a in A      5.0
SUB (:IND)   call of subroutine Indexer              127.5 (= 28 instructions)
F = MA       value of a[i, j] in F                   7.5
```

summing up to 157.5 microsecond.

This minimal use of stacking operations in the ALGOL 60 implementation for the EL X8 should be contrasted with their use in the implementation of the language for the EL X1. There every value was saved in the stack and used by fetching it from the stack. The translation of the term "$a[i, j]$" ran as follows (denoted in the assembly language for the EL X8):

```
B = :@a        address of a in register B                        36 microsecond
SUB1 (:TRAS)   call of subroutine Take Real Address Static       500 ( 9 instructions)
B = :@i        address of i in register B                        36
SUB1 (:TIRS)   call of subroutine Take Integer Result Static     532 ( 9 instructions)
B = :@j        address of j in register B                        36
SUB1 (:TIRS)   call of subroutine Take Integer Result Static     532 ( 9 instructions)
SUB1 (:IND)    call of subroutine Indexer                        3196 (59 instructions)
SUB1 (:TAR)    subroutine call Transform Address into Result     1032 (20 instructions)
```

Together 5900 microsecond, that is more than 37 times slower. Subroutines "TRAS" and "TIRS," having as parameter the address of a variable in register B, wrote their results to the stack. Subroutine "IND" took the required data from the stack and delivered the element address in the stack.

Register C, the one-bit condition register, with value 0 for **true** and 1 for **false**, was the natural place for logical values. C was assigned a new value by instructions with a condition-setting variant and used by instructions with a condition-following variant. A simple example of this is the translation of "**if** $i = 10$ **then** S," with "S" some statement:

$$
\begin{array}{ll}
G = M[@i] & \text{load the value of } i \text{ in register F} \\
F - 10, Z & \text{subtract 10 from F; resulting in 0?} \\
N, \text{GOTO} (: L) & \text{if not, skip the code for } S \text{ by jumping to L} \\
\ldots & \text{translation of statement } S \\
L: &
\end{array}
$$

It was self-evident to reserve a complete word of store for the value of scalar variables of type **Boolean**, using the most significant bit, the sign bit, for the logical value. In a logical expression the value of variable "bl" could then be loaded into C by one condition-setting instruction:

$S = M[@bl], P$ load the value of bl in register S. Is that value positive?

The assignment of the value of C to variable "bl" is another story: how to get the value of C in the sign bit of register S? We knew that bit d_{18} of store location 62 contained the value of C. We wished it had been bit d_{26}, the sign bit, of M[62]! We addressed Electrologica with the request to move the value of C to the sign bit. Our request was honored in the sense that the value of C was present in both bits of M[62]. Consequently the assignment of C to variable "bl" could be executed by the instructions:

$S = M[62]$ make the sign bit of register S equal to the value of register C
$M[@bl] = S$ write the value of register S to variable bl

We were at that time apparently blind for a simpler solution:

$Y, M[@bl] = $ B   write the value of the stack pointer to variable bl
$N, M[@bl] = -B$ write the value of the stack pointer negatively to variable bl

using the fact that stack pointer B permanently contained a (positive) address. This solution was even slightly faster: 7.5 μs instead of 8.75 μs!

A considerable part of the time is consumed by the design of the parameter mechanism of a procedure or function. On the one side you have the declaration of the procedure that determines the requirements that are posed on each (formal) parameter, and on the other side you have the procedure calls, in which every parameter has certain properties.

Here our ambition to allow that formal parameters that were "called by name," need not to be specified, caused lots of worries to us. We provide some examples to give an impression of the difficulties that our ambition gave us. Consider a procedure "assign" with declaration:

> **procedure** *assign* (x, y);
> **begin** $x := y$ **end**;

A call of this procedure now can read both "*assign*$(x, 3.14)$," with "x" a variable of type real, and "*assign*(bl,**true**)," with "bl" a variable of type **Boolean**. For the first assignment, however, quite other instructions have to be executed than for the latter one. It is clear that some form of interaction needs to be created between the code of the procedure body and the code for the procedure calls.

For procedure "*call*," declared by:

> **procedure** *call* (q, n);
> **begin** $q(n)$ **end**;

no other property of "n," the actual parameter of "q," is known than that it is an unspecified formal parameter of "*call*."

Also the potential presence of integer labels can be problematic. Suppose that somewhere in a program a statement is labeled by label "3." In a call of a procedure with "3" as one of its actual parameters it is not clear whether number "3" or label "3" is meant.

Of course we wanted to guarantee that programs that did not use the extra facilities offered by our ambition would not get any trouble of these extras and that their execution would not be slowed down.

Ultimately we arrived at the following construction. Each actual parameter is characterized in the translated ALGOL 60 program by an Actual Parameter Descriptor (APD). In the code the APDs follow directly upon the procedure call. An APD takes up one word, of which 6 bits for the parameter kind (code value 21 was not used):

0 simple real variable	4 real number ≥ 0.0
1 simple integer variable	5 integer number ≥ 32768
2 simple Boolean variable	6 logical value
3 simple string variable	7 integer $\in [0..32767]$
8 real array	12 switch
9 integer array	13 integer $\in [-32767.. - 0]$
10 Boolean array	14 label
11 string array	15 formal parameter
16 real array element	20 arithmetic expression
17 integer array element	
18 Boolean array element	22 logical expression
19 string array element	23 string expression
24 real procedure	28 designational expression
25 integer procedure	29 integer or designational expression
26 Boolean procedure	30 non-type procedure
27 string procedure	31 expression van unknown type
32 element of a formal array (type unknown) or switch designator	

Mostly these APDs are followed by small pieces of code which are referred to by the APDs and that can be used by the evaluation of the parameters.

Upon entrance of a procedure during execution of a program a new block cell is added to the stack for the link data, the actual-parameter words, and the local variables of the procedure. The actual-parameter words (called Actual Parameter Instruction Cell or shortly APIC) take up 4 or 2 words of store, depending on whether values are assigned in the procedure to the parameter or not (in the first case the corresponding actual parameter has to be a variable, this is checked during execution of the program). An APIC is constructed from the corresponding APD, which can be found via the procedure link. The first APIC word contains an instruction for the evaluation of the actual parameter, in many cases a subroutine call to one of the pieces of program following the APDs. The second APIC word contains the code number from the APD together with information about the addressing in the environment of the call. The eventual third and fourth APIC words contain instructions that play a role in assignments to the actual parameter.

An instruction from an APIC is executed by means of an execute instruction that refers to the APIC. Upon our request an instruction "DOS(M[. . .])" was added to the hardware in addition to the already existing instruction "DO(M[. . .])." That new instruction executes not only the instruction at location "M[. . .]" but delivers, as a side effect, the address of that location in register S. This made it possible to find the APIC immediately when necessary.

Frequently, subroutine calls occur in the object code of a translated program. Above is an example of the subroutine "IND", a subroutine of 18 instructions. The run-time support system contained some 16 subroutines with 627 instructions in total. Another example of such a subroutine is "CRV", Call Real by Value, called during the entrance of a procedure for a formal parameter from the value list with specification "real". The subroutine first constructs an APIC of two words on the stack by means of subroutine "CEN", Call Expression by Name, evaluates thereupon the corresponding actual parameter by executing the instruction in the APIC (this is done by the "DOS(M[B−2])" instruction in CRV) with result in register F and overwrites lastly the APIC by the value of F. The value of A should be kept and is saved temporarily to the stack. Subroutine CEN puts its link in store location M[8], the link of CRV is put on the stack on account of the possibility that the evaluation of the actual parameter also uses such fixed store locations.

CRV: MC = A	save A in the stack
SUB (:CEN)	construct a two-word APIC on the stack
DOS (M[B−2])	evaluate the corresponding actual parameter
A = MC[−3]	restore A
S = MC[−3]	load the subroutine link in S
M[B−2] = F	overwrite the APIC with the value of F
GOTO (:MS)	leave the subroutine via the subroutine link

May 1964 the mapping from ALGOL 60 programs to machine code was fixed and the run-time support system written. The results were laid down in a draft by Jan Nederkoorn and Frans Kruseman Aretz and internally circulated as R989, "Prolegomena to X8 ALGOL," but it never made it to a publication as a Mathematical Center Tract.[11] The distribution of the rough copy was restricted to the Computation Department and a few intimates.

During the execution of an ALGOL 60 program a number of checks against errors were carried out, such as against division by zero, access to a non-existing array element, assignment of a value to a formal parameter of which the corresponding actual parameter was not a variable, assignment of a value to a variable of type integer outside the integer capacity of $-67108863 \cdots + 67108863$, and some others. The programmer's manual mentions 15 cases.[12]

When the mapping was fixed testing could start using some short ALGOL 60 programs that we compiled by hand. For this testing we could gratefully use the EL X8 emulator for the EL X1 that Barning had completed in the meantime.[13] These tests had to be done during nights: they required quite an amount of computation hours on the EL X1, since emulation of a machine runs very slowly.

[11] Staff of Computation Dept. 1964. *Prolegomena to X8 ALGOL*. Internal report MCCD 64 R-989. Mathematisch Centrum, Amsterdam.

[12] Kruseman Aretz, Frans E.J. 1966a. *Het MC-ALGOL 60-systeem voor de X8; Voorlopige programmeurshandleiding*. Report MR 81. Mathematical Centre. Amsterdam.

[13] Barning, Freek J.M. 1964. *X8-simulator, simulatieprogramma voor het uitvoeren van X8-programma's met behulp van de X1*. Mathematisch Centrum report R 917. Amsterdam: Mathemathical Centre.

5.5.3 The Construction of the Compiler

Well before completing the design of the mapping from source text to object text, I started to think about the compiler. I found the method that Dijkstra and Zonneveld used for it rather complicated. In that method repeatedly a small piece of the program was read, just unto and including the next delimiter which then was interpreted on the basis of that delimiter and some six variables in which was kept in what kind of language construction that piece of text occurred, the so-called context. At context change one or more of these context variables were saved in a compiler stack in an ad-hoc manner.

It is unbelievably clever that they managed to build a working compiler in this way as firsts in the world. The compiler did almost nothing to check whether an ALGOL 60 program satisfied all grammar rules. Dijkstra and Zonneveld had considered that of little importance: programming in ALGOL 60 was so much easier than programming in machine code that probably no errors would be made. The experience was soon a different one.

But it was not that easy to insert a decent error check to the compiler method used by them. As apology for the lack of checks in their compiler one should realize that it was already a miracle that an ALGOL 60 compiler could be made that fitted in a computer of 4096 word of store; adding code for error checks had been impossible for certain.

As mentioned before the context-free grammar of ALGOL 60 was defined rigidly and formally by means of Backus-Naur Form, which allowed an extreme recursive definition. As an example of this I gave the grammar rule for a factor:

$$\langle factor \rangle ::= \langle primary \rangle \mid \langle factor \rangle \uparrow \langle primary \rangle$$

ALGOL 60 as programming language knew also recursion: procedures can be used recursively. I had seen many beautiful examples of this, first in the lectures Numerical Mathematics of Van Wijngaarden and later during my work at the Mathematical Center: the three towers of Hanoi, Hoare's Quicksort, a program for numeric quadrature, and others. Through these examples I was familiar with recursion and it was almost self-evident to use the recursive programming technique for the analysis of a syntax that was defined with recursion. For the grammar rule for factor given above it looks like[14]:

---

[14] ttp was the name of a variable with the internal representation of symbol $\uparrow$ as value. ttp (and TTP) stand for "to the power."

procedure *factor*; **begin** *primary*; *nextprimary* **end** *factor*;

procedure *nextprimary*;
begin if *lastsymbol* = ttp
    then begin macro(STACK); *nextsymbol*; *primary*; macro(TTP);
                nextprimary
        end
end *nextprimary*;

where "macro(STACK)" generated instruction "MC = F" and "macro(TTP)" instruction "SUBC(:TTP)," a call of the subroutine TTP from the complex.

I proceeded to write the complete translation program for arithmetic expressions and showed it to Van Wijngaarden. He was enthused and urged me to publish it. I called the paper "ALGOL 60 translation for everybody,"[15] expressing how really trivial I found the approach. Little did I realize that I had independently invented an important analysis technique—to me it had been so obvious to do it this way. The technique later came to be called "recursive descent" and was applicable to LL1 grammars. Even if the grammar rule for factor is not in LL1 form, it can be brought into LL1 form by a transformation that would become known as "elimination of left recursion." I applied that transformation automatically, again unwittingly.

The new compiler technique showed to have another advantage besides its simplicity and comprehensibility: it was not only simple to detect grammatical errors in the program to be compiled, but also to continue the analysis thereafter in order to detect, if possible, all other errors in one and the same scan of the program text.

One of the alternatives in the syntax rule for a primary reads:

$$(\langle arithmetic\ expression\rangle)$$

with analysis code:

if *lastsymbol* = open
then begin *nextsymbol*; *arithexp*;
        if *lastsymbol* = close **then** *nextsymbol* **else** *errormessage*(302)
    end

Apart from the error notification the code acts as if a missing closing parenthesis is present and it continues the analysis as customary.

It was decided that I would proceed along the route taken; Nederkoorn would investigate another method.

---

[15] Kruseman Aretz, Frans E.J. 1964. ALGOL 60 translation for everybody. *Elektronische Datenverarbeitung* 6:233–244.

In retrospect we may discern four elements of novelty in the approach:

- the compiler was designed and tested completely in a higher-level programming language;[16] after completion it could be re-coded to machine code by hand in a few weeks;
- the top-down analysis of ALGOL 60 programs, a technique that later became known as recursive-descent parsing;
- the treatment of the identifier table in a way that later became known as abstract data type, with complete separation between the what and the how; only after it was known what questions had to be answered by the identifier table and what information had to be added to the identifier table its structure was designed and the operations coded upon it;
- a macro processor with a number of tasks, such as the determination of the proper addressing variant of variables, the application of peep-hole optimizing, in which up to three successive macros sometimes could be united to one instruction, and the determination of the maximally needed stack space at block introduction.

During the generation of the translation the data of the "defining occurrence" of an identifier, such as its declaration or its appearance as label of a statement, have to be available at any "applied occurrence" of it, even if its application precedes its definition. The easiest solution, already applied in the ALGOL 60 compiler for the EL X1, is to collect in a preceding scan of the program text a block-wise oriented identifier table. The compilation scan becomes thereby the last text scan of two (or more) scans. I started by writing that last scan. In this way I could also determine what other information had to be gathered beforehand.

Naturally it seemed wise to determine the exact structure of the identifier table only when all questions that possibly had to be answered were known. This was solved in the following way. One of the alternatives for a *primary* was an *identifier*. In that case its type had to be acceptable for use in an arithmetic expression. An identifier was read by the compiler by the statement "$n := identifier$," that assigned to "n" the address in the identifier table of the data of the identifier, where-after the statement "**if** *Nonarithmetic*(n) **then** *ERRORMESSAGE*(304)" catered for the test and, if necessary, the error message.

In fact this approach turned the identifier table into a prototype for an "abstract data structure," in which the determination of the *what* was independent of the determination of the *how*. Again, I could not help considering this approach self-evident.

For the testing of the translation scan I used originally an ad-hoc implementation for procedures like "Nonarithmetic," making the type of an identifier dependent on its first letter or of the number of letters.

If a primary was a simple variable of type real the code was generated by the statement "macro2(TRV,n)." The procedures "macro" and "macro2" formed part of the macro processor, a part of the translation scan. Procedure "macro" had one

---

[16] Kruseman Aretz, Frans E.J., P.J.W. ten Hagen, and H.L. Oudshoorn. 1973. *An ALGOL 60 compiler in ALGOL 60, text of the MC-compiler for the EL X8*. Mathematical Centre tracts 48. Mathematical Centre, Amsterdam.

argument, a macro name (or more correct, the number of a macro), procedure "macro2" had two arguments, a macro name and a macro argument, often an address in the identifier table. The macro processor generated from the macro name one to three instructions, depending on the macro. In the case of macro "TRV" (Take Real Value) one instruction was generated of the form "F = M[...]," "F = MD[...]" or "F = Mp[q]" (with $0 \leq p \leq 57$ and $0 \leq q \leq 255$), depending on the addressing type of the variable. A few of the macros defined in R989[17] had more than three instructions or more than one macro argument. That was remedied by splitting the macro in two separate macros.

The macro processor had yet another task: peep-hole optimizing. If possible it replaces a number of successive instructions by one other one. An example: the compiler generated for "×3.14" (in an arithmetic expression) successively the macros: "STACK", "TRC(3.14)", and "MUL", corresponding to the instructions "MC = F", "F = M[3.14]", and "F × MC[−2]", but the macro processor reduced this succession to macro "MULRC(3.14)" with instruction "F × M[3.14]".

At the time that the growing translation scan became too long for executing partial tests on the EL X1 with the ALGOL 60 compiler of Dijkstra and Zonneveld it was fortunately possible to use the second ALGOL 60 implementation for the EL X1 made by Nederkoorn and Van de Laarschot.[18] Yet, testing took much longer, because the second compiler would generate machine code for an hypothetical bit machine emulated on the EL X1.

After the completion of the translation scan the conception of the pre-scans could be attacked. It proved useful to make two of them, the first one purely composing the identifier table on the basis of all defining occurrences of identifiers, and the second one that gathered further information about blocks and identifiers. These were relatively quickly written by taking the code of the translation scan, erasing much of it (e.g., all that had to do with syntax checking or code generation), and to supply it with the intended investigations. Among other things the use of formal parameters was investigated. If "b" was an unspecified formal name parameter one could from an ALGOL 60 construction "**if** b **then** ... " draw the conclusion that "b" had to be of type **Boolean** and make a record in the identifier table. Thereupon, in the translation a call "*Nonarithmetical(n)*" with "n" pointing to "b" would result in **true**.

All together many checks were incorporated. The programmer's manual[19] mentioned 139 distinct possible errors, of which 31 were found in prescan0, 5 in prescan1, and 103 in the translation scan.[20]

---

[17] Staff of computation dept (1964), Prolegomena.

[18] Laarschot, Piet J.J. van de, and Jan Nederkoorn. 1963. *Text of the second ALGOL 60 translator for the X1*. Technical Report MR 61. Mathematisch Centrum, Amsterdam.

[19] Kruseman Aretz (1966a), MC-ALGOL 60-systeem.

[20] The ALGOL 60 compiler for the EL X1 of Dijkstra and Zonneveld halted at the first error detection; 7 stops had to do with lack of store capacity, 2 stops with too large floating-point numbers, and 8 stops with unacceptable punchings in the paper-tape roll. Only 1 stop had to do with the grammar of ALGOL 60: use of an identifier without declaration, even without mentioning what identifier; Kruseman Aretz (2003), Dijkstra-Zonneveld compiler.

When the pre-scans were completed and tested, I could start coding the whole compiler into machine code by hand.[21] In response to a question from Electrologica, asking how many instructions the compiler would take in all, I had done the exercise of coding a small part. Based on that experience, I estimated that the compiler length would be 5000 instructions and during the recoding of the remaining part I saw to it that that number was not exceeded. After all, the coding in machine code was relatively simple since I had not made use of complex language constructs anywhere in my ALGOL 60 version of the compiler and especially restricted myself to procedures with a small number of arguments. In general the latter could be presented to the corresponding subroutines as register values.

As an example of the machine code, the coding of the ALGOL 60 procedures "*factor*" and "*next primary*" given above is presented below. The tail recursion of "*next primary*" has been replaced by iteration and subroutine "NXT PRIM" returns to the calling context of "FACTOR" via the subroutine link in the stack which is put there by the call of "FACTOR."

FACTOR:	SUBC (:PRIMARY)
NXT PRIM:	S = *last symbol*
	U, S −69, Z
	N, GOTOR (MC−1)
	A = 0
	SUBC (:MACRO)
	SUBC (:NXT SBL)
	SUBC (:PRIMARY)
	A = 7
	SUBC (:MACRO)
	GOTO (:NXT PRIM)

The ALGOL 60 version of the compiler counted 90 pages, of which

    16 for the general purpose procedures (used in several parts),
     8 for prescan0,
    20 for prescan1, and
    46 for the translation scan.

The lengths of these four parts in the machine-code version were:

general purpose procedures:	669 instructions,
prescan0:	509 instructions,
prescan1:	894 instructions, and
translation scan:	2761 instructions and table words
together	4833 words

---

[21] Kruseman Aretz, Frans E.J. 1966b. *The ELAN source text of the Mathematical Center ALGOL 60 system for the EL X8*. Mathematisch Centrum rapport MR 84, Mathematical Centre. Amsterdam.

I did the coding into machine code directly on a Flexowriter. As mentioned before it was not necessary to be really ingenious. The work was finished in a couple of weeks. That means a daily production of something like 250 instructions.

The machine-code version could be assembled on the EL X1 by means of an assembler written at the Utrecht University in EL X1 code, and be tested by means of the EL X8 emulator that Barning made for the X1.[22] Barning also wrote the code for the standard functions (sqrt, sin, cos, exp, ln, arctan)[23] and Mailloux and Van Berckel produced the conversion routines for input and output.

5.6 Text Editing Anno 1960–1965

The Friden Flexowriter, depicted in Fig. 5.5, was at that time our standard text editor. It was a typewriter of a kind that also had a paper-tape punch station and a paper-tape read station.

Fig. 5.5 A Friden Flexowriter

---

[22] Barning (1964), X8-simulator.

[23] Barning, Freek J.M. *Standard functions in X8 assembleercode ELAN*. Mathematical Centre report R 1942. Amsterdam: Mathematical Centre; Kruseman Aretz, Frans E.J. 2001. Uit de oude doos van de X1 en de X8 (over de berekening van sinus en cosinus). In *Liber Amicorum Jos Jansen*, edited M.J.H. Anthonisse. Eindhoven: Eindhoven University of Technology.

Using the Flexowriter, one could produce, while typing, a paper tape in 7-hole Flexowriter code. One could also make a print of an existing paper tape in Flexowriter code by means of the read station. One could even, while reading, printing, and punching, make a copy of the paper tape. It did make sense to insert a piece of blank tape between paragraphs (for normal texts) or between procedures (for programs) by means of the button "tape feed." This made it easy to cut out an incorrect piece of text and insert an improved version. One could even copy and print a paper tape, make a stop just before the incorrect text, type (and punch at the same time) an improved version and skip a piece of the old version in the read station by hand. Of course, one had to know the Flexowriter code by heart, which we all did.

5.7 Closing Remarks and Evaluation

First of all, the Electrologica X8 was a nice computer to program. It had a rather smart instruction set, far more convenient to use than the instruction sets of, e.g., IBM 360 or Philips P1000 series. It was particularly helpful that almost every instruction came with an addressing variant, a condition-setting variant, and a condition-following variant. The condition register C kept its value as long as no instruction with a condition-setting variant was executed and its value could be used in the meantime by more than one instruction (by condition-following variants). Among the addressing variants the (un)stacking variant was important, among which the subroutine-call instruction "SUBC" which laid its subroutine link on top of the stack. After using the machine code of the EL X8 for compilers and operating systems for more than five years, programming compilers and operating systems in the assembly language of the P1000 series was a major step back.

The implementation of ALGOL 60 on the EL X8 was, however, a tough piece of work. Apart from the mental work, the manual labor was strenuous, as the reports were long. The unpublished R915 comprised 102 pages, the internal report R989 45 pages, including 14 pages of runtime-support routines, and 26 pages of standard procedures and functions (input/output conversion included).[24] With that, I have not even mentioned the work by Barning, constructing an EL X8 emulator,[25] and that of Mailloux and Van Berckel, developing the PICO operating system. We did type and edit all the pages by ourselves on Flexowriters.

Lack of information and lack of tools posed a recurring problem. As our project started, the assembly language for the EL X8 still had to be decided upon. All Nederkoorn and I could do at that point was to start by describing the mapping from source language to object language in terms of the EL X1 instruction code. Admittedly, "F = MA" reads much easier than "2Y 30464 X0 C." Even runtime-support routines were coded in that way. Only for testing on the EL X1 it was an advantage having

---

[24] Staff of computation dept (1964), Prolegomena.

[25] Barning (1964), X8-simulator.

it written in the EL X1 instruction code. Our code could immediately be assembled by the EL X1 assembler.

Our work was not done in isolation. Universities, the Mathematical Center, laboratories and Electrologica cooperated in the Z8 committee, to construct the system software for the EL X8. Once the Z8 committee decided upon ELAN as the assembly language for the EL X8, the Dr Neher laboratory, the research lab of Dutch PTT, was assigned the construction of an ELAN assembler. In the end, alas, our only option to assemble the whole system was to use an assembler constructed at Utrecht University by Sietse van der Meulen.

Rarely did our knowledge of the hardware come directly from the manufacturer, Electrologica. Many details we learned through EWDs, the informal series of reports by Edsger Dijkstra who was closely involved in the hardware design.[26] We were never allotted test time on an EL X8 at the Electrologica factory in Rijswijk. Only after the delivery of the first EL X8 to Utrecht University, in the summer of 1965, were Mailloux and I able to install our system. Within two mornings the system operated next to flawlessly.

At a late stage, it became clear that the operating system that Electrologica was constructing would not be available in time, not to mention that we had no specification of it at all. Therefore, Mailloux and Van Berckel developed a minimal operating system on very short notice,[27] using the communication instructions for the input/output devices as described in one of the EWDs.[28] That system, named "PICO," was solely intended to support the ALGOL 60 system. In fact, it transformed the EL X8 into a pure ALGOL 60 machine that had to compile and execute ALGOL 60 program after ALGOL 60 program in succession, and nothing else. At several places the EL X8 remained an ALGOL 60 machine forever.

We held the explicit aspiration to bother the users as little as possible with detailed knowledge of the system. Thus, the programmer's manual did not even speak of compilation, only of syntax checking. For the user object programs did not exist. During execution of a program, the detection of an error would lead to the breaking down of the execution, followed by an error message specifying not only the kind of error but also the line number in the ALGOL 60 program in which the error had occurred.[29] It made "debugging" software almost superfluous.

---

[26] Dijkstra (1965c), drijvende arithmetiek.

[27] Kruseman Aretz, Frans E.J. 1974. Doelstellingen en achtergronden van de operating systems PICO, MICRO en MILLI. *Informatie* 16:672–678; Kruseman Aretz, Frans E.J. 2013. *On the design of two small batch operating systems 1965–1970*. CWI report SwAT, Centrum Wiskunde & Informatica, Amsterdam.

[28] Dijkstra, Edsger W. 1965d. *Documentatie over de communicatieapparatuur aan de EL X8*. [EWD140] Available at https://www.cs.utexas.edu/users/EWD/transcriptions/EWD01xx/ EWD140.html and a revised version [EWD149] https://www.cs.utexas.edu/users/EWD/ transcriptions/EWD01xx/EWD149.html.

[29] Kruseman Aretz, Frans E.J. 1971b. On the bookkeeping of source-text line numbers during the execution phase of ALGOL 60 programs. In: *MC-25 informatica symposium: [symposium on the occasion of the 25th anniversary of the Mathematical Centre, Amsterdam, 06-07.01.1972]*, edited De Bakker et al. Mathematical Centre tracts 37. Amsterdam: Mathematical Centre.

In the end, the compiler system ran so flawlessly that only a few corrections of the system were required. It proved to be a wise design decision to make compilation of a program stop at the end of prescan0 if the block structure of that program was too corrupt.

In order to get an impression of how the ALGOL 60 implementation spent its time, I made provisions to determine what the EL X8 at Philips Research was doing, by registering every few minutes during two days of September 1971 the value of the instruction counter and noting the instruction to be executed as well as the two preceding and two succeeding instructions. The result was the following table:

array-indexing	23 %
arithmetic expressions	14 %
block/procedure entrance/exit	12 %
compilation	12 %
input/output-conversion	10 %
sqrt/exp/ln/sin/cos/arctan	10 %
for clauses	4 %
logical expressions	4 %
assignments	2 %
all other constructions	3 %
waiting	7 %

The table yields that for almost 30% of its time the machine was busy doing real calculations. It is also striking that array-indexing took a considerable portion of computer time, of which perhaps some might have been saved by giving one- and two-dimensional arrays a separate treatment.

Was there more that could have been done better? Sure. To mention several points:

- It would have been better to do the checks of syntactic correctness of a program completely in prescan0, to the effect that for programs with an excessively corrupt block structure as many further errors as possible would be reported in advance.
- ALGOL 60 has three kinds of expressions: arithmetic, logical, and designational expressions. During a top-down analysis it is, however, not always clear what kind of (partial) expression is to be expected. A logical expression, e.g., can be a relation and therefore start by an arithmetic expression. And for actual parameters in expression form, it is totally unknown what type of expression will appear. The analysis may be done top-down but is probably carried out more conveniently bottom-up, as is done in the Pascal P compiler.
- We did not expect that our EL X8 would have more than two cabinets of core store. After a while, however, the third cabinet was installed, creating a memory size of 49152 words. But the words with addresses over 32767 were reachable only by indirect addressing, typically by means of an index register. It took only a few modifications to allow the execution stack, the working space of programs, to grow beyond 32767. For the object code of programs it was not that simple and it was never tried.

For the standard functions for square root, sine, and cosine I wrote faster and more accurate versions.[30] The error in the square root could be reduced to less than 1 bit (consequently the exact value was obtained if that square-root value was exactly representable as a floating-point number), the absolute value of a sine or cosine never exceeded 1 and the value of "$\sin(x)/x$" was 1 for small enough values of "x."

The ALGOL 60 system was completed well in time. The coincidence that the first delivery of an EL X8 was way beyond schedule made it easy on us. Utrecht University had been offered an EL X1 by Electrologica to make up for the late delivery of the EL X8. I provided Utrecht with a version of the load-and-go system of the ALGOL 60 implementation of Dijkstra and Zonneveld for their EL X1, a version that could work in a core store of 8192 words only. The ALGOL 60 system for the EL X8 was used at many institutions with an EL X8. To mention a few: the Mathematical Center, Utrecht University, THE (Eindhoven University of Technology), Fokker, Dr Neher Laboratory, Philips Research,[31] RCN (Reactor Center Nederland), the Technische Hochschule Kiel (of which some parts are now in the national Museum Boerhaave in Leiden), and Karlsruhe University.

An Electrologica employee once confided to me that the system had for some time been the fastest ALGOL 60 implementation in the world. That achievement was certainly indebted to the nice collection of instructions of the EL X8 and the use made of it in the implementation. For us it was quite impressive to see programs that had required a full hour of execution time on an EL X1 be completed in one minute on an EL X8. Nevertheless the EL X8 at the Mathematical Center was fully occupied within a few months!

My conclusion is that, after the success of the world's first ALGOL 60 implementation, the Dijkstra-Zonneveld compiler for the EL X1, the Mathematical Center continued its achievements with the implementation of ALGOL 60 for the EL X8. It is marvelous to see this piece of Dutch computer history kept alive by the preservation of an Electrologica X8 machine in Rijksmuseum Boerhaave in Leiden.

---

[30] Kruseman Aretz (2001), Liber Amicorum Jos Jansen.

[31] Zonneveld, Jaap A., and Frans E.J. Kruseman Aretz. 2016. *The NatLab computer center WAA, 1967–1983. Some photos.* Philips Research Technical Note TN-2016/00026, Eindhoven.

Chapter 6
History of Dekker's Algorithm for Mutual Exclusion

A Personal View

Theodorus J. (Dirk) Dekker[1]
Emeritus Informatics Institute, University of Amsterdam, Amsterdam, The Netherlands

Abstract The author describes where, when, and how Edsger Dijkstra presented to him the problem of mutual exclusion for two processes as an open problem, and how he solved this problem within a few days. Furthermore, some variants of solutions are described with some emphasis on fairness and finally, a new algorithm for any number of processes is presented.

6.1 Introduction

In January 1960 the algorithmic language ALGOL 60 was defined. And in the same year Edsger Dijkstra and Jaap Zonneveld produced, for the Electrologica X1 computer, the first ALGOL 60 compiler.[2] Also in that year Edsger Dijkstra posed to me the problem of mutual exclusion and after a few days I presented him my solution.

We, Dijkstra, Zonneveld and I, were then employed at the Mathematical Center, Amsterdam, in the Computation Department ("Rekenafdeling") headed by Aad van Wijngaarden. The department consisted of two sections, the Numerical section headed by Zonneveld and the Programming section headed by Dijkstra. I was a staff member in the Numerical section (Fig. 6.1 and 6.2).

In this configuration, one day, Dijkstra presented to me the problem of mutual exclusion for two processes as an open problem. Fortunately, he did not mention that

---

[1] Paper presented at Electrologica X8 symposium, Rijksmuseum Boerhaave, Leiden. March 24, 2018.

[2] Dijkstra, Edsger W. 1963a. An ALGOL 60 translator for the X1. *Annual Review in Automatic Programming* 3:329–345; Dijkstra, Edsger W. 1963b. Making a translator for ALGOL 60. *Annual Review in Automatic Programming* 3:347–356; Kruseman Aretz, Frans E.J. 2003. *The Dijkstra-Zonneveld ALGOL 60 compiler for the Electrologica X1*. CWI Report SEN-N301. Centrum voor Wiskunde en Informatica. Amsterdam, The Netherlands; Naur, Peter, ed. 1960. J.W. Backus, F.L. Bauer, J. Green, C. Katz, J. McCarthy, A.J. Perlis, H. Rutishauser, K. Samelson, B. Vauquois, J.H. Wegstein, A. van Wijngaarden, M. Woodger, Report on the algorithmic language ALGOL 60. *Num. Mathematik* 2:106–136.

Fig. 6.1 Dirk Dekker in Ostia, 1958

some people in his environment, himself included, had doubts whether the problem might be solvable at all.[3] Moreover, Dijkstra presented a precise definition of the problem, which, I think, is important—say half the work—to find a correct solution.

The problem was clear to us. Dijkstra had developed a system of communication between one processor, Electrologica X1, and various peripheral devices. This was the subject of his doctor's thesis in 1959.[4] So, we could very well imagine a situation

---

[3] Dijkstra, Edsger W. 1962. Over de sequentialiteit van procesbeschrijvingen (Dutch 1962–64) [EWD35]. http://www.cs.utexas.edu/users/EWD/ewd00xx/EWD35.PDF English version: About the sequentiality of process descriptions, at http://www.cs.utexas.edu/users/EWD/translations/EWD35-English.html.

[4] Dijkstra, Edsger W. 1959a. *Communication with an automatic computer*. [PhD Thesis. October 28, 1959. Universiteit van Amsterdam]. Excelsior, Rijswijk.

Fig. 6.2 Dirk Dekker and Aad van Wijngaarden at the Mathematisch Instituut, Roeterstraat 15, 1970s

where two (or more) processes would communicate with some common device, which obviously would require mutual exclusion. Unfortunately, we did not consider at that time to publish my solution. I had solved a nice problem (a "curiosity" as Dijkstra later called it, see below) and that was it.

Dijkstra published my solution in two internal reports of the Technological University Eindhoven, referring to me as "dr. T.J. Dekker" or "the Dutch mathematician Th.J. Dekker."[5] In 1962, Dijkstra stated that Dekker had solved the problem in 1959.[6] I think I solved it in 1960, formulating my algorithm in ALGOL 60, but it may very well be that for Dijkstra the problem dates back to 1959. Moreover, he states that for him this problem had been a "curiosity" for some years and suddenly gained urgency in 1962. Dijkstra wrote: "The problem had by now changed drastically. In 1959, the question was of whether the described capability for communication between two machines made it possible to couple two machines such, that the execution of the critical sections was mutually excluded in time." In 1962, a much wider group of issues was considered and the question had also changed to "What communication possibilities between machines are required, to play this kind of games as gracefully

---

[5] Dijkstra (1962), sequentialiteit van procesbeschrijvingen, page 17; Dijkstra, Edsger W. 1964. Cooperating sequential processes, [EWD123] http://www.cs.utexas.edu/users/EWD/ewd01xx/EWD123. PDF; Dijkstra, Edsger W. 1965a. Co-operating sequential processes. In *Programming languages*, edited F. Genuys, 43–112. New York: Academic Press.

[6] Dijkstra (1962), sequentialiteit van procesbeschrijvingen.

as possible?"[7]. This, subsequently, led to the introduction of semaphores in that paper.

In the sequel, I shall first describe the definition of the problem as Dijkstra presented it to me, subsequently—to the best of my reminiscence, using EWD123 as an aid to memory[8]—describe my solution in the original form which I presented to Dijkstra. Next, I will discuss some variants and finally comment upon the generalized problem for any number of processes and present a new algorithm.

6.2 Definition of the Mutual Exclusion Problem for Two Processes

Two processes use a common critical section one or more times under the following conditions:

1. Mutual exclusion: at each time only one process can use the critical section.
2. No deadlock: the processes must never wait forever to enter the critical section.
3. No starvation: each process must be enabled within finite time to use the critical section.
4. The protocol to enter the critical section must work correctly irrespective of the relative speed of the processes and the speed must not be zero (certainly within the critical section, because the other process would then suffer starvation); moreover, one process must be able to use the critical section more than once in succession when the other process is not interested; for instance, it is not acceptable if the critical section can only be used alternatingly.
5. Reading and writing to common variables used for communication are to be regarded as indivisible operations, i.e. if the two processes simultaneously access a common variable, then the final value of writing must be one of the assigned values and the result of reading must be the value before or that after assignment by the other process, and nothing else.

6.3 Dekker's Algorithm for Mutual Exclusion

I use the language ALGOL 60, because we used this language for communicating algorithms. The algorithm needs some variables which are commonly accessible by the processes. In this language one can assign a value to a variable (assignment

---

[7] Dijkstra (1962), sequentialiteit van procesbeschrijvingen, page 10, quoted from the English translation. "De probleemstelling was inmiddels wel drastisch veranderd. In 1959 was het de vraag of de beschreven communicatiemogelijkheid tussen twee machines het mogelijk maakte om twee machines zodanig te koppelen, dat de uitvoering van de critische trajecten elkaar in de tijd wederzijds uitsloten. In 1962 werd een veel wijdere groep problemen bekeken en werd bovendien de vraagstelling veranderd in "Welke communicatiemogelijkheden tussen machines zijn gewenst, om dit soort spelletjes zo sierlijk mogelijk te spelen?"

[8] Dijkstra (1964), Cooperating sequential processes.

symbol ":="), and one can obtain the actual value of a variable. And these operations are considered to be indivisible operations.

We introduce a control variable for each process, c_1 for process 1 and c_2 for process 2, indicating if the process is interested in the critical section ("active," value 1) or not ("passive," value 0), and a precedence variable *turn* indicating which process has precedence when the processes both are interested. The variables c_1 and c_2 are used to ensure mutual exclusion and the variable *turn* is used to prevent deadlock and starvation.

The initial situation is $c_1 = 0$, $c_2 = 0$ and *turn* = 1 (or 2); this means that, to begin with, processes are passive, i.e., not interested in the critical section, and process 1 (or 2) has precedence. Conditions which hold (and must hold for the sequel) are presented between brackets.

```
begin comment process 1;                      begin comment process 2;
in: part_not_using_critical_section;          in: part_not_using_critical_section;
w0: c1 := 1;                                  w0: c2 := 1;
w1: if c2 = 1 then                            w1: if c1 = 1 then
      begin if turn = 1 then goto w1;               begin if turn = 2 then goto w1;
          c1 := 0;  {turn = 2, c2 = 1}                  c2 := 0;  {turn = 1, c1 = 1}
          comment wait for precedence;                  comment wait for precedence;
w2:       if turn = 2 then goto w2;           w2:       if turn = 1 then goto w2;
          goto w0;                                      goto w0;
      end;          {c1 = 1, c2 = 0}                end;          {c2 = 1, c1 = 0}
      critical_section;                             critical_section;
      turn := 2; c1 := 0;                           turn := 1; c2 := 0;
      goto in;                                      goto in;
end                                           end
```

Proof. To enter the critical section a process first shows interest by assigning the active value 1 to its control variable. The process then asks if the other process is active. If not, it can enter immediately. The entrance condition, i.e., the condition to enter the critical section, is: the own control variable (c_1 or c_2) has the active value 1 and thereafter the control variable for the other process (c_2 or c_1) has the passive value 0. This ensures mutual exclusion. Note that a process must first set its own control variable and then get the value of the other one. The value of *turn* plays a role only when the processes both are interested in the critical section. Then the process not having precedence assigns the passive value 0 to its control variable, thus temporarily not showing interest, in order to yield the right of way to the other process which will then enter after finite time because its speed is non-zero. This ensures that no deadlock occurs. After completing and leaving the critical section, a process assigns a value to the variable *turn* yielding precedence to the other process and thereafter finally assigns the passive value 0 to its own control variable so that the other process can enter. Thus, no starvation occurs.   □

Note that the two processes can never change a variable simultaneously. Each process can change only its own control variable, and variable *turn* is only changed by a process leaving the critical section before it assigns the passive value 0 to its control variable.

Remarks.

1. Designing my algorithm, the choice of the three commonly accessible variables was obvious to me. I think that the crucial step in this algorithm is that a process not having precedence temporarily holds back, i.e. it temporarily assigns the passive value to its control variable in order to enable the other process to enter. Subsequently, after finite time the process will get precedence and can enter as described above.
2. This algorithm is not fair, i.e. does not satisfy "first come first serve." Especially when the speeds of the processes differ considerably, it may happen that a fast process enters the critical section several times before the other process finds that it has precedence, then assigns the active value to its control variable and enters when the other process is ready, all within finite time.

6.4 Variants

An Equivalent Variant. Here, an equivalent variant of the algorithm is given. It just may have been the case that I simply used the variable names a, b, and c, instead of c_1, c_2, and *turn*. The presented text is conforming to that in Dijkstra[9], except for the values 0 and 1 of the control variables. Dijkstra had 1 for "passive" and 0 for "active." It strikes me as somewhat unnatural and I think that, at the time, I chose the values as presented above.

In 1962 Dijkstra presented the algorithm (with values "true" and "false" for the entrance variables) in the form of a flow diagram.[10] It had the advantage of presenting program pieces, the pieces liable to be executed simultaneously, next to each other, visually in parallel. The downside of the flow diagram presentation was that, in ALGOL 60 and other programming languages, one must write the program pieces in some sequential order.

I am not sure which order I chose in my original formulation. Placing the waiting cycle for non-precedence first, followed by the cycle for precedence, is an equivalent choice. Moreover, the latter cycle jumps back to label w_0, which, I think was my original formulation. The version chosen here, however, allows a slightly improved variant: the cycle with precedence does not need to test the value of *turn* anymore and can therefore be represented as a separate cycle jumping back to label w_2, as elaborated for process 1 presented below. Doran and Thomas offer the same variant, adding a comment that they prefer two successive loops over the nested loops.[11]

---

[9] Dijkstra (1964), Cooperating sequential processes; Dijkstra (1965a), Co-operating sequential processes.

[10] Dijkstra (1962), sequentialiteit van procesbeschrijvingen.

```
begin comment process 1;
in: part_not _using_critical_section;
w_0: c_1 := 1;
    if c_2 = 1 then
    begin if turn = 2 then                    {turn = 2, c_2 = 1}
        begin c_1 := 0; comment wait for precedence;
        w_1: if turn = 2 then goto w_1;
            c_1 := 1;
        end; comment from now on turn remains 1;
    w_2: if c_2 = 1 then goto w_2;
    end;                                      {c_1 = 1, c_2 = 0}
    critical_section;
    turn := 2; c_1 := 0;
    goto in;
end
```

A Fair Variant. Next, let me provide a fair algorithm. It may have been that I have considered whether more than two different values for c_1 and c_2 would be needed or useful. My conclusion was that two different values, say 0 and 1, suffice. However, adding a third value may yield a valuable improvement, namely fairness. In the above algorithm value 1 means that a process is interested in the critical section, but value 0 means either that the process is not interested or is waiting for precedence. Thus, it makes sense to use three values, say 0 for passive, i.e., not interested, 1 for requesting, i.e. waiting for precedence, and 2 for active. This leads to the following variant:

```
begin comment process 1;
in: part_not_using_critical_section;
w_0: c_1 := 1;
    if c_2 > 0 then
w_1:    if turn = 2 then goto w_1;           {turn = 1 or c_2 = 0}
    c_1 := 2;
    if turn = 2 then
        begin if c_2 > 0 then goto w_0       {turn = 2, c_1 = 2, c_2 = 0}
        end
    else
w_2:    if c_2 = 2 then goto w_2;            {turn = 1, c_1 = 2, c_2 < 2}
    critical_section;
    turn := 2; c_1 := 0;
    goto in;
end
```

[11] Doran, R.W., and L.K. Thomas. 1980. Variants of the software solution to mutual exclusion. *Information Processing Letters* 10(4):206–208.

Note that in this variant two different entrance conditions are used depending on the precedence. The condition for process 1 to enter the critical section is $c_1 = 2$ and thereafter $c_2 = 0$ if $turn = 2$ or $c_2 < 2$ if $turn = 1$. Here three loops are used and the second loop jumps back to label w_0 to ensure this entrance condition. This algorithm is roughly similar—but not equivalent—to that by Knuth for two processes, which first tests $turn$ and then the control variable of the other process, and also takes precedence by changing the value of $turn$ ($k := i$ in his notation) before entering the critical section.[12] De Bruijn presents an improved version (for N processes) changing $turn$ after leaving the critical section, but doing so only in favor of other process(es).[13] In all these variants the other process cannot sneak into the critical section another time when a process is interested. So, the algorithms are fair.

Another Fair Algorithm. The algorithm of Peterson is also correct and, as Raynal remarks: "an elegant and simple solution to this problem."[14] The main differences are that in this algorithm each process has only one waiting cycle, only two values are used for the entrance variables and variable $turn$ plays a different role. Here my translation of Peterson's algorithm into ALGOL 60 follows.

```
begin comment process 1;                    begin comment process 2;
in: part_not_using_critical_section;        in: part_not_using_critical_section;
    c₁ := 1; turn := 1;                          c₂ := 1; turn := 2;
w₀: if c₂ = 1 and turn = 1 then             w₀: if c₁ = 1 and turn = 2 then
        goto w₀;                                     goto w₀;
    {c₁ = 1, c₂ = 0 or turn = 2}                 {c₂ = 1, c₁ = 0 or turn = 1}
    critical_section;                            critical_section;
    c₁ := 0;                                     c₂ := 0;
    goto in;                                     goto in;
end                                         end
```

The entrance condition for each process is that its control variable is set active and then either the other process is passive or the value of $turn$ equals the number of the other process, indicating that the other process is later. So, this algorithm is also fair. Note that in this algorithm $turn$ indicates not which process has precedence, but which process has latest assigned to $turn$ and thus has no precedence.

[12] Knuth, Donald E. 1966. Additional comments on a problem in concurrent programming control. *Communications ACM* 9(5):321–322.

[13] Bruijn, Nicolaas G. de. 1967. Additional comments on a problem in concurrent programming control. *Communications ACM* 10(3):137–138.

[14] Peterson, G.L. 1981. Myths about the mutual exclusion problem. *Information Processing Letters* 12(3):115–116; Raynal, M. 1986. *Algorithms for mutual exclusion*. Oxford: North Oxford Academic.

6.5 Mutual Exclusion for Any Number of Processes

Algorithms to solve this problem for any number of processes have been presented by Dijkstra, Knuth, De Bruijn, Lamport, and Peterson.[15] Knuth remarks on Dijkstra's algorithm that "there is a definite possibility that one or more of the computers which wants to execute its critical section may have to wait 'until eternity' while other programs are executing theirs." De Bruijn remarks on Knuth's solution for N processes: "It is not quite easy to check that any computer waiting for its critical section has to wait at most 2^{N-1} turns." Subsequently, he presents a slight modification of Knuth's algorithm such that the upper bound "can be reduced to $\frac{1}{2}N(N-1)$, with the extra advantage that for this new program it is easier to see why and how it works." In general, the algorithms mentioned differ mainly in how the order of precedence of the processes is defined.

A New Algorithm. I propose a new algorithm using a linked list of precedence. After completing the critical section a process places itself at the bottom of the list and moves the other lower ranking processes one place upward. Thus, I claim, the upper bound for waiting is reduced to N. I think that this algorithm is more in the spirit of Dekker's algorithm for two processes. However, this algorithm uses three values for the control variables in order to ensure fairness.

The moves in the list must be done such that always all processes in the list remain visible for the other processes. Hence, the process placed at the bottom of the list temporarily occurs twice in the list. Consequently, the bottom element cannot be used to indicate the end of the list. Therefore, the penultimate element is used instead, the bottom element being defined as the one next to it.

We assume for N processes that, besides N, the following variables are commonly accessible:

integer *top, penult*; **integer array** $c[1:N]$, *next*$[1:N]$;

and that the initial situation is as follows:

top $= N$, *penult* $= 2$, and for $j = 1, \ldots, N$: $c[j] = 0$ and *next*$[j] = j - 1$.

This means that, to begin with, all processes are passive, i.e., not interested in the critical section, and the order of precedence of the processes corresponds to their process number j, where process N has highest priority. (Any other ordering would do, we choose this for simplicity.)

Starting from this initial situation, procedures *process*(i) for $i = 1, \ldots, N$ are executed in parallel:

---

[15] Dijkstra (1965a), Co-operating sequential processes; Dijkstra, Edsger W. 1965b. Solution of a problem in concurrent programming control. *Communications ACM* 8(9):569; Knuth (1966), a problem in concurrent programming control; Bruijn, de (1967), problem in concurrent programming; Peterson (1981), Myths; Lamport, Leslie. 1974. A new solution of Dijkstra's concurrent programming problem. *Communications ACM* 17(8):453–455.

procedure *process* (**value** i; **integer** i);
begin integer *pre, previous, post, pos, subtop, bottom*;
in_0: part_not_using_critical_section;
w_0: $c[i] := 1$;
w_1: *pre* := *top*;
in_1: **if** *pre* $\neq i$ **then**
    begin if $c[pre] > 0$ **then goto** w_1;
        pre := *next[pre]*; **goto** in_1
    end;   {all $c[pre] = 0$}
    $c[i] := 2$; **comment** same loop with $c[i] = 2$;
    pre := *top*;
in_2: **if** *pre* $\neq i$ **then**
    begin if $c[pre] > 0$ **then goto** w_0;
        previous := *pre*; *pre* := *next[pre]*; **goto** in_2
    end;   {$c[i] = 2$, all $c[pre] = 0$}
    comment $c[i]$ remains 2: preceding processes ready or not interested,
                wait until posterior processes ready;
    if (**if** $i = top$ **then true else** *previous* $\neq$ *penult*) **then**
w_2: **begin** *post* := i;
    in_3: *pos* := *post*; *post* := *next[post]*; **if** $c[post] = 2$ **then goto** w_2;
        if *pos* $\neq$ *penult* **then goto** in_3
    end;   {$c[i] = 2$, all $c[pre] = 0$, all $c[post] < 2$}
    critical_section;
    bottom := *next[penult]*; **comment** place process i at bottom;
    if $i \neq bottom$ **then**
    begin *next[bottom]* := i; *penult* := *bottom*;
        subtop := *next[i]*;
        if $i = top$ **then** *top* := *subtop* **else** *next[previous]* := *subtop*;
    end;
    $c[i] := 0$; **goto** in_0;
end

Note that this algorithm treats the preceding processes and the posterior processes differently. The condition for process i to enter the critical section is $c[i] = 2$, thereafter $c[pre] = 0$ for the preceding processes and finally $c[post] < 2$ for the posterior processes. So, this algorithm is fair. This algorithm works correctly for $N > 2$. For $N = 1$ it is meaningless and does not work trivially. For $N = 2$ the algorithm is equivalent to the first fair algorithm presented above for two processes.

Acknowledgements The author is grateful to Gerard Alberts and Peter van Emde Boas for their encouragements and valuable comments.

Chapter 7
The Electrologica X8 and the BOL Detector

Networking, programming, time-sharing, and data handling in the Amsterdam nuclear research project "BOL," a personal historical review

René van Dantzig[1]
National Institute for Subatomic Physics (Nikhef), Amsterdam, The Netherlands

Abstract From 1967 to 1974, an Electrologica X8 computer was installed at the Institute for Nuclear Research (IKO) in Amsterdam, primarily for online and offline evaluation of experimental data, an application quite different from its "brother's," X8's. During that time, the nuclear detection system "BOL"[2] was in operation to study nuclear reactions. The BOL detector embodied a new and bold concept. It consisted of a large number of state-of-the-art detection units, mounted in a spherical arrangement around a target in a beam of nuclear particles. Two minicomputers performed data acquisition and control of the experiment and supported online visual display of acquired data. The X8 computer, networked with the minicomputers, allowed fast high-level data processing and analysis. Pioneering work in both experimental nuclear physics as well as in programming, turned out to be a surprisingly good combination. For the network with the X8 and the minicomputers, advanced software layers were developed to efficiently and flexibly program extensive data handling.

---

[1] This review is dedicated to the memory of my dear brother Émile C. van Dantzig, who started his career in information technology with the X8 at the Mathematical Center in 1968 and moved to IKO in 1972, where he enthusiastically and skillfully managed the X8 and the succeeding DEC system-10 until 1979.

[2] 'BOL' is Dutch for 'SPHERE'.

7.1 Introduction and Background

The establishment of the Mathematical Center (MC)[3] and of the Institute for Nuclear Research (IKO)[4] was firmly rooted in the post-World War II revival of science in Europe. One of the many important ramifications was the groundbreaking development of computers at the MC, in conjunction with a large-scale nuclear detection system at IKO. As described in this article, direct and indirect links between these two successful institutes proved to be extremely fruitful, for IKO in particular.

It was in the summer of 1953, when I was 16 years old, that I had the opportunity to spend six weeks in the computing department of the MC, where I was able to "assist" in assembling and testing circuits for the second version of the ARRA computer[5]. There, I met prof. Adriaan van Wijngaarden, Bram Loopstra, Carel Scholten, Edsger Dijkstra, and Jaap Zonneveld, the team responsible for a decade of inventive computer developments[6] at the MC, the early pioneers of Dutch information and computer technology in hardware as well as in software. Their work was continued at the first Dutch computer manufacturer, Electrologica[7].

The initial series of Electrologica computers was the "EL-X1," an early copy of which was installed at the MC in 1960. The MC offered courses on coding the X1 machine. These courses were open to people from outside the MC, and I, at the time a physics student at IKO, attended these, receiving a coding certificate in 1961. On top of that, Van Wijngaarden's inspiring classes in numerical mathematics at the university of Amsterdam made me and others at IKO familiar with programming techniques in the ALGOL 60 language. This turned out to be quite relevant for IKO, since in the early 1960s the need for data reduction, analysis, and theoretical modeling increased significantly. For me, it meant that my use of the very noisy mechanical Monroe and Friden motor driven calculators was steadily replaced by

---

[3] The Mathematical Center (MC) was founded in 1946 and housed in a school building in East Amsterdam. The first director was Johannes van der Corput. The MC installed a Computation Department in 1947, led by Adriaan van Wijngaarden. In 1983 the name was changed to Center for Mathematics and Informatics (CWI).

[4] IKO was established in 1946 in buildings of a former gas factory in East Amsterdam. The founding partners were Philips, the Foundation for Fundamental research on Matter (FOM), and the City of Amsterdam. The first director was Cornelis J. Bakker, who later became director of CERN, the institute currently known as European Center of Particle Physics (Cern) in Geneva. In 1975, IKO became part of NIKHEF, the National Institute for Nuclear- and High-Energy Physics—later renamed the National Institute for Subatomic Physics (Nikhef).

[5] This "job" was arranged for me by prof. David van Dantzig, mathematician, statistician, MC department head, one of the founders of the MC, and my father, who paid me the equivalent salary of a simple holiday job at an enterprise (my original intention), because he thought that staying at the MC would be better for my future. He was right.

[6] At the MC the first Dutch computers were developed: i.e., vacuum tube machines ARRA-I (1952), ARRA-II (1954) and FERTA (1955); later the partly transistorized ARMAC (1956) and the fully transistorized X1.

[7] Electrologica was founded in 1956 by A. van Wijngaarden, B.J. Loopstra and C.S. Scholten from the MC, and J. Engelfriet, from the assurance company Nillmij. Electrologica developed and produced the X1 (1959) and finally the "eightfold" faster X8 (1965). In 1968 Electrologica was taken over by Philips and renamed "Philips-Electrologica."

silent programming. The MC had created an open shop service for the EL-X1 computer, which allowed us physicists and technicians to write our programs during daytime and run these ourselves at the MC during evenings and nights. We spent nights running programs on the X1 with a portable radio on the memory cabinet: the beeping and crackling of the radio interference kept telling us how far the data processing had progressed.

Our institute, IKO, had been set up to house a synchro-cyclotron[8], the first circular accelerator of nuclear particles in Europe and at that time the second largest in the world. The cyclotron, based on principles developed in the USA, had been constructed by the Philips company. It became operational in 1949, enabling irradiations inside the cyclotron. Accelerated particles of various types[9] with various energies could hit a target inserted at the edge of the cyclotron. Nuclear collisions produced radioactive nuclei inside the target, which was removed after irradiation[10] for radiochemical and nuclear spectroscopy studies, as well as for medical purposes.

Not long before I started as a student at IKO in 1959 the cyclotron had been equipped with an external beam system to guide nuclear particles to a target far outside the cyclotron, where they collided with the target nuclei. Generally, nuclear particles can fly away from such collisions in "any" direction. When caught in special detectors near the target in a vacuum scattering chamber, detected particles can reveal aspects of the collision process, of the nuclear reactions that occur and of the structure of the nuclei involved.

The IKO "nuclear reaction group," also called "deflection group," in which I participated for the experimental part of my study, had been responsible for the extraction and deflection of the beam from the cyclotron and its use for nuclear reaction experiments. In addition to the internal irradiations, the external beam with various instrumental setups made it possible to perform a range of nuclear experiments, including the one for my own master's thesis in 1962.

In the first few years of the 1960s, a second accelerator was built at IKO, the linear electron accelerator "EVA." All the activities relating to both accelerators were part of a broad and fruitful research program that was a rich source for publications in international journals over the years. In this article, we will concentrate on parts of the work with the cyclotron.

---

[8] In principle, a circular accelerator can reach much higher energies for charged particles than a linear accelerator. In a synchro-cyclotron, the high frequency/high voltage acceleration mechanism is adapted to the relativistic mass increase of particles with increasing energy; Heyn, F.A., and J.J. Burgerjon. 1952. Het synchro-cyclotron te Amsterdam. *Philips Technisch Tijdschrift* 14:291–307; Luijckx, Guy. 1980. Het cyclotron. *Philips Technisch Tijdschrift* 39(10):274–276.

[9] Originally only deuterons and alpha-particles (^{4}He-nuclei) could be accelerated, later also protons and ^{3}He-nuclei.

[10] In 1966, the 15,000th internal irradiation took place.

7.2 The BOL Project

In 1964, I returned to the nuclear reactions group after a one-year stay abroad[11]. By that time, measurements at IKO as well as in laboratories elsewhere had shown the importance of detecting two or more particles emerging simultaneously from the same nuclear collision, called "coincidences." These provided much more detailed information on the ongoing nuclear reactions and on the structure of the colliding nuclei compared to the more common "singles" measurements. This was particularly true for "few body reactions," which could be well described theoretically and give information about nuclear dynamics and forces.

After various feasibility studies, initiated by our group leader, Leo A.Ch. Koerts, a broad instrumental development was set up to construct a brand new type of detection system to measure coincidences.[12] The system would include a then revolutionarily shaped, spherical scattering chamber around the target, containing many detection units, the whole resembling an inverted insect's eye. This became the BOL project.[13]

One underlying idea was that the number of pairs of detection units rises almost quadratically with the number of detection units. Therefore, also the probability to catch coincident particles would rise quadratically with that number. Another principal idea was that the detection units, when placed in a spherical arrangement, could sample nearly the entire measurement space at the same time.

An ambitious team of enthusiastic physicists and technicians, the BOL team, was formed around Koerts, the founding father and overall coordinator of the BOL project. Three very motivated physicists in their twenties, Karel Mulder, Jona E.J. Oberski, and myself, coordinated the developments of, respectively, mechanical and detection hardware, electronics and computing hardware, and software. However, all three of us were more or less involved in all BOL activities. This meant that we had a broad spectrum of unofficial duties and responsibilities, although none of us had a PhD yet. These were different times from today! We had a semi-permanent employment contract at IKO and were not supposed to write our PhD theses until we had obtained our own significant physics results, whatever time it would take. Building the equipment to obtain these required many years' work, including substantial delays! Gradually, the team was expanded with younger PhD students, master's students, and technicians. Most of them made vital contributions to our project. From the beginning, we operated in a remarkably free environment, based on mutual trust and equality, without any authoritarian hierarchy or bureaucracy.

The BOL detector was mainly designed and constructed during the years 1964–1966. The apparatus came into operation with a steadily growing number of rocket-shaped detection units, ultimately 64 in all. When mounted, each had its silicon

---

[11] At the Weizmann Institute of Science, Rehovot, Israel, I studied nuclear theory and made an analysis of my master's thesis measurements. This was made possible by a stipend from the Dutch organization for scientific research (ZWO).

[12] Koerts, L.A.Ch., K. Mulder, J.E.J. Oberski, and R. van Dantzig. 1971. The BOL nuclear research project. *Nuclear Instruments and Methods* 92:157–160.

[13] Dantzig, René van. 2017. Project BOL (1964–1977), Historical overview. https://www.nikhef.nl/history/bol-EN.

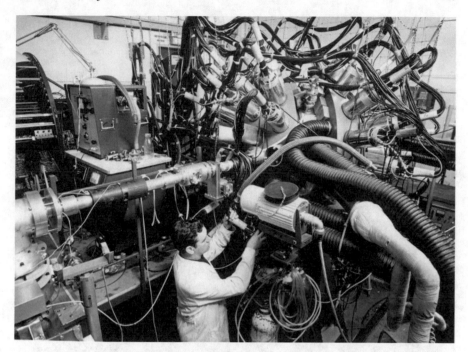

Fig. 7.1 The BOL detector, with technician Wil Verlegh at work. The particle beam can pass through the pipe coming from the left side

semiconductor "detector telescope" in a vacuum scattering chamber, cooled at minus 20 °C and pointing at the target; the external part contained air-cooled front-end electronics (Fig. 7.1).

BOL was the first "4π-type"[14] nuclear physics multi-detector system in the world that simultaneously covered largely all scattering angles and could determine the "type" of the detected particles. It was equipped with state-of-the-art detectors developed in close collaboration with the BOL team by the Philips NatLab Nuclear Detection group.[15] An essential innovation was the Checkerboard detector, which made it possible to determine a particle impact position with millimeter precision, corresponding to typically 1 degree in scattering angle. This detector turned out

---

[14] "4π-type" means sampling all 4π steradians, the total maximum solid angle (the surface of a unit sphere) by an internally directed omnidirectional looking fine-meshed "fly's eye." The coverage for detection was typically 10% for single particles and 1% for coincidences, values experimentally unprecedented at that time.

[15] Dantzig, René van. 1980. BOL. *Philips Technisch Tijdschrift* 39/10:286–291 (Dutch, English and French edition). The Philips NatLab Nuclear Detection group led by dr. Wim Hofker included Piet Bakker, Jarich Politiek, Dick Oosthoek, and others. It was housed at the IKO campus.

to be a first step in the development of detectors currently essential in high-energy particle physics experimentation.[16]

Fig. 7.2 BOL electronics for one of the 64 detection channels: (**a**) detection unit, from top to bottom: detector telescope, pre-amplifiers, vacuum-air separating flange, processing electronics for the analog signals; (**b**) printed circuit board that contains the logic and control electronics; (**c**) printed circuit board that digitizes the detection signals

In line with the complexity and the new detection methods, the technical realization of BOL implied new approaches and specialized expertise[17] on the design, testing, and production of a massive and at the same time delicate electronic system.[18]

---

[16] Heijne, Erik H.M. 2003. Semiconductor detectors in the low countries. *Nuclear Instruments and Methods in Physics Research* 309:1–16.

[17] The electronics were designed and developed with indispensable ingenuity and perseverance by Rein F. Rumphorst, head of the electronics group, assisted by Johan Dieperink, Erwin Kok and others.

[18] Oberski, Jona E.J., et al. 1971a. Electronics of the BOL system. *Nuclear Instruments and Methods* 92:177–187.

Each of the 64 detection channels consisted of electronics for (a) preprocessing the signals inside the detection units, as well as two large printed circuit boards with (b) system logic and (c) digitization using several analog-to-digital converters (ADCs). One of these—as a masterpiece—was a 4096-channel high-precision highly linear ADC operating at 100 MHz, a marvel far ahead of its time. The 2×64 boards (Fig. 7.2) were radially mounted in adjacent cylindrical frames, the "double drum." To illustrate that all the hard work was not without humor, each ADC-board carried a motto, which freely translated to: "Computer at any speed, this ADC will floor it indeed."

Fig. 7.3 BOL control panels at left, display station and PDP8-B with teletype at right, and the cyclotron control console with the operator at the back

Compared to what was available commercially those days, the resulting BOL electronics were unrivaled in terms of precision, measurement speed, and size.[19] Each of the 64 detector units had its own electronic channel with manual control of several voltage parameters (Fig. 7.3). All channels had at the-back end a 72-bit register. This held all digital data of one detected particle, a "single particle event." The 72 bits were made-up of "bites," each containing a measured value—for

---

[19] In total, the BOL electronics contained about 40,000 transistors, 100,000 passive components, 35 m^2 circuit board, and 13 km of cabling, all of which were huge quantities at that time for such equipment.

instance, an energy signal from the detection telescope (12 bits), a similar signal from the checkerboard detector (7 bits), a mark to indicate which single particle events belonged together to form a coincidence event, and others. The "event data" were read out from the detection channels through a sequencer by a minicomputer (see Sect. 7.7), part of a dedicated computer network.

From 1965 onwards, the BOL detector and its infrastructure were gradually produced, assembled, and commissioned. Creating BOL gave rise to a variety of technological challenges for IKO, and the project involved about half of the staff of the institute. Their joint effort: assembling a complex mechanical construction with subtle cooling and vacuum hardware, fragile detectors, and the intricate electronics system. For everyone involved, these years offered a wealth of experience. A lot of details had to be thought through in advance, while it was not yet clear how matters would turn out.

In 1968, we obtained the first results with successively 10, 20, and 30 detection units. From that time on, the system was systematically expanded, debugged, and increasingly used for experiments with day and night data recording periods and subsequent analysis. This continued until the summer of 1973, when BOL was put on stand-by.

Innovative as they were, BOL and the cyclotron had their limitations. In order to avoid overload by accidental coincidences, the BOL experiment could handle only a low-intensity beam, matching the limited properties of the nearly two decades-old cyclotron, which was by itself no longer competitive with the modern cyclotrons that appeared elsewhere in Europe. For a decade BOL contributed significantly to the useful life of the "aged" IKO-cyclotron, which was switched off in 1975.

7.3 Why and How the X8 Came to IKO

At the beginning of my work at IKO in 1960, before the BOL project, nuclear measurements were visualized online as 1-dimensional (1D) or 2-dimensional (2D) distributions of the number of detection signals (pulses) as a function of their height, "pulse-height spectra"[20]. These distributions were obtained with a "kicksorter" or "pulse-height analyzer," which contained one or two ADCs coupled to core memory. In tandem with the recording process, a cycling process went along all memory addresses and displayed the spectrum dynamically on a CRT (cathode ray tube) display. Thus, we could visually follow during the experiment various spectra, corresponding to detection signals. Whenever a typical spectrum reached sufficient significance, we stopped the accumulation, studied the spectrum in detail and decided if it was what we wanted. If not, the experiment was readjusted and the procedure was repeated. The spectra could be printed, punched, or saved on magnetic tape.

In general, a physics measurement with many adjustable elements in the system needs continuous monitoring and supervision of the system behavior. In addition, at

---

[20] The pulses were sorted according to their height in bins and counted per bin.

the start-up of the measurement and at any time when changes are to be made, correct parameter adjustments or re-adjustments depend on adequate feedback concerning the system functions.

When we learned of small online computers in the USA, it was immediately clear to us that replacing a kicksorter with a small general-purpose computer would be of tremendous advantage. The latter could do all of the data handling of the kicksorter much better, with much more flexibility and capacity!

When Digital Equipment Corporation (DEC)'s PDP-8 minicomputer[21] came on the market, we immediately purchased one for the data acquisition[22] in the BOL project. We remember the wooden crate that came by plane from the USA, from which a gleaming half-transparent PDP-8 computer emerged. All of us immediately fell in love with it! A second one, also for BOL, followed soon; several more were bought for other IKO research groups. From the beginning, perhaps because of our X1 coding experience, some of us were fascinated by programming these machines. The PDP8 4K Disk Monitoring System that came with them was primitive and not well-suited to our data acquisition needs. I initiated several developments, some of which are discussed in Sect. 7.1. Although both PDP8 machines offered us remarkable possibilities and were certainly essential for data acquisition and for experiment control, their capacity was far from sufficient for the needs we anticipated for online data handling for BOL.

From 1962, at all of IKO, the steadily growing computing requirements were annually evaluated and reported. A committee was appointed to prepare a plan on how to meet the future calculation needs. It was anticipated that the necessities for experiments at both IKO accelerators would be enough reason to seek funding for an in-house general-purpose computer. Up to that time, the offline calculations had practically all been done on the X1 at the MC. In 1964, it was foreseen that an online computer would ultimately be needed in 1966 to cover all IKO computing work.

In December 1962, Lout Jonkers, already acquainted with many aspects of computing, started his master's study at IKO on our in-house computer issues. In 1964, after his first year of orientation and study, he wrote an internal report[23] concerning computer requirements for the various experimental setups in operation, in which he called for minicomputers as a solution to the experimental problems. At that moment, it was not yet clear at the laboratory level how fast new instrumentation (BOL) could change the requirements. In a slightly later report,[24] he argued that: "for the sake of

[21] This "Classic" "Programmable Data Processor," PDP-8, was the first real minicomputer (1965) having 4K 12-bit memory (32 pages of 128 words) and direct addressing within a page. The machine came with a Teletype ASR-33 serving as a console as well as paper tape punch and reader. Our machine also had a DF32 fixed head disk system with a storage capacity of 32k 12-bit words. In this article, we will refer to PDP-8 as "PDP8."

[22] Dantzig, René van, et al. 1971a. Data acquisition with the BOL nuclear detection system. *Nuclear Instruments and Methods* 92:199–203.

[23] Jonkers, H.L., W.T.H. van Oers, and H.R.E. Tjin A Djie. 1964a. Discussie rond huidige en toekomstige behoefte aan rekencapaciteit van het IKO. IKO internal report Interiko 64. Archived at the National Museum Boerhaave, Leiden and at Nikhef, Amsterdam.

[24] Jonkers, H.L. 1964c. Computer requirements of the Institute for Nuclear Physics Research. IKO informal report. Archived at the National Museum Boerhaave, Leiden and at Nikhef, Amsterdam.

following the experiment and experimental control, the immediate interpretation of preliminary results requires complicated computations and data processing. Large quantities of information will have to be stored with high speed and in such a manner that later offline data reduction by a computer can be done economically." This report also addressed the need for "multiprogramming with hardware program relocation and multi-level indirect addressing" and stated that "it is highly desirable that there will be close cooperation between the manufacturer and our laboratory." We fully agreed with all of these points, and his discussions with us may have fleshed out the particulars.

The X8 in development at Electrologica had already been in the picture as a possible future IKO-machine since 1963. An ad hoc comparison[25] between the X8 and the CDC 3200 from Control Data Corporation, a US company particularly active in Europe, showed advantages[26] for the X8—partly because of its appealing broader functionality and partly due to the possible support of Electrologica on hardware and software development. For comparison, offers were requested from several US computer manufactories, including CDC. It turned out that only the least expensive machine, the CDC 3200, was at all affordable. In 1964, the X8—almost ready for rent or lease—became the anticipated (dreamed) machine for BOL as well as for other IKO applications, and consultations took place.

On the basis of the above evaluations, in 1964, IKO requested funding for the fiscal year 1965 from the overarching research agencies FOM (Foundation for Fundamental Research on Matter) and ZWO (the Dutch organization for pure scientific research) for the procurement of an electronic computer.[27] Almost at the same time, the high-energy physics (HEF) community at the Zeeman Laboratory in Amsterdam requested funding along the same route for a computer, online and offline, for equipment measuring high-energy particle tracks on pictures taken at Cern. Unfortunately for us, the IKO request for 1965 was not approved; that year, high-energy physics was prioritized[28] with a rented CDC 3200.

Still, at the same time, the online coupling of the computer to BOL became the spearhead of an updated funding request specifically for the X8, with convincing arguments being made for the X8, in comparison with the foreign (US) alternatives.

---

[25] Wapstra, A.H., H.L. Jonkers, and L.A.Ch. Koerts. 1964. Internal note 'Rekenmachine'. https://ub.fnwi.uva.nl/computermuseum/pdfs/Wapstra.pdf; Jonkers, H.L. 1964b. A comparison EL-X8 and CDC-3200 for on-line use. IKO internal report Interiko 64/5. Archived at the National Museum Boerhaave, Leiden and at Nikhef, Amsterdam. https://ub.fnwi.uva.nl/computermuseum/pdfs/X8vsCDC3200.pdf.

[26] Although the X8 cycle time was longer, the instruction set was considered considerably more powerful.

[27] Wapstra, A.H., H.L. Jonkers, et al. 1965. Voorstel tot aanschaffing van een electronische rekenautomaat ten behoeve van het fysisch werk op het Instituut voor Kernfysisch Onderzoek. Internal report IKO-2168. https://ub.fnwi.uva.nl/computermuseum/pdfs/X8aanschafvoorstel.pdf.

[28] The competing demands in 1966 for expensive computing facilities from the side of the high-energy physics (HEF) community as well as from IKO, the nuclear physics institute, prompted FOM to propose to ZWO to combine both in one national institute of nuclear and high-energy physics. However, it was not until almost a decade later, in 1975, that this institute, NIKHEF was created, where at that moment my employment contract with FOM was continued.

This time, the request was honored! Delivery would be in 1966; it actually turned out to be 1967, two years later than we had originally planned. On the other hand, such delays also occurred in other parts of our project, so we had gotten used to this.

7.4 Setting up the Computing and Network Infrastructure

As mentioned, before online computers were available, we would check and adjust the performance of our experimental setups using "measured data" from an online kicksorter on an oscilloscope display. We realized that, making the transition to work with BOL, we were bound to change our habits and base our adjustment decisions on more significant "preliminarily analyzed data," to be delivered by a computer. In this spirit, hardware and software for the approved EL X8 were prepared. In 1965, the contract was signed between IKO/FOM and Electrologica, in which it was agreed that in addition to the standard computer with various peripherals, a hardware buffer interface, "IKOB," with accompanying software and several software packages would be supplied by Electrologica according to mutually agreed specifications.

In conjunction with Electrologica staff and together with my collaborators, I had interrupted my involvement on the PDP8s (see Sect. 7.7) in order to specify the X8 packages. Similarly, my close collaborator, Jona Oberski, in consultation[29] with Electrologica, came up with the specifications for the network communication between the X8 and the PDP8s. None of us had experience with large software packages or with networking for an X8, but that was also true for most of the BOL-developments: the learning curves were steep. We were told by Electrologica that the communication principles and design specifications for IKOB had to be formulated by us within three months; otherwise, the X8 delivery would be substantially delayed. Despite Electrologica's expectation that this would be impossible for us, the deadline was met! Perhaps that is why Electrologica could not meet the scheduled delivery.

In planning for the data processing and data analysis, we realized that BOL would produce large amounts of individual, non-reproducible events, for each of which a set of quantities would be measured simultaneously. On these raw event measurements, a range of criteria and conversions would have to be applied. Ultimately, not these event data themselves would be the final goal, but rather a "bundled" representation of them. Additionally, such bundled data, "spectra" in a broad sense, needed to be processed further, in order to obtain the final results of the experiment that allowed physics interpretations.

Concerning the network communication, our point of departure was that the burden of the "clerical control" should primarily be carried by the X8, since that machine was equipped with sophisticated input/output (I/O) facilities. On the other hand, a PDP8 machine incorporated in the network would have to give final permis-

---

[29] In particular, with Philip Seligmann from Electrologica.

sion before any data transfer, even if it had taken the initiative. In the box in Fig. 7.6, we give a synopsis of the network communication guidelines.[30]

To help carry over the data, the X8 contained a dedicated micro-programmable I/O-processor, called Charon. Although the Greek mythological ferryman Charon would row his passengers across the Styx to the other world himself, the X8-Charon could delegate the actual "rowing" between computers to IKOB together with the fast direct-memory-access (DMA) mechanism of the X8 (fast-channel-selector, SKK) and of the PDP8s (data-break).

Fig. 7.4 The X8-room with programmer Anton Mars. From right to left: X8-console, magnetic tape drives, punched paper tape boxes, paper tape reader, and paper tape punch

The installation of our X8 configuration[31] started in late 1966 and was completed at the beginning of 1967 (Fig. 7.4). Thereafter, the machine was also integrated

[30] Toenbreker, S.J.A.M., P.G. van Engen, R. van Dantzig, L.A.Ch. Koerts, K. Mulder, and J.E.J. Oberski. 1965. De toepassing van een EL X-8 op het IKO. IKO internal report Interiko 65/9. Archived at the National Museum Boerhaave, Leiden and at Nikhef, Amsterdam. https://ub. fnwi.uva.nl/computermuseum/pdfs/X8opIKO.pdf; Oberski, Jona E.J., R. van Dantzig, K. Mulder, L.A.Ch. Koerts, and F. van Hall. 1965. IKOB, koppeling van PDP8 en X8. IKO Internal report. Archived at Nikhef, Amsterdam.

[31] The X8-configuration consisted of the basic unit with central processor (CRO), operator console, magnetic core memory 32k (later upgraded to 48k) 27-bit words (+parity bit) with cycle time 2.5 μs, a memory access multiplexer, Charon—the I/O-processor, fast-channel-selector (SKK), Bryant magnetic drum with 512k memory of 27-bit words and a cycle time of 20 ms, real time clock/alarm clock, console for manual control, Siemens teletypes, line printer 1-5 lines/s and for paper tape: a 1000 ch/s EL 1000 reader and a 150 ch/s Facit punch.

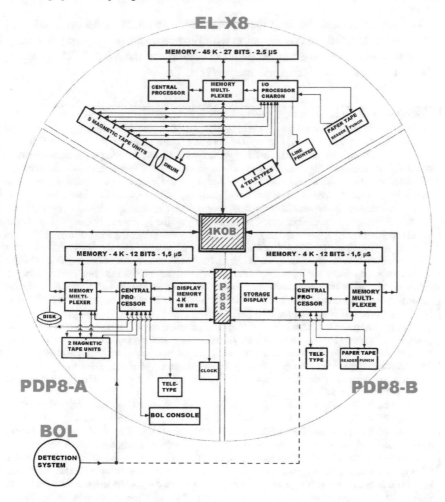

Fig. 7.5 Diagram of the triangular computer network realized for the BOL-system

into the triangular BOL network with IKOB and the two PDP8s connected by the homemade interface P88 (Fig. 7.5).[32] Shortly after, measurements with BOL were sent to the X8s and secondary data coming from the X8 appeared on one of the display units with which the PDP8s were equipped. From that time onward, adequate insight into the experimental situation and the quality of the measurements of the functioning BOL-system was available to the physicist overseeing the experiment. Our coupling of a complex nuclear physics detection setup to a computer network for the online control and data handling may well have been a European first.

[32] Oberski, Jona E.J., et al. 1971a. Electronics of the BOL system. *Nuclear Instruments and Methods* 92:177–187; Oberski, Jona E.J, L.A.Ch. Koerts, R. van Dantzig, and K. Mulder. 1967. Toelichting op de computers in BOL. IKO internal report Interiko 67/9. Archived at the National Museum Boerhaave, Leiden and at Nikhef, Amsterdam. https://ub.fnwi.uva.nl/computermuseum/pdfs/computersBOL.pdf.

The next three sections describe aspects of the innovations we designed or developed at IKO, partly in collaboration with Electrologica, on the computer side of our installation: the time-sharing operating system and the X8 and PDP8 software essential for the data handling and analysis (Fig. 7.6).[33]

The communication between the X8 and a PDP8 is to be set up as a series of block transfers, denoted 'conversations', that can be initiated by any of the three machines. Two types of sentences can occur in the conversations: 'introductory sentences' and 'main sentences'. An introductory sentence is a short data block of fixed length and with a fixed format, providing information about at most one following main sentence. Main sentences have a variable length and structure. Charon always has at its disposal addresses in memory space, where current sections for input or output are located in all three machines. These memory sections are called 'repositories'.

If a machine wants to communicate with another machine by sending an introductory sentence, it offers a communication request to Charon, specifying the addressed machine. Charon then checks whether IKOB is 'not busy' and – if so – investigates whether the addressed machine gives 'input permission', implying that this machine has an input repository ready to receive a block transport. Then Charon arranges a data transfer through IKOB from the 'output repository' of the source machine to the 'input repository' of the target machine. The PDP8s have fixed repositories for input and output of introductory sentences. A flag (flip-flop/bit) in IKOB indicates whether the input repository is available. Transfers always involve an even number of PDP8-words of 12 bits being packed in 24 bits, on the X8-side fitted into a 27-bit word.

The repositories in the X8 are chains of relocatable memory sections, connected by address pointers and provided with chain counters. When a subsequent request comes before the current repository is available, the next section in the chain is used. Upon a communication request, Charon reads the address of the repository and arranges the transfer. When the introductory sentence has been transferred in DMA-mode, with a word transfer counter in IKOB, the latter informs Charon with a dedicated flag.

Also, if the X8 takes the initiative, a main sentence is handled by Charon only following a request from a PDP8. In that case, the PDP8 is 'invited to invite' Charon to send an introductory sentence with the required PDP8 details included. When a main sentence DMA transfer has been completed, IKOB notes this in this case, too, and informs Charon with a dedicated flag.

Because, on the PDP8 (experiment) side, the available memory is restricted and speed is important, a single main sentence can be transferred in 'stutter-mode', implying that the transfer is split up in parts separated by a pause, such that the PDP8 can use the same memory section a number of times, thus saving space. The stutter mode does not allow the transfers to be checked rigorously and thus cannot be used if even an exceptional error cannot be tolerated, such as with transfers of programs. For measurement data from BOL, this mode is considered acceptable.

The simplest and fastest mode is 'unsolicited reading' of PDP8 memory by the X8. In this case, as long as IKOB is 'not busy', the X8 can read a specific part of PDP8 memory (a section with measurement data) and is supposed to know how to handle the obtained data.

Software drivers for IKOB are needed on both types of machines in such a way that data transfers satisfy standards already existing for the data streams to and from the magnetic tapes. This is important in order to facilitate data handling procedures independent of the specific input and output channels.

Fig. 7.6 Summary of the PDP8 ↔ X8 ↔ PDP8 network communication guidelines/requirements, in accordance with informal reports by Toenbreker (1965) and Oberski (1965)

---

[33] Dantzig, René van, et al. 1971b. Analysis of multidimensional nuclear data (BOL). *Nuclear Instruments and Methods* 92:205–213.

7.5 Time-Sharing

Almost all computers in the 1960s relied on "batch processing" or "unitasking," where one job is executed after the other. "Time-sharing" (TS)[34], where a number of users can work in parallel, each of them having access to essentially all system resources, had been developed in the USA. Worldwide, the first TS system became fully operational in 1961 at MIT in Cambridge. A little later, several TS systems in the USA were described in the literature, but—as far as we know—no such systems were available in Europe at that time.

As installed, the X8 operating system, called "Monotor," provided only batch processing. When, in the course of 1967, the system became intensively used, the shortcomings of batch processing were felt more and more. Often, time was lost with a change of user. Immediate high priority access to the computer was rarely possible, and conversational control of programs was hardly allowed, because it was considered inefficient and it would preclude access by another user for quite some time.

Fortunately, within one year, Pieter van Engen and Rolf Meesters of the IKO Software Group[35] developed a time-sharing system, called "Wammes,"[36] which included a few parts of Monotor, such as magnetic tape drivers. On starting this project, the authors were inspired by the work of Edsger W. Dijkstra[37] on "semaphores" and "mutual exclusion"[38] to safely guide concurrent processes through "critical sections" that had the risk of—for example—a "deadlock."

Wammes became fully operational in March 1969 and allowed users to load, assemble, execute, trace, stop, and inspect programs simultaneously at each of the four terminals. The system and the programs it could handle were written in the X8 assembler macro-code ELAN[39]. The assembly of a program resulted in a binary relocatable[40] file, which could be appended to the system library, including the program text. In the absence of discs, the file system was a mixed system of the drum

---

[34] Time-sharing implies "multitasking" and "multiprogramming," but the converse is not necessarily true. In the latter cases, jobs submitted in batch mode can overlap in time and in system resources, but there is not necessarily a possibility for multiple users working parallel to each other. The first Dutch application here was the "THE"-multiprogramming system developed by E.W. Dijkstra, where jobs are submitted in batch mode, but run as much as possible interleaved, to gain overall runtime.

[35] The IKO software group led by Pieter van Engen included Anton Mars, Rolf Meesters and Pim Biekman.

[36] Engen, Pieter G. van, and Rolf Meesters. 1969. WAMMES, een time-sharing systeem voor de EL-X8: gids voor gebruikers. Archived at the National Museum Boerhaave, Leiden. https://ub.fnwi.uva.nl/computermuseum/pdfs/WAMMESgebruikersgids.pdf.

[37] Dijkstra, Edsger W. 1968. The structure of the THE-multiprogramming system. *Communications of the ACM* 11(5):341–346. https://www.cs.utexas.edu/users/EWD/ewd01xx/EWD196.PDF.

[38] Mutual exclusion for concurrent processes is discussed by Th.J. Dekker. See Chap. 6 in this volume.

[39] 'ELAN' is discussed by F.E.J. Kruseman Aretz, The Mathematical Center, Algol 60 and the Electrologica X8. See Chap. 5 in this volume.

[40] Upon assembly, the resulting machine program was, using a simple trick, equipped with "relocation information" to be used at start-up time.

and magnetic tapes. A user could create a file on the drum and dump it onto the central library, a magnetic tape, from which it could be retrieved later.

The system was based on a carefully operating swapping method. If possible, a program was loaded in an unoccupied core area or elsewhere on the drum. When a program in core memory was blocked, only the part that was needed for another program was swapped. Except for magnetic tape units, which a program had to reserve in advance for its own use, all other programs could use every input/output device virtually simultaneously. This was achieved by buffering the I/O data on the drum. A driver program corresponded to any output device, selecting the next "closed" file for actual output. Every program could use dynamic storage allocation routines which operated in the working space of the program.

One of the benefits was that the time necessary for programming was considerably reduced due to the editing, debugging and library facilities, making more time available to more users. The possibility to split and run a program in segments, as we developed for the PDP8 (see Sect. 7.7), and as often done in other TS systems, was not possible for the X8. Every program could only be relocated in its entirety.

Priorities and machine time allocation to logged-in users were essential. The starting point was the democratic principle that all users get the highest priority, and in turn, the same slice of processor time. However, there were a few other rules, too. For example, the response time at terminals was—as much as possible—within seconds. When a program was involved in semi-real-time data processing for the BOL experiment, it had "urgency priority," which meant that it got all the processor time it needed and could get and would not be swapped out, unless manually by the operator. If there were two urgent programs, the first one received the highest priority.

An important software debugging facility, which came to full fruition in Wammes, was "dynamic program tracing." It was available on our X8 exclusively, and originated from one of the early meetings with Electrologica, where we reported our positive experience with PDP8 program debugging using our own development of "tracing" under dynamic supervision. We had discovered that a very simple trick made this possible and we asked Electrologica whether something similar could be done for the X8. The method, which we called "delayed self-interrupt" (see Sect. 7.7), imposed only extremely simple requirements on the hardware. The program, while running, could be interlaced in time by a tracer interrupt routine, operating in the background of the program. It turned out that a similar trick was also possible for the X8 and a program to be tested could run under the control of the programmable tracer, while after the execution of essentially any machine instruction,[41] the status of registers and addresses could be checked on the basis of flexible criteria in the tracer interruption routine. In a report[42] of a BOL-Electrologica meeting, it was written that "This tracing facility would in the first instance be applied especially for IKO."

---

[41] Only instructions executed within a system program, where the X8-interrupt was switched off, could not be traced, obviously.

[42] Note added to a brief Electrologica report by Th.R.C. Bonnema of a meeting end 1965, with present: Nossbaum, Seligmann, Bonnema from Electrologica, and Koerts, Van Dantzig and Oberski from IKO, with the title translated as: "Coordination facilities for a tracer."

Wammes was a "bomb-proof" time-sharing system: all user programs ran in a mode where it was impossible to write outside their own memory space. This was realized thanks to X8's top-of-the-line, hardware feature, write-protection to be set and cleared for blocks of 512 words by system routines running in kernel mode. Even if a user got stuck in a loop, there was a clock interrupt at the end of the current time slice to finish the user task.

The Wammes developers promised a bottle of good wine to the user who succeeded in "hanging" Wammes. JEP de Bie, one of the physicists/programmers, accomplished this the next day with a program having a single instruction: "Program Boom; Loop: do Loop; end Boom." The "do" command executed the instruction indicated in the address field—in this case, this instruction itself. Thus a single instruction was trapped in an endless recursive loop, the system being immune for any clock interrupt. As a result, the "blinking lights" on the console glowed continuously. The only recourse was to hit the on/off switch and do a full reboot. Apparently, this possibility had been overlooked in the hardware design by Electrologica. JEP de Bie thus got his bottle of wine. I am not certain whether Electrologica corrected this. Anyway, deliberately hanging Wammes was rewarded only once; it became banned and no such anomaly ever showed up in normal user programs.

When we consider Wammes from the user's point of view, in principle we could start, pause, and stop programs on the teletype as if the entire X8 were freely at our disposal. Mostly, that worked out well, although it could happen that the system refused a program because it would need too much drum memory or tape units, some of these having already been reserved by other users. Basic characteristics of time-sharing systems, such as the parallel use of peripherals by different users and the simultaneous use of both the foreground and a background memory, were clearly present. The goal, to build a system that could efficiently run essentially the same programs as in batch mode, had been realized. The X8 with Wammes became a more pleasant and better manageable machine.

7.6 Developing Data Reduction and Analysis Software

Soon, we became strongly committed to the design of an overall data reduction system that would be as simple as possible, and could flexibly be programmed without complications from I/O. To achieve our goals, we would "mold" our event data into a universal structure according to a set of rules, the "BOL format." The main idea was that the data structure would have "levels" in substructure and that operations at the various levels could be programmed separately, independent from where they came and where they would go. Once in this BOL format, the events could be subjected to several user-programmed "passes" with checks, alterations, rejections, selections, and calibrations, ending up on tapes as experimental sets of "validated data."

All data were supposed to remain in accordance with the format during all the processing. The BOL format had seven levels of nested data subsets, "quanta" of information.[43] For primary BOL data at the deepest level, the elementary quantum was a "record," specifically, an "event record" that contained data from a measurement of one or more detected particles resulting from one collision. At the next level, and only for practical reasons,[44] a number of records were packed in a "block" (without a particular meaning). A series of records (in blocks) would combine into a "train"; trains into a "net"; nets into a "group"; groups into a "file"; and finally, files into a "repfile." Trains, nets, groups, and files were separated by special blocks. Different quanta were meant to have a specific meaning. For instance, a train (of blocks of records) might contain homogeneous data, measured under exactly the same experimental conditions. A net (of trains of blocks of records) might correspond to the same target with different beam conditions. The largest quantum at the highest level was a "repfile," a series of files, representing all data from one full experiment.

To obtain an overview and analysis of what was measured, we would have to "bundle" validated event data. Bundling meant that certain combinations of values derived from the event data were "sorted and counted" on a multidimensional (mD) grid in order to produce mD "spectral arrays,"[45] "spectra" for short. A spectrum was characterized by the numbers and the widths of the mD grid cells, together with the number of counts collected in each cell. The coordinates corresponding to the central values of the grid cells represented derived "physics values."[46]

The BOL format was defined in such a way that it could be used for spectral arrays as well, to make these suitable for our standard data processing. An array element then became an "array record," a row of the array became a train, a column of rows became a net, and so on. A file thus could embody a series of 3D-arrays or a 4D-array. For event data, the sequence of quanta within their next higher quantum was irrelevant, while for array data, this sequence was fixed by the positions (coordinates) in the array.[47]

In that same design phase, we realized that for our anticipated measurement accuracy (0.1–1%), the size of mD arrays, in whatever representation, would be far too large to be stored in their entirety in the X8 core memory. However, we could use the drum memory, which was 16 times larger! It was helpful that the number of counts in large spectral arrays would often be low in average and distributed in-homogeneously, crowded in relatively small regions (peaks or mountain ranges)

---

[43] Dantzig, René van, et al. 1967a. Kwantisering van infostromen: draft. Leiden: Archived at the National Museum Boerhaave.

[44] Memory buffering and writing on external media like magnetic tape.

[45] A train represented a 1D array, that was a row of array records (0D-arrays), a net, a series of trains (1D arrays, rows, or a single 2D array), a group, a series of nets (2D arrays, or a single 3D array), and a file, a series of groups (3D arrays, or a single 4D array).

[46] For experimental data, the "physics values" are derived from measured values. For all experiments it is common to produce event data by a Monte Carlo (MC) random sampling method according to a theoretical model and all experimental effects taken into account. These MC-data are handled like experimental data and thus also can deliver "theoretical values," to be compared directly with their experimental counterparts.

[47] Therefore, "array quanta" to be rejected could not be removed, but at most administratively invalidated.

and almost or completely empty in large regions, partly even by definition.[48] High resolution would be only relevant in regions with good statistics. With this in mind, together with Electrologica, we made specifications for array-handling on drum store, allowing declaration and manipulation of groups of flexibly sized 3D-arrays with array elements of 3, 6, 12, or 24-bit bites. In cases where small bites would be chosen, a certain percentage of the array elements was allowed to "overflow." This was taken care of by successively assigning larger bites in a reserved overflow area. As opposed to the basic distributive[49] structure, the storage of these elements was associative.[50] At read-out, these cells were to be picked up together with the non-overflow elements in order to form the whole spectrum. A smart buffering and synchronization mechanism[51] was necessary to read and modify the content of the drum addresses in an optimally efficient way.

Based on the above ideas, Electrologica started to build the corresponding software layer, a package of subroutines that would take the format and structure rules as given and provide the appropriate basic functionality for the data processing for all future BOL experiments. This layer was called the "Window system" for the X8 (we here call it "WSX"),[52] and the specifications were finalized with Electrologica in 1966.[53]

The Window system with the drum array layer including documentation became available[54] in 1967.[55] From that moment on, it was central in our data processing. In the user programs ("passes"), data could easily be split, switched, and mixed between different I/O channels, and the programming was concentrated in "windows" at separate structure levels, dealing with the various information "quanta" described. The data at a given level would pass along the program window for that level. Program windows would only be opened for levels that were relevant in the current processing. A program window could read, alter, or reject a quantum of data before sending it to one or more output channels. ELAN was used to write both the system routines and the user's programs. From that moment on, essentially all BOL data handling was programmed and run in WSX.

---

[48] In many spectral arrays, the kinematics of the reaction restricts the coordinate regions that can be occupied by event counts at all.

[49] In general, the most compact build-up and storage of spectra can be 'distributive' or 'associative'. In the distributive—conventional—case, the memory space for the spectrum is completely and regularly structured beforehand such that all cells can be addressed directly given the coordinates.

[50] In associative storage, the structure in memory space is formed during the build-up and depends on details of the spectrum. Then, the coordinates of a cell are stored in an associated manner, i.e., together with—or pointing at—the cell content.

[51] The method amounted to (a) temporarily keeping the coordinates of the addressed array elements in core memory buffers that were associatively sorted according to drum tracks; (b) asynchronous transport of drum tracks to core memory and vice versa, giving highest priority to the tracks with most modifications. Access rates of 104 per second were achieved.

[52] In Sect. 7.7, a simplified Window system for the PDP8 (WSP) is introduced.

[53] Dantzig, René van, et al. 1967b. Window-processing for on-and off-line data-handling: draft specifications. Leiden: Archived at the National Museum Boerhaave.

[54] WSX was realized by Stef Toenbreker, Pieter G. van Engen and Hans Suys from Electrologica.

[55] Dantzig, René van, and Stef Toenbreker. 1968b. Vensterprogrammering. Leiden: Archived at the National Museum Boerhaave.

Even with the above-mentioned arrays on the drum, we thought that we would be unable to reach our overall required ultimate resolution, not even for only 2D array spectra. Therefore, together with Electrologica we made specifications for an additional package, called "counting in trees" or "associative counting." In this approach, 2D-trees, with a resolution consistent with a 4096 × 4096 grid, would be built up beginning in core memory and continuing on drum storage. The tree structure was defined so that each leaf of a tree contained an end node or maximally 4 pointers (2 for each dimension) to other leaves, each pointer corresponding to the value of a certain bit in both coordinates.

Since each coordinate had a maximum of 12 bits, at most 12 pointer levels would be needed to reach non-zero counts cells. In principle, an arbitrary number (maximally 32) of trees could be built simultaneously, restricted by available drum space. It was, all in all, a quite complex framework. A buffer and synchronization technique, algorithmically even smarter than for the WSX-arrays on drum storage, was made. The package was delivered by Philips-Electrologica[56] in 1969,[57] but there were challenges to its use. The package was large, complicated to handle and slow. Moreover, at that time we could already solve our problems with the available software and the required resolution was less than anticipated. If my memory is correct, despite the good work, this package may have been an instance where our ambitions were too high.

Within WSX, spectra could be sent to an output medium, or immediately further analyzed. The spectra could have peaks, valleys, flat parts, and empty parts, all of these together constituting the "spectral structure" for the chosen parameters and the chosen grid. Here, for the first time, we could judge whether the measurements looked comprehensible, and hopefully correct. If not, we had to go back to the data conversion passes and look for a possible explanation. When the validated data looked fine, the next crucial step could be taken, the identification of the detected particles (see the box in Fig. 7.7).

In our team, a conversational program language, "Simplex,"[58] influenced by ALGOL 60 had been developed for calculations within the WSX framework. This was particularly important in the final stage of the BOL data reduction and data presentation, where we wanted to easily and flexibly apply our instrumental and physics insights to prepare pictures for further study or for publication. Spectra could be presented on a graphics storage display with hard-copy read-out connected to a PDP8 (see Sect. 7.7). A useful extension of Simplex was the Lisp-based program Lisi,[59] which provided facilities for the graphics display with formula manipulation and symbolic processing of complex display structures.[60]

---

[56] In 1968, Electrologica was taken over by the Philips company.

[57] Pouls, M.P. 1969. Programma documentatie Associatief tellen. Electrologica report CS.69/64/582. Archived at the National Museum Boerhaave, Leiden.

[58] Simplex was developed by Bob J. Wielinga from the BOL team.

[59] Lisi was developed by Theo F. de Ridder from the BOL team, who had installed and extended the LISP program of Van der Poel and Van der Mey.

[60] Theo F. de Ridder. 1972. LISI, een LISP-SIMPLEX systeem met display faciliteiten, Informal IKO report. Archived at the National Museum Boerhaave, Leiden.

Measurements from the BOL detection telescopes had been calibrated and converted to the parameter values, E (detected particle energy) and ΔE (energy loss in the checkerboard detector). These parameters were characteristic for whether a detected particle was of the type proton, deuteron, triton, τ (He-3) or α (He-4) particle. In an $E \times \Delta E$ versus ΔE spectrum approximately parallel mountain ranges would appear, each range – if present – belonging to one of the particle types. The particle identification required the contours of the mountain ranges to be outlined and then made available to a new pass of event data. There, using these contours, we could determine for each event the type(s) of the detected particle(s), including the type: 'unknown', in case the particle(s) fell outside all contours. The unknown type could sometimes be resolved later using other information. From this point onward, physics definitely came into the picture! Suddenly, we could select a particular nuclear reaction process and study that in detail, by now bundling the data to the most meaningful representations. These were real physics results, energy spectra, angular distributions or correlations, and the like for a specific nuclear reaction. They could be interpreted, studied and compared with theoretical model predictions. A selection of these results would appear in our publications.

Fig. 7.7 Particle identification, an essential step in the data analysis

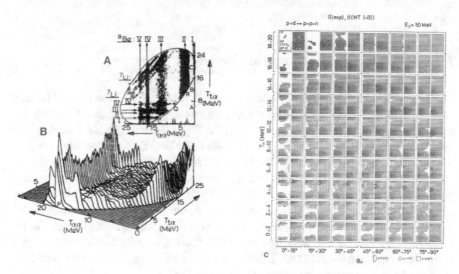

Fig. 7.8 Examples of published measurements in 2 and 4 dimensions. (**a**) 2D-topview of the measured reaction probability above a certain threshold for the reaction $^9\mathrm{Be} + d \rightarrow t + \alpha + \alpha$, where the energies and directions of all three particles in the final state were deduced from the data; (**b**) the same 2D data in a 3D isomeric display; (**c**) comparison between a measurement and the corresponding theoretical simulation in 4D for the reaction $p + d \rightarrow p + p + n$. The bin-averaged data are shown as a (10×12) 2D array of a double (15×15) 2D array (data, theory). The reaction probability is represented by special symbols for values in a 10-bin range. Only the lower half range in θ_n that means half of the data is here shown

For their physics interpretation, BOL results needed to be compared with theoretical model predictions. Mostly this meant that, assuming the validity of the model, we had to perform a full Monte Carlo computer simulation of the experiment, taking into account the detailed measurement situation, including all the mounted and correctly working detection units. Because of rotational symmetry around the beam axis, there was a lot of measurement redundancy, largely compensating for missing detection units (see Sect. 7.8). When considered individually, our data were often less accurate, both statistically and systematically, compared to measurements performed elsewhere with fewer detectors. However, they covered almost all of the kinematical final states of the nuclear reaction under study in a continuous way. And that was unique! As foreseen, this was particularly important for the study of "few body reactions." A discrepancy with simulated data would indicate "that"—and often "where"—the experiment showed deviations from the theory. A notable example was a comparison in full 4D between an experiment and a theory simulation (Fig. 7.8).[61]

The results obtained might clarify a known problem, but often new questions arose, leading to a follow-up experiment to shed light on the new questions. For the planning of new experiments, a crucial program[62] in ALGOL 60 was developed, applying relativistic kinematics for nuclear reactions.

7.7 Software for Minicomputer Network Nodes

The hardware and software functionality of the two network PDP8s (A and B) was very relevant in the X8 context. Our program developments for the PDP8s in the assembly language PAL/8 were of importance for choices in the X8 software and vice versa. Since interrupt handling was primitive for the PDP8 and we were starting on a basic programming level, in the interaction with peripherals, we worked with "waiting" for a ready "flag"[63] of each equipment, with one exception: tracing. An operating system, called Monikor, was built by us, physicists, around a linked list, containing all active waiting points and the corresponding values in the accumulator register, which also had to be restored as soon as the program was continued. Thus a compact and primitive multitasking system was created, without the use of interrupts, which for many years—with later I/O extensions—transferred all measurement data from the BOL-system to magnetic tape and/or to our X8.

The Monikor system enabled dynamic storage allocation, binary program allocation, multi-job processing with time-sharing and memory sharing, asynchronous data streams with semaphore mechanisms, dynamic program tracing, and a computer-computer (A↔B) conversational scheme. Compared with the software available for minicomputers at the time, most of these mechanisms were state of the art.

In our network, PDP8-A took care of reading the events from BOL, while including information from the physicist on duty, putting the data in the BOL format,

---

[61] Blommestijn, G.J.F., R. van Dantzig, Y. Haitsma and R.B.M. Mooy. 1981. The reaction $d(p, pp)n$ measured with BOL at E_p = 50 MeV. *Nuclear Physics A* 365:202–228.

[62] This program was developed by Ton Ypenberg from the BOL team.

[63] A flag was a "flip-flop" (bit) that could be set (1) and reset (0) externally and/or programmatically. It could be sensed by a PDP8-instruction: if flag is set, skip next instruction. When properly programmed, it could also give a program interrupt.

Fig. 7.9 The technician Theo Bijvoets at work with PDP8-A. At right the connected display station. The cathode ray tube with light pen is integrated into the desk

writing them on tape, and/or sending them to the X8 and/or to the autonomous display (Fig. 7.9) with "light pen."[64] Some changes to a M(emory)-unit of a kick-sorter[65] with help from Philips NatLab had made it possible to operate all previously manually steered functionality of the display by direct computer control of PDP8-A. With the light pen, we could mark channels independent of the PDP8. An interface between the M-unit and the display oscilloscope allowed "contour" and "isometric" 3D-display modes. In the latter case, this was achieved by turning the viewing angle around. Also, it became possible to make selections on channel address and/or channel content as well as to adjust the light intensity of each displayed point based on the memory content. A little later, a storage oscilloscope[66] with hard-copy read-out was interfaced to PDP8-B, thus making it the main display facility.

---

[64] When the light-sensitive pen touched the oscilloscope screen at an illuminated point, its electric pulses could be matched with register values determining the position of that point. These values could then be read-out by the PDP8.

[65] A 512 channel Nuclear Data 130 Analyzer, where the least significant 12 bits were used for data and the 6 most significant bits for logic functions like interrupting the PDP8, display permission, display intensifying or light pen flag.

[66] Tektronix Storage Oscilloscope Type T611. All interfacing (BOL detector, tape units and display units) was done by the IKO digital group led by Evert Kwakkel, which included Pier ten Kate, Jan Kraus, and others.

The PDP8's memory consisting of 32 "pages" of 128 words of 12 bits, allowed direct addressing within the same page. Memory sharing of asynchronous programs required a suitable dynamic storage technique. We divided the core memory into two regions of pages: the free region and the occupied region. The boundary between them was dynamic and in fact, the regions could overlap each other page-wise. The administration contained a list of page-status words. Two functions controlled the memory sharing administration: "get-page" and "put-page." Their calls had to be paired off, so that every job would finish only after giving up all space reserved during runtime.

Whenever a job program was loaded, it obtained the needed pages. The loader program itself was also a job program, active in parallel with other programs. Successively allotted pages were, in general, not contiguous. In order to use the dynamic storage allocation mechanism for programs, we had to allow programs to be relocatable by page rather than by program. We restricted references to other pages to jumps and subroutine calls. This was a limitation we could work with, while the relocation method could be straightforward and the formats could remain standard.

The format of data streams that have been implemented for the X8, as described in Sect. 7.6 in terms of the info-quanta (record, block, train, net, group, file, repfile), required a similar—though simplified—window processing layer (WSP) for the PDP8s. For this purpose, a general input-output file handling system,[67] tailored to the Monikor system, was built by our software group. This system covered all information channels like the BOL setup, tape units, the display units, and the X8. Interacting asynchronous input- and output-processes could "switch" information at the file level between one input channel and an arbitrary set of output channels. The data stream, which was divided into the info-quanta, could pass "window programs" as described for the X8. Specified at the highest protocol level, these could inspect and operate upon the data between input and output. Different I/O processes could run simultaneously, while output jobs waiting for input information did not take up processor time. Synchronization was accomplished using I/O semaphore-functions: the WSP system turned out to be sufficiently flexible and powerful.

As brought up in Sect. 7.5, the X8 tracer had been made in accordance with our simple method for the PDP8, the "delayed self-interrupt." It consisted of an external interrupt inducing flag (bit), which was cleared at the entry and set before the exit of a tracer interrupt subroutine, the latter with an intrinsic delay of about 5 μs. The delay time was chosen so that only one instruction of the program under tracing could be executed, at the completion of which, the flag provided a new program interrupt. While tracing a program, the interrupt subroutine (possibly adapted to personal needs) could, for example, cause a stop when the content of a selected register or memory address satisfied a preset condition. This provided an excellent new test facility for the in-house software development.

Around 1970, inspired by the design of Wammes and experienced in building the PDP8 Monikor and WSP system, Anton Mars, Jan Visschers, and Ruud van Wijk

---

[67] Biekman, W.C.M., and Anton J. Mars. 1968. PDP-8 IN-UIT-systeem. IKO informal report. Archived at the National Museum Boerhaave, Leiden.

developed a genuine time-sharing operating system AIDA[68] for a PDP8. I think, this was unprecedented for such a small machine. It could serve up to 12 users with time and memory sharing through alphanumerical terminals. Since the PDP8 was interfaced to the X8, these terminals also could serve programs running under Wammes, thus extending the number of simultaneous X8-users. Relocatable user programs, as described for Monikor, could be controlled and run independently and simultaneously on the PDP8. All this could be realized thanks to a hardware extension to the PDP8-processor, a memory protection unit, designed by the IKO digital group with specifications from the software group. This unit functionally blocked I/O- and halt-instructions as well as all memory reference instructions, writing outside certain dynamically specifiable areas of core memory. Upon occurrence of such a blocking, an interrupt was generated, enabling the operating system to take appropriate action. AIDA brought considerable satisfaction for the programmers as much as for the users. It has been used until the DEC-system 10 came into view.

Practically all of the PDP8 software mentioned above was reported at meetings of the Digital Equipment User Community (DECUS) Europe in 1968[69] and in 1972.[70]

7.8 Final Considerations and Conclusions

Over three decades the Philips Company and IKO had an invaluable collaboration that included construction and support of the cyclotron, support on building and maintaining an electron accelerator as well as the development and production of nuclear detectors.[71]

The Mathematical Center, meeting the growing computational requirements at IKO in the first half of the 1960s, was essential. The access to the X1 allowed IKO physicists and technicians to complete practically all of their computer work, amounting to many hundreds of hours each year.

The continuation of the MC computer developments within Electrologica led to the production of a substantial series of X8 machines, one of which found its way to IKO. To obtain the funding, our institute had a strong hand with the portfolio of its cyclotron, the 85 MeV linear accelerator, a much more powerful 300 MeV electron accelerator in the planning stage, and last but not least the immediate needs of the

---

[68] AIDA = Algemeen Interactief Data-analyse systeem.

[69] Dantzig, René van, et al. 1968a. Recent hardware and software developments for the PDP-8. In *Proceedings of the 4th European DECUS Seminar (1968)*. Leiden and at Nikhef, Amsterdam: Archived at the National Museum Boerhaave. See also https://ub.fnwi.uva.nl/computermuseum/pdfs/RecentHardwSoftwPDP8.pdf

[70] Mars, Anton J., J.L. Visschers, and R.F. van Wijk. 1972. AIDA—an operating system for the PDP-8. I. Software. In *Proceedings of the 8th DECUS Europe Seminar 1972*. Archived at Nikhef, Amsterdam; Kate, P.U. ten, and E. Kwakkel. 1972. AIDA - An operating system for the PDP-8. II. Hardware. In *Proceedings 8th DECUS Europe Seminar 1972*. Amsterdam: Archived at Nikhef.

[71] Waalwijk, J.M., N. Wiedenhof, G. Luijckx, G.A. Brinkman, W.K. Hofker, R. van Dantzig, H.J. Akkerman, P. Bakker. 1980. 35 jaar samenwerking met IKO. *Philips Technisch Tijdschrift* 39(10):269–312 (English, French and Dutch edition). All articles in this issue.

BOL project. Equally compelling was that Electrologica, as the first Dutch computer manufacturer, produced a first-class computer and had the ability and willingness to provide the necessary IKO special hardware and software at reasonable costs.

The X8 made it possible for us to dive into the then modern programming developments and, together with Electrologica, to create an avant-garde online network with data processing software. Programming in ELAN gave us great satisfaction because of its structure and power. In our view, this assembly language was very well thought-out!

The IKO software group, which was created with the arrival of the X8, was as enthusiastic and ambitious as we, the physicists and hardware technicians, were. A major result was Wammes. Time-sharing became indispensable for all of us in many respects. It gave us ample opportunity to "get at the machine," not only in cases of experimental urgency but also for efficient analysis as well as program development and online testing. Moreover, it allowed us to learn and employ new techniques, such as list-processing and formula manipulation, thereby accelerating and improving our work. Wammes may have been the first fully operational time-sharing system in Europe. Although only tailored to EL-X8-computers, Wammes was in several respects comparable to the AT&T Unix operating system which came into worldwide use a few years later.

There were no significant problems in building and operating the BOL network. This was quite remarkable, since there were two suppliers, the Electrologica staff involved on the X8 side, and IKO (the BOL team), on the PDP8 side. The two groups made an excellent match!

In the end, what really counted was the data processing and analysis. Of the main software packages programmed by Electrologica, the X8 Window system was the most general and indispensable one. It consisted of a set of subroutines and rules that could have been programmed in any computer language. The fact that there was no future for Electrologica, for Wammes and for the Window system is regrettable. On the other hand, we were early workers on—in contemporary jargon—"big data" and "data mining." That some of us then already got the opportunity to learn and apply early ideas of artificial intelligence,[72] is notable, considering that these three areas are now, half a century later, strongly intertwined.

After hearing the many positive things of BOL, one might wonder if everything was really so exciting and successful. Of course, there were setbacks and challenges. Parts of the project took much longer than foreseen or were not realized at all. The cyclotron beam was less intense and could not be focused on targets as well as had been anticipated. The complexity and size of the electronics required very time-consuming maintenance. We always had a number of detection units missing, because they were being repaired, or subtle errors turned up when mounted units were checked. However, we could live with this, thanks to a lot of redundancy in the measurement space and—importantly—by comparing the experimental data with adequately simulated theoretical data. In spite of the many problems, the whole

---

[72] An artificial intelligence study group was formed by, among others, Bob Wielinga and Theo de Ridder. Bob Wielinga became a professor at several universities and became well known for his AI research on the methodology of knowledge-based system design and knowledge acquisition.

concept of BOL worked; the results, often multidimensional, set a new standard and were fascinating! To report on our multidimensional results in articles and at conferences in a way comprehensible to colleagues not familiar with BOL, made that we had to develop special ways of presentation.[73]

Fig. 7.10 Physicists of the BOL team, 1967: from left to right: René van Dantzig, Ton Ypenberg, Henriette v/d Pijl (secretary), Wil Carton (X8-manager), Wim Hermans, Leo Koerts, Theo de Ridder, Jan Lindhout, José Magendans, Jan Waal, Gerard Blommestijn, JEP de Bie, Ton Sonnemans, Bob Wielinga, Karel Mulder, Jona Oberski (not visible), Jan Joosten (at the bottom)

We, physicists of the BOL team (Fig. 7.10), had a mood and attitude, that somehow belonged to the 1960s: everything was possible or at least should have been possible! That meant freedom and cooperation in daring experimentation in physics, electronics and programming. It also meant being smart, working hard and with dedication, and doing night shifts at the cyclotron or on the computer after a full day of work. We were eager to work at the forefront of science and technology, we read a lot

---

[73] On this we got advise from distinguished colleagues, in particular, prof. Ivo Šlaus, from Zagreb University.

of professional literature and we had our own colloquium and working group. There was a lot of liberty in choosing the subjects of learning and of experimentation, even if the connection to the project was uncertain. We became accustomed to "out of the box" thinking. Occasionally, some of us spent evenings and nights together and with friends, listening to contemporary pop music, while fleeting romances could arise with wine and cannabis as catalysts. In summary, I believe that the multifaceted open-minded spirit of our team contributed a great deal to the BOL project's success, on top of the acquired expertise, and, to be honest, quite a bit of good luck, too.

Fig. 7.11 The BOL 'monument' on the Science Park campus after 25 years, ready for dismantling

It was in 1971 that we, the BOL "triad," Karel Mulder, Jona Oberski and I, in a full afternoon marathon ceremony at the University of Amsterdam, successfully defended, one after the other, our Ph.D theses with BOL results. Our experimental work continued until 1973, when the measurements were stopped. A total of nearly 2000 data tapes remained. The data analysis was continued mainly by three graduate students and several undergraduates. The following year, the X8 was replaced by a model 10 computer from Digital Equipment Corporation (DEC).[74] The main

---

[74] Dantzig, René van, et. al. 1973. Voorstel tot vervanging van de EL-X8 computer configuratie van het IKO. Leiden: Archived at the National Museum Boerhaave. https://ub.fnwi.uva.nl/computermuseum/pdfs/X8vervanging.pdf; Wielinga, B.J., J.E.J. Oberski, R. van Dantzig et al. 1973. Toelichting op de aanvraag voor vervanging van de rekenmachine van het Instituut voor

functionality of the X8 software was reprogrammed in Fortran by staff from DEC. Analysis and preparations of publications continued officially until 1977. Our last publication appeared in 1982.[75] The BOL project might be summarized as a difficult and successful undertaking, with most of its significance at the forefront of few-body nuclear physics. It led to twenty publications in international scientific journals, three patents, six PhD theses, as well as many master's theses, conference articles, and laboratory reports.

As a whole, BOL with its full infrastructure can be viewed as an early precursor of modern particle physics setups, with its 4π-type detection "all around" the collision region, with its silicon detectors for "accurate" impact position measurements, with its "large" number of electronic channels, with a computer network online to the experiment and sophisticated software. All of these qualities are, in extremely scaled-up and improved fashion, characteristics of current high-energy particle physics experiments.

Fig. 7.12 Recovered essential parts of BOL on show for 14 years at Nikhef with an explanatory presentation. Visible are the two inner halves of the heart of the BOL-system together with the detectors and electronics for one of the 64 detection channels. In 2016, these parts were included in the collection of the National Rijksmuseum Boerhaave in Leiden

Kernphysisch Onderzoek (IKO) te Amsterdam. IKO informal report. Archived at the National Museum Boerhaave, Leiden. https://ub.fnwi.uva.nl/computermuseum/pdfs/vervanging1973.pdf.
[75] Blommestijn, e.a. (1981), reaction.

In 1977, the BOL detector was placed as a "monument" on our campus and stayed there for 25 years (Fig. 7.11). Shortly after the turn of the century, it was dismantled and the heart of the system with examples of its main elements were exhibited at Nikhef in a showcase with a continuously running presentation until 2016. In that year, the BOL remnants and our corresponding archive were transferred to the Dutch Science Rijksmuseum Boerhaave in Leiden (Fig. 7.12). That same Museum decided in 2018 to also include an X8, which had been kept elsewhere,[76] in the collection. It feels good that, now, a half-century later, our BOL and an X8 have been saved for posterity, together.

Acknowledgements Much of the chronological framework of this article could be retrieved thanks to IKO and FOM annual reports. The black-and-white photographs from the BOL-period, shown here, were taken by Hans Arnold. I am very much indebted to my former colleagues from the BOL and X8-period, who shared with me their recollections and provided useful comments on versions of this article, in particular, JEP de Bie, Gerard Blommestijn, Theo Bijvoets, Pieter van Engen, Anton Mars, Jona Oberski, Henk Peek, Theo de Ridder, Ton Sonnemans and Jan Visschers. I am especially grateful to David van Dantzig and Zachary Tobin for textual improvements. I feel honored to have been invited by Gerard Alberts, editor of the Springer series History of Computing, to compose this article, and I am very grateful for his support in realizing it.

---

[76] This X8 had been operational at the University of Kiel, Germany.

Chapter 8
An Early Experiment in Algorithmic Composition

Lambert Meertens

Abstract IFIP, the International Federation for Information Processing, held a computer-composed music competition in connection with IFIP Congress 68. The following describes how I wrote a program for composing music, which produced a string quartet that received a special mention from the jury. Included are a translation of (thus far) the only published paper presenting an in-depth description of the algorithmic principles underlying the program, which was originally written in Dutch and published in the journal *Informatie*, as well as the full text of the central procedure of the program, written in ALGOL 60.

8.1 Introduction

In 1967 I was employed as a programmer at the Mathematical Center, which gave me complete freedom to follow my passion: to explore the potential of programmable electronic computers. My first publication, in 1962, had been about an experiment in artificial intelligence: a program for solving such puzzles as finding a route through a maze, or the wolf, goat and cabbage problem, a well-known river crossing puzzle.[1] Many experiments were to follow, mainly in algorithmic art, but also in a variety of other areas.

8.2 Affix Grammars

Also in 1962, Kees Koster and I attended a seminar, organized by Evert Beth in the context of a Euratom project for machine translation. We read the book *Syntactic*

---

[1] Meertens, Lambert G.L.T. 1962. Kunstmatige intelligentie, een programma voor het optimaal oplossen van een klasse van problemen (Artificial intelligence, a program for optimally solving a class of problems). *Mededelingen van het Nederlands Rekenmachine Genootschap* 4:6–13. (*In Dutch*).

Structures by Chomsky,[2] in which he introduced "phrase structure grammars" to describe the structure of sentences in a natural language. While these grammars were new to most of the participants, Kees and I were familiar with them as being the same (at least in their simplest form, context-free grammar) as the so-called BNF grammar used in the ALGOL 60 Report[3] to describe the structure of "sentences" in the artificial language ALGOL 60. The very idea of using them to describe natural language was also new to us. Also, in the Chomskyan view, the function of these grammars was not merely to be *descriptive*—they were most of all meant to be *generative* grammars.

Fig. 8.1 Lambert Meertens in Teleac TV studio. Still from the TV course on statistics where Professor Jan Hemelrijk invited Lambert Meertens to explain about his computer-aided composition based on randomness and probability.

The participants in the seminar were expected to give presentations. Somewhat boldly, Kees and I took it upon ourselves to give a demonstration of the use of a phrase structure grammar to generate grammatically well-formed English sentences. Kees was to write the program (in machine code for the Electrologica X1), while my role was to supply the grammar. I did not want the grammar to be too simple. For the demonstration to be convincing, it had to show, for example, the possibility of recursion as seen in dependent clauses (*The dress that the girl who David likes is wearing is beautiful*). So, obviously, it should also produce basic sentences consisting of a noun phrase (the subject), a verb form, and an optional second noun phrase (the object), such as:

- *the boy falls*
- *mice like grains*

A phrase structure grammar that will generate these sentences is given by:

---

[2] Chomsky, Noam. 1957. *Syntactic structures*. Mouton: The Hague.

[3] Naur, Peter, ed. 1960. J.W. Backus, F.L. Bauer, J. Green, C. Katz, J. McCarthy, A.J. Perlis, H. Rutishauser, K. Samelson, B. Vauquois, J.H. Wegstein, A. van Wijngaarden, M. Woodger, Report on the algorithmic language ALGOL 60. *Num. Mathematik* 2:106–136.

$$
\begin{aligned}
\text{SENT} &\rightarrow \text{NP VERB} \\
\text{SENT} &\rightarrow \text{NP VERB NP} \\
\text{NP} &\rightarrow \textit{the boy} \\
\text{NP} &\rightarrow \textit{mice} \\
\text{NP} &\rightarrow \textit{grains} \\
\text{VERB} &\rightarrow \textit{falls} \\
\text{VERB} &\rightarrow \textit{like}
\end{aligned}
$$

This grammar delivers as promised. However, it does too much. It also produces ungrammatical sentences:

- *the boy like
- *the mice falls

These sentences do not obey subject–verb agreement. A singular object needs a singular verb form, and a plural subject a plural verb form. This can be solved by making copies of the sentence rules for each combination of grammatical numbers:

$$
\begin{aligned}
\text{SENT}_{sg} &\rightarrow \text{NP}_{sg}\ \text{VERB}_{sg} \\
\text{SENT}_{pl} &\rightarrow \text{NP}_{pl}\ \text{VERB}_{pl} \\
\text{SENT}_{sg} &\rightarrow \text{NP}_{sg}\ \text{VERB}_{sg}\ \text{NP}_{sg} \\
\text{SENT}_{sg} &\rightarrow \text{NP}_{sg}\ \text{VERB}_{sg}\ \text{NP}_{pl} \\
\text{SENT}_{pl} &\rightarrow \text{NP}_{pl}\ \text{VERB}_{pl}\ \text{NP}_{sg} \\
\text{SENT}_{pl} &\rightarrow \text{NP}_{pl}\ \text{VERB}_{pl}\ \text{NP}_{pl} \\
\text{NP}_{sg} &\rightarrow \textit{the boy} \\
\text{NP}_{pl} &\rightarrow \textit{mice} \\
\text{NP}_{pl} &\rightarrow \textit{grains} \\
\text{VERB}_{sg} &\rightarrow \textit{falls} \\
\text{VERB}_{pl} &\rightarrow \textit{like}
\end{aligned}
$$

The extended grammar now generates the two example sentences we started with, but not the ungrammatical ones marked with asterisks. It does generate some strange sentences (*grains like the boy*), but that is fine, as long as the sentence is grammatical. By no means do the added rules provide a full solution. We still have some ungrammatical productions:

- *the boy falls mice
- *grains like

Next to number agreement, a grammar for English also needs to be cognizant of transitivity (transitive; intransitive; either), person agreement (1st-person-sg: *I am*; 2nd-person-sg: *thou art*; 3rd-person-sg: *it is*; ...), cases for pronouns (*he knows them*; *they know him*), tenses (*goes*; *went*; *has gone*; *will go*; ...), and so on. To take account of these requires, for each, to replace rules by multiple copies, and multiple copies of multiple copies, and multiple copies of multiple copies of multiple copies, a combinatorial explosion.

It soon dawned on me that producing a grammar was not going to be so simple as I had naively assumed. If each basic rule was going to spawn dozens of agreement-obeying rules, I foresaw three problems. The first was that I was not going to finish on time for the promised and already scheduled demonstration. The next was that even if I somehow did manage to finish in time, we would not have time to debug the bloated grammar. The worst problem, as I saw it, was that producing the expanded grammar was going to be excruciatingly boring. For some time I considered the possibility of writing a program to expand the grammar. It would need input from a set of production rule schemas, such as

$$\text{SENT}_N \rightarrow \text{NP}_N \; \text{VERB}_N$$
$$\text{SENT}_N \rightarrow \text{NP}_N \; \text{VERB}_N \; \text{NP}_{N'}$$
$$N, N' \rightarrow \text{sg}$$
$$N, N' \rightarrow \text{pl}$$

Then it occurred to me that this expansion step could be fused with the generation process, so that only one (more complicated) program would be needed. The whole grammar was written in one night, using the term "affix" for the entities written above as subscripts, which serve to coordinate different branches of the parse tree—so to speak a form of entanglement, "spooky action at a distance." The next day I made a neater copy and presented it to Kees, more or less expecting that he would be unhappy with the extra complication—but he was, in fact, enthusiastic. The demonstration went without a glitch, but no one expressed any interest in this newfangled variant of a phrase structure grammar. Kees, on the other hand, kept working with affix grammars, using them for parsing sentences in natural languages,[4] as well as the basis for the programming language CDL, an initialism for "Compiler Description Language."[5]

The head of the Computing Department of the Mathematical Center was Adriaan van Wijngaarden—for us Professor van Wijngaarden—a position he kept when he became director of the institute. He read the Mathematical Center reports before they were printed, as well as the reports of our departmental meetings, in which Kees presented his work. I wonder if any of this served as a source of inspiration for his two-level grammars, used in the description of ALGOL 68,[6] where they serve a similar coordinating role as in the affix grammar from 1962. In any case, this was to

---

[4] Koster, Cornelis H.A. 1965. *On the construction of Algol-procedures for generating, analyzing and translating sentences in natural languages*. Mathematical Centre report MR 72. Mathematical Centre. Amsterdam.

[5] Koster, Cornelis H.A. 1971. *A Compiler Compiler*. Mathematical Centre report MR 127/71. Mathematical Centre. Amsterdam.

[6] Wijngaarden, Adriaan van. 1969. Peck, John E.L., Mailloux, Barry J., and Koster, Cornelis H.A. (eds). Report on the algorithmic language ALGOL 68. *Num. Mathematik* 14:79–218.

the best of my knowledge the first two-level grammar of any kind, earlier than the first van Wijngaarden grammar,[7] which preceded Knuth's Attribute Grammars.[8]

Although I did not continue working on the affix grammar formalism, their usefulness in coordinating different branches of a parse tree remained in my mind. Among the things I had realized is that they became much more powerful if even a modest amount of computation on the affixes was allowed. Then they could be used like Lindenmayer systems to describe successive generations of finite approximations of, for example, the Thue–Morse sequence 0110100110010110..., or of fractal patterns. The original program for generating English sentences had been written in machine code, but by now I programmed such excursions in ALGOL 60, making good use of recursion, using procedures to model nonterminals, with parameters taking the role of the affixes. I experimented with affix grammars for generalizing schemas of familiar song forms, such as the ABAC and AABA forms. Then I realized I could actually use this method to generate a melodic line at the same time if I allowed a random element in the computations applied to the affixes. Initially consisting of a sequence of notes of all the same duration, the generated melodies soon were enriched with rhythm, produced together with the melodic line using computationally enhanced affix grammars.

I can read a music score the way most Dutch people can read a book written in Basque: you can read all the letters, and yet you don't know how their combination is supposed to sound. Someone, I don't remember who, but it may have been someone from the University of Leyden Central Computing Institute, had written a program that made the X1 perform computations that produced a recognizable melody (one voice only). When the X1 computer was executing a program, fetching and storing data in its magnetic core memory generated electromagnetic pulses, which could be made audible by keeping a transistor radio close to the cabinets containing the memory modules, or "mats" as they were colloquially called. That made it possible for me to listen to the melodies generated by my experiments. The program had no notion of an underlying harmony, but the melodies were quite singable.

8.3 The IFIP Competition

During the Christmas holidays of 1967 I was skimming through computer-science journals in the library of the MC and leafing through a back issue of the journal *Computers and Automation*, when an announcement of a computer-composed music competition caught my eye. The competition was held by the International Federation for Information Processing, in connection with the upcoming IFIP Congress, which was held every four years. Entries had to be submitted in the form of either a

---

[7] Wijngaarden, Adriaan van. 1965. Orthogonal Design and Description of a Formal Language. *Reports Stichting Mathematisch Centrum* MR 76. Mathematisch Centrum, Amsterdam. [https://ir. cwi.nl/pub/9208] cf. https://en.wikipedia.org/wiki/Van_Wijngaarden_grammar.

[8] Knuth, Donald E. 1966. Semantics of context-free languages. *Mathematical Systems Theory* 2(2):127–145.

recording, or a score for a string quartet. I would not know how to produce a recording, but coming up with a score seemed within the realm of possibilities. Unfortunately, the issue was already several months old, and the deadline for submitting an entry was now only a month away, so I decided there was no way I could meet it.

I had been interested in exploring the possibilities of writing programs for composing music, not so much in a modern idiom, such as the computer-composed *Illiac Suite*,[9] but in specific styles, such as Gregorian chant, or the Classical-period style of Haydn. Lacking a background in music theory, this had always appeared a hopeless undertaking to me, but now I felt a sharp regret at not being able to take up this challenge. The next day the regret was only worse, and I thought, why not give it a try? Not even trying would feel like a worse failure, I thought, so let me see this as a fun opportunity, whatever the result. So I started by writing a small library of music-oriented functions such as for representing tones and scales. I dove into the Amsterdam Music Library as soon as it re-opened after the Christmas and New Year's closure and for a week checked out every day as many books about music theory as I was allowed. From a book on the string quartets by Haydn I gleaned some useful information about their structure, but for the rest this turned out to be a huge disappointment. About melody I did not find anything useful, except some statistical data about the frequency of occurrence of intervals between successive notes of a melody. There were books about harmony that I could not make heads or tails of, which was all the worse since they gave me the tantalizing feeling there was some algorithmic content hiding in the inscrutable texts. Just as I was beginning to despair, I found a booklet by Paul Hindemith with exercises for students of traditional harmony that gave very concrete instructions on what to do and what not to do in terms of constructing chords and chord progressions.[10] I immediately set out to translate this into code. Unfortunately, after the second of two brief chapters, I had to give up because I could no longer understand the instructions. At least I had something for the harmonic part. (For readers who have some knowledge of chord progressions, this explains why there is not much else going on harmonically than an interminable repetition of I–IV–V–I chords.)

Next, I checked out a collection of scores of Haydn quartets and looked at them. I could visually identify many things I had not read about, such as that the two middle voices (second violin and viola) regularly played together in the same rhythm, different from the melody carried by the first violin and the bass line of the cello. I already had a skeleton in place for the main procedure, which I had given the name *compose*, which was based on my earlier experiments with a musical affix grammar. Each time I saw a recognizable pattern, I added a piece of code to *compose*, which usually required adding another affix in the form of a parameter. These parameters were passed down in the recursion process, but in a modified form, where the modifications were controlled by chance, but also by the values of other parameters.

---

[9] Hiller, Lejaren, and Isaacson, Leonard M. 1959. *Experimental music: Composition with an electronic computer*. New York: McGraw-Hill.

[10] Hindemith, Paul. 1949. *Aufgaben für Harmonieschüler* (translation to German of the English original "A concentrated course in traditional harmony", 1943), B. Schott's Söhne, Mainz, Edition 3602.

In doing so, I was in a way making up on the fly, in a completely *ad hoc* way, (possibly Haydn-specific) musical theory that I had been unable to find in the library books. The whole thing became a convoluted and bloated piece of code, with no obvious way of making it more modular.

It became time to start testing it, which I did on the Electrologica X8—the program had become too large for the X1. Preciously little time remained before the deadline. It became apparent very soon that testing a program whose behavior was intrinsically non-deterministic, controlled as it was by a random number generator, was a nightmare. No debugging tools were available; everything was processed in batch mode, and for a week each run terminated with a program abort, with a usually not very informative error message. After a bug was found and seemed to have been fixed, another ostensibly innocuous and unrelated minor change could make it reappear. I myself had no idea what the combined effect of all this code ought to be, so inasmuch as something was produced, I could not see how much of it conformed to the intentions behind all the code snippets added one by one, and how much was due to erroneous code.

There was another problem that I had not yet given much thought to. My entry had to be submitted in the form of a score. But the only output medium, apart from punched paper tape, was a line printer, which could not even print lower-case letters, let alone print a score. The X1 had a Calcomp plotter attached, and data could be exchanged between the X8 and X1 using paper tape, but writing a program for plotting a score was going to take far too much time. I came up with a poor man's solution, which was to abuse the line printer as if it was a plotter, printing the music turned by 90 degrees, so that the staves ran vertically, by printing | | | | | for each of the four voices on each line, or, by using the possibility of overprinting characters, something like | Φ | | | to represent a *g* note above middle *c* (for a staff with treble clef). These patterns, stacked, simulated the unbroken lines of a staff. If you held the printout a meter or two from your face and squinted your eyes, you just could imagine this represented a score—provided you had a powerful imagination.

Then the moment came of a completed run of all four parts of the string quartet: *Allegro–Andante–Minuetto–Finale*. It should not have been a day later. I grabbed the printout, went to the post office early the next morning, and had the whole thing sent off by registered express mail to the IFIP Congress Office in London. It weighed over 5 kg (about 12 lbs) and cost me a small fortune. It was thus a poor man's solution indeed. (The idea of asking the MC to reimburse the cost did not occur to me.) I had no clue what I had sent off, in terms of how it would sound if performed. Would it even sound like music? Would I ever find out?

A letter came from the jury, politely saying, all good and well, but would I send them a human-readable score as soon as possible, preferably yesterday. I procured an ample amount of blank music sheets (blank except for the preprinted staff lines) and undertook the laborious work of manually copying the music from the hard-to-read printout to the sheets, using a fine pen. Working 16-h days, this took me a week—I had to be very careful not to make mistakes, and my hand was untrained for the task of drawing notes. I know now that composers are content with drawing the filled note heads of crotchets not as an oval but as a fat stripe, which would have saved a lot of time; instead, I tried to produce the appearance of a printed score as faithfully as I could.[11] In any case, the jury accepted this late completion of my submission, because I received a letter stating that the work had been found worthy of a special mention and would be performed during a concert, scheduled as a special event during the IFIP Congress, held in August 1968.

8.4 The Musical Result

At the concert, the quartet was not performed by a group of four musicians, as is usual for string quartets, but by the full strings section of the Pro Arte Orchestra of Edinburgh. This was the first time it was performed in public, but I had attended a repetition and therefore knew already how it sounded: like "real" classical music— not in any way great and inspired music, but not robotic either. (Much later I heard a Quartetto for Three Violins and Cello composed by Benjamin Franklin—who was a contemporary of Carl Philipp Emanuel Bach—that reminded me of my own string quartet, but was actually more robotic. In spite of all his genius, there is a reason why the polymath Franklin is not remembered as a composer.)

The President of IFIP, Ambrose P. Speiser, who was a member of the jury, told me after the concert that there had been a total of fifteen qualifying entries, and that the judgement of the jury had been based on a performance of inferior quality. In his mind, there was no doubt that it should have been awarded at least the third prize. In primary school our report cards showed not only grades for accomplishment but also a grade for diligence. I think my work deserved a prize for diligence, in at least trying.

It is hard to tell how much of the evident shortcomings of the composition is due to the remaining programming errors, how much is due to the rudimentary understanding of harmony theory encoded in the program, how much is a matter of yet undeveloped musical theory, and how much of it can be ascribed to a lack of inspiration that requires the sensibilities of a human composer. As to the latter, nowadays there are AI-based programs that use neural networks to produce music for which it is not possible to tell it was not composed by a human. Unfortunately, we will not learn anything about musical theory from this; whatever theory has been extracted from the pieces of (human-composed) music that were used to train the networks is distributed over the synapses in an undecipherable way. To me, it feels like cheating.

The only descriptions until now of the way the procedure *compose* works have been in Dutch, except for an extremely summary description included in the Proceedings of the 1968 IFIP Congress.[12] For historical interest, a translation is appended of a publication from 1968, based on a lecture I then gave for the Nederlands Reken-

---

[11] Published as: Meertens, Lambert G.L.T. 1968. *Quartet No. 1 in C Major for 2 Violins, Viola and Violoncello*. Mathematical Centre Report MR 96. Mathematical Centre. Amsterdam.

[12] Meertens, Lambert G.L.T. 1969. The imitation of musical styles by a computer. In *Information Processing 68*, Proc. IFIP Congress 1968, Vol. 1, xxv–xxvi. Amsterdam: North-Holland Publishing

machine Genootschap (Dutch Computer Society). It could only describe the grand lines. The detail can be seen in the ALGOL 60 source text of the procedure, also appended. Obviously, it is not self-contained, extensively making use of a library of music-oriented functions, yet it will offer an appreciation of what went into the making and baking of the cake.

Company; Andriessen, Louis, Leo Geurts, and Lambert Meertens. 1969. Componist en computer. *De Gids* 132:304–311.

Appendix 1: Composing with a Computer

Lecture for the Nederlands Rekenmachine Genootschap on 23 September 1968.[13]

0. *Introduction*

Computers can be used to compose music. This unusual application is a response to the challenge of realizing a creative process with the help of a computer, a challenge that is probably as old as the computer. Taking advantage of the possibilities offered by a computer, a composer can achieve something that otherwise could not be realized because of the large amount of work involved.

However, this is not the only goal of composing by computer. If a theory regarding music in a particular style is sufficiently formalized, one can "translate" that theory into a program and next compare pieces composed by the program with original music in that style. In this way it can be determined to what extent that theory is able to explain the beauty and inventiveness that we experience in the original music, and how much remains to be explained.

Unfortunately, most theories in the field of music do not lend themselves well to formalization. About the subject of "melody," of paramount musical importance, little more can be found than that smaller intervals, with the exception of the relatively rare prime interval, are more common than larger ones, that a large jump is preferably filled up by steps in the reverse direction, and that an increase and decrease of the melodic line generates and dissolves tension.

A program that composes in a traditional style must therefore incorporate a great deal of newly formed theory. This article outlines how such a program was realized in ALGOL 60.

1. *Harmony*

Among the components of musical theory, harmony is the one that is most susceptible to formalization. The program described here used a book by Hindemith, "Aufgaben für Harmonieschüler."[14] It sets out clear rules for a successive pair of four-voice chords.

Some of these rules are constructive, but the majority are in the form of a restriction. A constructive rule is: resolve a diminished fifth or augmented fourth in a chord (e.g., in a dominant seventh chord) by moving one voice up by one second and the other down by one second, so that a third or a sixth is formed. Figure 8.2 shows how an augmented fourth between the soprano and the tenor is resolved. A restrictive rule is: two voices in a chord that form a fifth may not form a fifth again by changing in the same direction to the next chord. Figure 8.3 shows "parallel fifths" between the soprano and the bass.

---

[13] Translation of: Meertens, Lambert G.L.T. 1968. Componeren met de computer. *Informatie* 10:418–421.

[14] Hindemith (1949), course in harmony.

	first chord	second chord
soprano:	f ♯	g
alt:	d	d
tenor:	c	b
bass:	d	g

Fig. 8.2 Resolving an augmented fourth between soprano and tenor

	first chord	second chord
soprano:	c	d
alt:	f	d
tenor:	a	b
bass:	f	g

Fig. 8.3 Parallel fifths between soprano and bass

Two problems had to be solved in converting these rules into program form. The first was that in the aforementioned book by Hindemith, rules are sometimes introduced, presumably for some reason, only to be suddenly abolished a few pages later. The second was that it is not clear in advance that a series of chords progressing according to the rules of the art, could not enter a dead-end path and finally reach a chord from which no legitimate continuation is possible.

The first difficulty has been addressed by interpreting the restrictions such that some restrictions apply very strongly, while others indicate rather that a certain phenomenon should preferably be avoided, but may occur, if need be, in cases where it is hard to go around it. The strength of each restriction is expressed in a number, the corresponding "penalty."

In the program, the harmonic part is laid down in a procedure named *harmonic adviser*. One of the input parameters of this procedure is the last chord.

Harmonic adviser generates, according to constructive principles, a large number of new chords, being candidate successors of the last chord. Each of these chords is tested in turn against each restrictive rule included in the procedure. When a chord is found to violate a restriction, it is imposed the corresponding penalty. The penalties for a chord are added up; the chord with the least total penalty is returned in an output parameter. This method also offers a solution for the second difficulty: in a difficult case, the least bad continuation is still chosen.

The chord to be formed can already have been partially fixed in advance, because a few voices have already been filled in, or because the root of the chord is given.

Moreover, by using *Jensen's device*[15] an arbitrarily complex request can be taken into account for each call of *harmonic adviser*. This is achieved by assigning each generated candidate chord to the output parameter, and then adding the result of the evaluation of a parameter *special fine* to the total penalty. Thereby, if so desired, it can be ensured that the soprano and the bass are in contrary motion, or that the soprano and the alto move in parallel thirds and sixths.

Some examples of restrictions with their penalties are:

restriction	penalty
parallel fifths	100 000
doubled third	30 000
bass not doubled	5 000
crossing voices	2 000
change in the middle voices	100 to 200 for every second difference

This last restriction rule replaces the constructive rule that the middle voices (alto and tenor) move over the smallest possible intervals, since a larger jump in the middle voices is far preferable to a parallel fifth.

To save time, the soprano and bass are always pre-filled in the program; this drastically reduces the number of chords generated.

2. *Melody*

The composition principles given in this section are all, as far as known, original. A recursive procedure is used to compose a passage, which can be described very sketchily as follows:

```
procedure compose (duration, parameters);
if further subdivision undesirable then output else
begin  calculate left duration;
       calculate left parameters;
       compose (left duration, left parameters);
       right duration := duration − left duration;
       calculate right parameters;
       compose (right duration, right parameters)
end
```

This is how the rhythm and melody are generated.

---

[15] Note added in translation: see Dijkstra, Edsger W. 1961. Letter to the editor: Defense of ALGOL 60. *Communications of the ACM* 11(4):502–503; https://en.wikipedia.org/wiki/Jensen's_device.

2.1. *Melodic line*

The principle underlying the formation of the melodic line stems from the following, very general, aesthetic rule:

In a piece of music there should be a regular alternation of tension and relaxation.

Many composing principles can be formulated in terms of tension and relaxation, and then fall under this rule. In the melodic line, tension is evoked by a climax, and relaxation follows when it falls. However, if successive maxima repeatedly fall on the same note, this has a decidedly trivial effect. It is better if they differ slightly. This can quite well be achieved as follows:

Each passage reaches its highest note somewhere. When this passage is divided into two, each of these sub-passages also has a highest note, and the highest note of at least one of these two sub-passages is the same as that of the whole passage. It is now sufficient to make sure that the highest note of the other sub-passage is slightly lower. This procedure applied to the entire passage is similarly applied to the two sub-passages.

In ALGOL 60:

```
procedure compose (duration, highest note);
value duration, highest note; integer duration, highest note;
if duration = 1 then output (highest note) else
if RANDOM < 1/2 then
begin compose (duration/2, highest note);
       compose (duration/2, highest note − 1)
end else
begin compose (duration/2, highest note − 1);
       compose (duration/2, highest note)
end
```

The expression $RANDOM < 1/2$ occurring in this code needs some explanation. $RANDOM$ is a function procedure that for each call returns a different real number r satisfying $0 \leq r < 1$, in such a way that, for $0 \leq p \leq 1$, the expression $RANDOM < p$ has a "probability" of (almost) p of being true. Moreover, in successive evaluations of $RANDOM < p$, no other regularity can be detected than already follows from the magnitude p of the probability of the outcome "true."

So we can use $RANDOM$ as a kind of die. Instead of actually rolling the dice and asking: *thrown eyes* = 6, we can ask: $RANDOM < 1/6$. Thus, in melodic lines generated using the above procedure, the highest point of the passage will fall approximately equally often in the left as in the right half of the passage.

An example of a melodic line that could have been generated by the call *compose* (16, 4):

$$1 \quad 0 \quad 1 \quad 2 \quad 1 \quad 2 \quad 3 \quad 2 \quad 1 \quad 2 \quad 3 \quad 2 \quad 3 \quad 4 \quad 3 \quad 2$$

or, using note names:

$$d \quad c \quad d \quad e \quad d \quad e \quad f \quad e \quad d \quad e \quad f \quad e \quad f \quad g \quad f \quad e$$

Purely by coincidence, all intervals in this example are seconds.

The call *compose* (16, 4) in this example resulted in the calls *compose* (8, 3) and *compose* (8, 4), and these again resulted in *compose* (4, 2), *compose* (4, 3), *compose* (4, 3), *compose* (4, 4), etc.

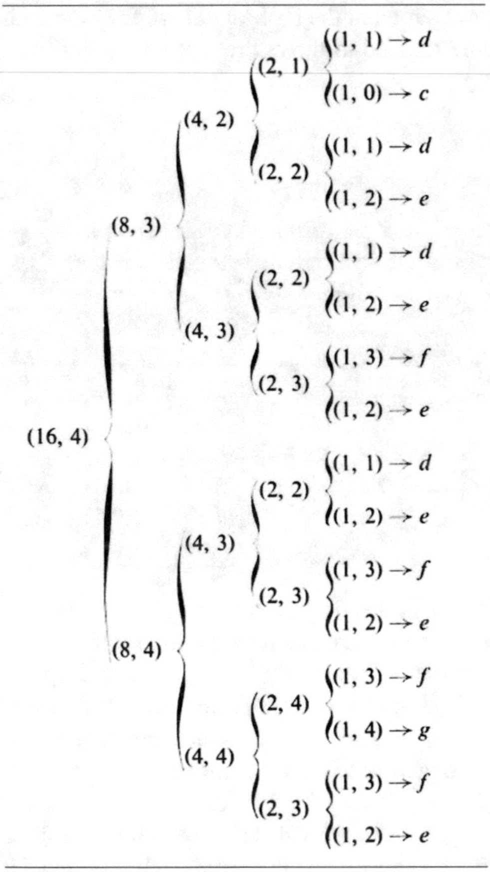

Fig. 8.4 Example of generating a melodic line

The complete process is shown in Fig. 8.4.

It is nice to compare the frequencies of occurrence of the intervals for the melodic lines generated by this principle with the intervals from classical music. Figure 8.5 shows the tallied frequencies for a generated sequence of 128 notes. This appears to agree quite well with what was stated in the introduction. In addition, of the 19 occurring jumps, 17 were followed by a second in the opposite direction. So it turns out that this simple principle, based on an aesthetic consideration, explains *en passant* two known, seemingly independent phenomena.

interval	number of occurrences
prime	25
second	83
third	14
fourth	5
≥ fifth	0

Fig. 8.5 Frequency of intervals in a generated series

2.2 *Rhythm*

The rhythm can be generated by the following procedure:

```
procedure compose (duration, level);
value duration, level; real duration; integer level;
if RANDOM ≥ level/4 then output (duration) else
begin compose (duration/2, level − 1);
        compose (duration/2, level − 1)
end
```

In this procedure, depending on the value of *level*, we have the following probabilities of subdivision:

level	duration	probability of subdivision
≥ 4	> 1	1
3	1	$\frac{3}{4}$
2	$\frac{1}{2}$	$\frac{1}{2}$
1	$\frac{1}{4}$	$\frac{1}{4}$
0	$\frac{1}{8}$	0

An example of a rhythm that could have been generated by the call *compose* (8, 6):

$$1 \mid \frac{1}{2} \; \frac{1}{8} \; \frac{1}{8} \; \frac{1}{4} \mid \frac{1}{2} \; \frac{1}{8} \; \frac{1}{8} \; \frac{1}{4} \mid 1 \mid \frac{1}{8} \; \frac{1}{8} \; \frac{1}{4} \; \frac{1}{2} \mid \frac{1}{4} \; \frac{1}{4} \; \frac{1}{4} \; \frac{1}{4}$$

2.3. *Synthesis of rhythm and melodic line*

The melodic line and rhythm procedures can very easily be combined into one melody procedure:

```
procedure compose (duration, level, highest note);
value duration, level, highest note;
real duration; integer level, highest note;
if RANDOM ≥ level/4  then output (highest note, duration) else
if RANDOM < 1/2 then
begin compose (duration/2, level − 1, highest note);
        compose (duration/2, level − 1, highest note − 1)
end else
begin compose (duration/2, level − 1, highest note − 1);
        compose (duration/2, level − 1, highest note)
end
```

In the program this procedure *compose* is much more complicated than the above text would suggest. For example, the procedure uses 28 parameters, 17 of which have an intensive role in the recursion process. For the sake of clarity, and in addition because the entire text of the procedure would take up a few pages, only the simplest aspects have been touched upon here.

It should also be mentioned that the procedure, by manipulating with the set of *RANDOM* values, manages to make the same sequence of decisions in the rhythm splitting process in different bars, creating the effect of rhythmic motifs. An attempt to do something similar with the melody failed due to a programming error.

The way in which a synthesis is reached between harmony and melody in procedure *compose* is still unsatisfactory: the harmonic function and the melody are determined independently, and in case of incompatibility the melody is slightly changed.

3. *Macrostructure*

The macrostructure of the composition is that of a classical string quartet. Although there is no difficulty in principle to allow for variations in the macrostructure on a case-by-case basis, the following sequence of four parts is defined in the program:

part I	*Allegro*	$\frac{3}{4}$ time	C major
part II	*Adagio*	$\frac{6}{8}$ time	a minor
part III	*Minuetto*	$\frac{3}{4}$ time	C major
part IV	*Finale*	$\frac{2}{2}$ time	C major

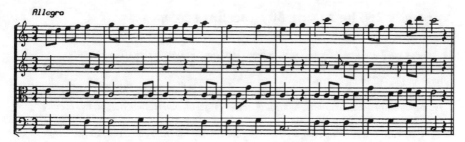

Fig. 8.6 First sentence of the Allegro

Part I is composed in the sonata form, consisting of exposition (repeated), development and recapitulation. Due to the drastic nature of the variation technique used, very little of the original thematic material can be discerned in the development. The minuet is in a form often used by Haydn. The macrostructure of the composition is obtained by calling procedure *compose* several times with suitably chosen parameters. It is striking how pieces of very different character can be composed this way.

4. *Results*

The program described here was run on the ELECTROLOGICA X8 of the Mathematical Center and produced the score for a string quartet. The entire process, from the design of the program to the end result, took place within a month in great haste. It was therefore not possible to find all programming errors in the program. In fact, the string quartet composed is the result of the first run without premature termination of the program due to errors; also up to now its last run. It was entered for the 1968 IFIP computer music competition and received a special mention.

To conclude, Fig. 8.6 shows an example from the string quartet, composed and drawn by computer.[16]

---

[16] Note added in translation: This fragment was plotted using the Calcomp plotter attached to the X1 of the Mathematical Center. The plottable shapes for the clefs, notes, and other musical signs, together with the plotter moves for drawing them, were designed by Leo Geurts.

Appendix 2: The ALGOL 60 Procedure *compose*

procedure *compose* (*melodic voice, num beats, left function code, right function code,*
   steady function, cadence, bars to go, constant, new start, figurating, melos, rhythm, others,
   max height, left branch, beat strength, right beat strength);
value *melodic voice, num beats, left function code, right function code, steady function, cadence,*
   bars to go, constant, new start, figurating, melos, rhythm, others, max height, left branch,
   beat strength, right beat strength;
integer *melodic voice, num beats, left function code, right function code, bars to go,*
   beat strength, right beat strength;
real *melos, rhythm, others, max height*;
Boolean *steady function, cadence, figurating, left branch*;
Boolean array *constant, new start*; **comment** [*soprano* : *bass*];
begin integer *voice, bass voice, voice 2, round, left right function code, right left function code*;
   Boolean array *split up*[*soprano* : *bass*]; **Boolean** *some split up, last of cadence*;
   real *left melos, right melos, left rhythm, right rhythm*;

   bass voice := **if** *melodic voice* = *bass* **then** *tenor* **else** *bass*;
   round := (*left function code* − *right function code*) / 3 + (*num beats* − 1) / *mean cycle beats*;
   right function code := *right function code* + 3 × *round*;
   if *right function code* < *left function code* **then** *right function code* := *right function code* + 3;
   left right function code := (*left function code* + *right function code*) ÷ 2;
   if *cadence* ∧ *num beats* = *bars to go* × *bar beats* ∧ *bars to go* ≥ 9 **then**
   begin *right left function code* := *right function code* − *bars to go* ÷ 2 + 1;
     maxim (*left right function code, right left function code* − 1)
   end else
     right left function code := (*left function code* − *left right function code* +
       right function code);

   last of cadence := *cadence* ∧ *bars to go* = 1;
   for *voice* := *soprano, alto, tenor, bass* **do**
     split up[*voice*] := **if** *constant*[*voice*] **then false else**
       if *left function code* ≠ *right function code* **then true else**
       if *last of cadence* **then true else**
       if *voice* = *melodic voice* ∧ *figurating* **then true else**
         (**if** *voice* = *melodic voice* **then** *next random* (*rhythm*) **else** *next random* (*others*)) <
           (**if** *voice* = *bass voice* **then** (*num beats* − 1) / *bar beats* **else**
           (*num beats* + *bar beats* − 1) / (2 × *bar beats*));
   for *voice* := *soprano, alto, tenor, bass* **do**
     if *voice* = *bass voice* **then else**
     if *split up*[*voice*] = *split up*[*melodic voice*] **then else**
     for *voice 2* := *soprano, alto, tenor, bass* **do**
       if *voice 2* = *melodic voice* ∨ *voice 2* = *bass voice* **then else**
       if *next random* (*others*) ≥ .50 **then** *split up*[*voice 2*] := *split up*[*voice*];
   some split up := *split up*[*soprano*] ∨ *split up*[*alto*] ∨ *split up*[*tenor*] ∨ *split up*[*bass*];

   left melos := *perm01* (*next random* (*melos*)); *left rhythm* := *perm01* (*next random* (*rhythm*));
   right melos := *melos*; *right rhythm* := *rhythm*;
   if ¬ *left branch* **then** *left branch* := **true else**
   begin *left branch* :=
      next random (*melos*) < *bar beats* / (*bar beats* + *num beats*);
     if *next random* (*melos*) < .5 **then**
     begin *melos* := *right melos* := *left melos*;

```
        rhythm := right rhythm := left rhythm
    end else
    if next random (rhythm) < .5 then
        rhythm := right rhythm := left rhythm
end;


if num beats = 1 ∨ ¬ some split up then
begin integer step, function, turning point, keynote of chord, prop mel, koc, int;
    Boolean established, establishable, dominant seventh possible, improper,
        some internote requested;
    integer array proposed, internote, alternote[soprano : bass];
    Boolean array filled in[soprano : bass];

    function := left function code − left function code ÷ 3 × 3;
    function := if function = tonic code then tonic else
        if function = subdominant code then subdominant else dominant;
    if tritone (last output) then resolution required := true;
    turning point := quotus (last output[melodic voice]) − octave;
    maxim (turning point, quotus (lowest note of[melodic voice]));
    for voice := soprano, alto, tenor, bass do proposed[voice] := last output[ voice];
    step := − second;
    if new start[melodic voice] then proposed[melodic voice] := max height;
    if function ≠ tonic then tonic required := false else
        if last of cadence then tonic required := true;
    established := function = last function ∧ last function established;
    establishable := beat strength > right beat strength + 1 ∧ num beats = 1 ∧ steady function ∧
        ¬ tonic required ∧ ¬ constant[melodic voice];
    int := if last output[melodic voice] = rest ∨ last output[bass voice] = rest then rest
        else qred (abs (last output[melodic voice] − last output[bass voice]));


test proposed note :
    for keynote of chord := if function = dominant then tonic else function − third, function do
    begin integer thirds in mel;
        if tonic required ∧ keynote of chord ≠ function then go to end keynote;
        if ¬ major (key) ∧ keynote of chord = second then go to end keynote;
        proposed[bass voice] := if ¬ established then function else keynote of chord;
        if function = dominant ∧ proposed[bass voice] ≠ function then go to end keynote;
        dominant seventh possible := keynote of chord = dominant ∧ ¬ steady function;
        if proposed[bass voice] ≠ keynote of chord ∧ ¬ establishable then go to end keynote;
        thirds in mel := thirds in (proposed[melodic voice] − key − keynote of chord);
        improper := thirds in mel >
            (if dominant seventh possible then thirds in seventh else thirds in fifth);
        if function ≠ keynote of chord ∧ thirds in mel ≥ thirds in (function − keynote of chord)
            then go to end keynote;
        if improper ∧ ¬ (establishable ∧ keynote of chord = function) then go to end keynote;
        proposed[bass voice] :=
            nearest to (if last output[bass voice] = rest then middle[bass voice] else
                last output[bass voice] + sign (quotus (middle[bass voice] −
                    last output[bass voice])) × second,
                bass voice, proposed[bass voice] + key, key);
        if int ≠ rest ∧ proposed[bass voice] ≠ last output[bass voice] then
        begin integer int 2;
            int 2 := qred (abs (proposed[melodic voice] − proposed[bass voice]));
            if int 2 ≠ prime ∧ int 2 ≠ fifth then else if int 2 = int then go to end keynote else
```

```
        if sign (proposed[melodic voice] − last output[melodic voice]) ≠
            sign (proposed[bass voice] − last output[bass voice]) then else
        if int < int 2 then go to end keynote else
        if int 2 = prime ∧
            abs (quotus (proposed[melodic voice] − last output[melodic voice])) ≥ third ∧
            abs (quotus (proposed[bass voice] − last output[bass voice])) ≥ third then
        go to end keynote
        end;
        if new start[bass voice] ∧ proposed[bass voice] ≠ last output[bass voice] then
            go to end keynote;
        go to new chord;
end keynote :
    end;

    if proposed[melodic voice] ≥ turning point then step := second;
    proposed[melodic voice] := proposed[melodic voice] + step;
    if proposed[melodic voice] ≥ quotus (highest note of[melodic voice]) ∧
        new start[melodic voice] then go to test proposed note;
```

```
    NLCR; PRINT TEXT ('programming error dump ');
    PRINT (function + 1); PRINT (melodic voice);
    bpr ('tonic required', tonic required); bpr ('establishable', establishable);
    bpr ('established', established); bpr ('steady function', steady function);
    bpr ('new start[bass voice]', new start[bass voice]);
    ber ('new start[melodic voice]', new start[melodic voice]);
    EXIT;

new chord :
    for voice := soprano, alto, tenor, bass do filled in[voice] := ¬ new start[voice];
    filled in[bass voice] := true;
    filled in[melodic voice] := ¬ (resolution required ∨ tonic required);
    prop mel := proposed[melodic voice]; koc := keynote of chord;
    harmonic advisor (last output, proposed, general rest, melodic voice, bass voice, filled in,
        koc, true, dominant seventh possible, key,
        (if tonic required ∨ reduced (proposed[melodic voice] − key) = unison then 0 else 10000)
            + (if resolution required then 10000 × abs (quotus (last output[melodic voice] −
                proposed[melodic voice])) +
                1000 × abs (quotus (prop mel − proposed[melodic voice])) else 0));

    some internote requested := false;
    for voice := soprano, alto, tenor, bass do if internote requested[voice] then
    begin integer q1, q2, z;
        some internote requested := true;
        q1 := quotus (last output[voice]); q2 := quotus (proposed[voice]);
        internote[voice] := proper (if abs (q1 − q2) = second then 2 × 2 − q1 else
            if q1 = q2 then q1 − second else q1 + sign (q2 − q1) × second, key);
        alternote[voice] := proper (if abs (q1 − q2) = second then 2 × q1 − q2 else
            if q1 = q2 then q1 + second else q2 + sign (q1 − q2) × second, key);
        if internote[voice] ≠ safe (internote[voice], voice) then
            internote[voice] := alternote[voice] else
        if alternote[voice] ≠ safe (alternote[voice], voice) then
            alternote[voice] := internote[voice];
        for voice 2 := soprano step 1 until voice − 1 do if internote requested[voice 2] then
        begin z := qred (abs (internote[voice 2] − internote[voice]));
```

```
         if z ≠ prime ∧ z ≠ fifth then else
         if qred (abs (last output[voice 2] − last output[voice])) ≠ z ∧
            qred (abs (proposed[voice 2] − proposed[voice])) ≠ z then else
         if internote[ voice] ≠ alternote[voice] then internote[voice] := alternote[voice] else
         internote[voice 2] := alternote[voice 2]
      end
   end;

   if some internote requested then
   begin integer offenders, off min, keynote, optimal keynote;
      Boolean array good[soprano : bass];
      off min := max int;
      for voice := soprano, alto, tenor, bass do if ¬ internote requested[voice] then
         internote[voice] := last output[voice];
      for keynote := qred (proposed[bass voice]), keynote − third, keynote − third do
      begin offenders := 0;
         for voice := soprano, alto, tenor, bass do
         if thirds in (internote[voice] − keynote) > thirds in fifth then
            offenders := offenders + 1;
         if offenders < off min then
         begin off min := offenders;
            optimal keynote := keynote
         end
      end;

      for voice := soprano, alto, tenor, bass do good[voice] := true;
      for voice := melodic voice + 1 step 1 until bass, soprano step 1 until melodic voice do
      if off min ≥ 1 then else
      if ¬ internote requested[ voice] then else
      if thirds in (internote[voice] − optimal keynote) > thirds in fifth then
      begin good[voice] := false; off min := off min − 1 end;
      keynote := optimal keynote − key;
      harmonic advisor (last output, internote, proposed, melodic voice, bass voice, good,
         keynote, true, false, key, SUM (voice, soprano, bass,
            500 × abs (quotus (internote[voice] × 2 − (last output[voice] + proposed[voice]))))));
      produce output (intertime, internote requested, internote);
      for voice := soprano, alto, tenor, bass do internote requested[voice] := false
   end;

   if num beats ≠ 1 then else
   if next random (others) ≥ .75 then
   for voice := soprano, alto, tenor, bass do
   if voice = melodic voice ∨ voice = bass voice then else
   if ¬ new start[voice] then
   begin new start[voice] := true; proposed[ voice ] := rest end;
   produce output (time, new start, proposed);
   tonic required := false; resolution required := tritone (last output);

   if some split up then
   begin intertime := time + (if (if split up[melodic voice] then next random (rhythm) else
      next random (others)) < prob34 then 3/4 else 1/2) × dur beat;
      if (if split up[melodic voice] then next random (melos) else next random (others)) <
         prob do it yourself then
      begin integer array preserve[soprano : bass];
```

```
        for voice := soprano, alto, tenor, bass do filled in[voice] := ¬ split up[voice];
        harmonic advisor (last output, proposed, general rest, melodic voice, bass voice,
            filled in, koc, false, dominant seventh possible ∧ ¬ resolution required, key, 0);
        if resolution required then for voice := soprano, alto, tenor, bass do
            preserve[voice] := last output[voice];
        produce output (intertime, split up, proposed);
        if resolution required then for voice := soprano, alto, tenor, bass do
            last output[voice] := preserve[voice]
    end else
        for voice := soprano, alto, tenor, bass do internote requested[voice] := split up[voice]
    end;

    improper := thirds in (last output[melodic voice] − key − keynote of chord) > thirds in fifth;
    if function ≠ last function then
    begin last function := function; last function established := false end;
    if ¬ last function established then
        last function established := keynote of chord = function ∧ ¬ improper;
    if improper then resolution required := true;
    time := time + num beats × dur beat
end else

begin integer left beats, right beats, preserve bar beats; real preserve dur beat;
    real array max h[1 : 2];

    preserve bar beats := bar beats; preserve dur beat := dur beat;
    if num beats = bar beats then
    begin if ¬ figurating then figurating := next random (rhythm) < prob figur;
        if dur beat ≥ min dur beat then else if next random (rhythm) < prob double speed then
        begin num beats := num beats × 2; bar beats := bar beats × 2; dur beat := dur beat / 2 end;
        if last of cadence then else
        if next random (rhythm) < (expansion factor − 1) / (3 × expansion factor − 1) then
        begin integer rep, voice, v; real r;
            r := perm01 (rhythm);
            rep := 1 + entier (3 × next random (r));
            for v := melodic voice step −1 until melodic voice − rep do
            begin voice := if v ≥ soprano then v else v + bass − soprano + 1;
                compose (voice, num beats, left function code, right function code,
                    if v = melodic voice − rep then steady function else
                        left function code = right function code,
                    cadence, bars to go, constant, new start, figurating, melos, rhythm, others,
                    max height + suggested max height[voice] − suggested max height[melodic voice],
                    left branch, beat strength, right beat strength);
                go to end compose
            end
        end
    end;

    right beats := if num beats > bar beats then num beats ÷ (2 × bar beats) × bar beats else
    num beats × preserve bar beats ÷ bar beats ÷ 2 × bar beats ÷ preserve bar beats;
    left beats := num beats − right beats;
    if num beats > bar beats then right beat strength := beat strength;
    for voice := soprano, alto, tenor, bass do
        constant[voice] := ¬ split up[voice] ∨ last of cadence;
    max h[1] := max h[2] := max height;
```

max h[1 + entier (2 × *next random* (*melos*))] :=
    max height − (**if** *figurating* **then** *octave* / 3 **else** *second*);
if *last of cadence* **then** *max h*[1] := *least jump* (*melodic voice, key, key*);
compose (*melodic voice, left beats, left function code, left right function code,*
    left right function code = *right left function code, cadence, bars to go, constant, new start,*
    figurating, left melos, left rhythm, next random (*others*), *max h*[1], **true**, *beat strength,*
    right beat strength − 1);
if *num beats* = *bar beats* ∧ *left beats* ≠ *right beats* **then**
    right beat strength := *right beat strength* − 1;
if *last of cadence* **then**
begin *produce output* (*time, all* **true**, *general rest*); *time* := *time* + *right beats* × *dur beat* **end**
else *compose* (*melodic voice, right beats, right left function code, right function code,*
        steady function, cadence, bars to go − *left beats* ÷ *bar beats, constant, split up,*
        figurating, right melos, right rhythm, perm01 (*others*), *max h*[2], *left branch,*
        right beat strength, right beat strength − 1);
end compose :
    bar beats := *preserve bar beats*; *dur beat* := *preserve dur beat*
  end
end

References

[1] Alberts, G., and P.C. Baayen. 1987a. Ingenieur van taal. Interview met A. van Wijngaarden. In *Zij mogen uiteraard daarbij de zuivere wiskunde niet verwaarloozen*, eds. Alberts G., F. van der Blij, and J. Nuis, 276–288. Amsterdam: CWI.

[2] Alberts, G., and P.C. Baayen. 1987b. De hoeder van de stichtingen. Interview met J.H. Bannier. In *Zij mogen uiteraard daarbij de zuivere wiskunde niet verwaarloozen*, eds. Alberts G., F. van der Blij, and J. Nuis, 101–114. Amsterdam: CWI.

[3] Alberts G., F. van der Blij, and J. Nuis, eds. 1987c. *Zij mogen uiteraard daarbij de zuivere wiskunde niet verwaarloozen*. Amsterdam: CWI.

[4] Alberts, G., H.J.M. Bos, and J. Nuis, eds. 1989. *Om de wiskunde. Stimulansen voor toepassingsgerichte wiskunde rond 1946*. Amsterdam: CWI.

[5] Alberts, Gerard. 1998a. *Jaren van berekening. Toepassingsgerichte initiatieven in de Nederlandse wiskunde-beoefening 1945–1960*. Amsterdam: Amsterdam University Press.

[6] Alberts, Gerard. 1998b. Optimaal regelen. In *De opkomst van de informatietechnologie in Nederland*, ed. E. van Oost e.a., 103–117. Amsterdam: Amsterdam University Press.

[7] Alberts, G. 2006. De geboorte van de Nederlandse informatica in Londen – Aad van Wijngaarden. *Informatie* 48(1): 46–50.

[8] Alberts, Gerard, and Huub T. de Beer. 2008a. De AERA. Gedroomde machines en de praktijk van het rekenwerk aan het Mathematisch Centrum te Amsterdam, *Studium* 2, 101–127. Amsterdam: Amsterdam University Press.

[9] Alberts, Gerard, and Huub T. de Beer. 2008b. Interview met A.W. Dek, directeur van de Nillmij en commissaris van Electrologica, gehouden op 8 januari 2008, unpublished.

[10] Alberts, G. 2010 Appropriating America: Americanization in the history of European computing. *IEEE Annals of the History of Computing* 32(2):4–7.

[11] Alberts, G. 2014a. Algol culture and programming styles; guest editor's introduction, algol culture and programming styles. *IEEE Annals for the History of Computing* 36(4):2–5, special issue.

© The Author(s), under exclusive license to Springer Nature Switzerland AG 2022
G. Alberts, J. F. Groote (eds.), *Tales of Electrologica*, History of Computing,
https://doi.org/10.1007/978-3-031-13033-5

[12] Alberts, G., ed. 2014a. Algol culture and programming styles. *IEEE Annals for the History of Computing* 36(4), special issue.

[13] Alberts, G., and E. Daylight. 2014c. Universality versus locality: the Amsterdam style of ALGOL implementation. *IEEE Annals for the History of Computing* 36(4): 52–63.

[14] Alberts, Gerard, and Bas van Vlijmen. 2017. *Computerpioniers: het begin van het computertijdperk in Nederland*. Amsterdam: Amsterdam University Press.

[15] Alberts, G. 2019. Computerbouw in Nederland: ondernemende academici en bedachtzame industriëlen. *Studium* 12(1–3):48–69.

[16] Amdahl, Gene, Gerrit Blaauw, and Fred Brooks. 1964. Architecture of the IBM system. *IBM Journal of Research and Development* 8(2):87–101.

[17] Andriessen, Louis, Leo Geurts, and Lambert Meertens. 1969. Componist en computer. *De Gids* 132:304–311.

[18] Apt, K.R. 2002. Edsger Wybe Dijkstra (1930–2002): A portrait of a genius. *Formal Aspects of Computing* 14(2):92–98.

[19] Baayen, P.C., and J. Nuis. 1988. In memoriam A van Wijngaarden 1916–1987. *Nieuw Archief voor Wiskunde* 6(3):269–282.

[20] Bakker, J.W. de, and J.C. van Vliet, eds. 1981. *Algorithmic languages. Proceedings of the International Symposium on Algorithmic Languages*. Amsterdam: North-Holland.

[21] Bakker, M.S.C., and W.H.P.M. van Hooff. 1991. *Gedenkboek Technische Universiteit Eindhoven, 1956–1991*. Eindhoven: Technische Universiteit Eindhoven.

[22] Barning, Freek J.M. 1964. *X8-simulator, simulatieprogramma voor het uitvoeren van X8-programma's met behulp van de X1*. Mathematisch Centrum report R 917. Amsterdam: Mathemathical Centre.

[23] Barning, Freek J.M. *Standard functions in X8 assembleercode ELAN*. Mathematical Centre report R 1942. Amsterdam: Mathematical Centre.

[24] Beer, H.T. de. 2006. The history of the ALGOL effort, Master's thesis, Technische Universiteit Eindhoven.

[25] Beer, H. de (2008) Electrologica, Nederlands eerste computerindustrie. *Informatie* Informatie 50(10):30–37.

[26] Biekman, W.C.M., and Anton J. Mars. 1968. PDP-8 IN-UIT-systeem. IKO informal report. Archived at the National Museum Boerhaave, Leiden.

[27] Bindenga, A.J., and H.H.J. Nordemann. 1984. *Hoor en wederhoor: artikelen aangeboden aan prof. dr. A. B. Frielink bij zijn afscheid als buitengewoon hoogleraar*. Amsterdam: Vakgroep Bedrijfsinformatica en Accountancy van de Faculteit der Economische Wetenschappen van de Universiteit van Amsterdam.

[28] Blaauw, Gerrit A. 1952. *The application of selenium rectifiers as switching devices in the Mark IV calculator*. Dissertation, Harvard University (Mass.).

[29] Blaauw, Gerrit A., and Frederick P. Brooks. 1997. *Computer architecture: Concepts and evolution*. Boston: Addison-Wesley Pub.

[30] Blanken, I.J. 2002. *Een industriële wereldfederatie; Geschiedenis van Koninklijke Philips Electronics N.V., Deel 5* Zaltbommel. De Europese Bibliotheek.

[31] Blommestijn, G.J.F., R. van Dantzig, Y. Haitsma and R.B.M. Mooy. 1981. The reaction $d(p, pp)n$ measured with BOL at E_p = 50 MeV. *Nuclear Physics A* 365:202–228.

[32] Bogaard, Adriënne van den. 2007. De bijdrage van Philips (Research) aan de informatietechnologie in Nederland vanuit het perspectief van kenniscirculatie, 1945–2010. Eindhoven: Stichting Historie der Techniek [rapport vooronderzoek].

[33] Bogaard, Adriënne van den. 2008a. Styles of programming 1952–1972. *Studium* (Rotterdam, Netherlands) 1(2):128–144.

[34] Bogaard, Adriënne van den. 2008b. Stijlen van programmeren 1952–1972. In *Computers en hun gebruikers*, 128–144.

[35] Bogaard, Adriënne van den, and Gerard Alberts. 2008c. Inleiding, in Adriënne van den Bogaard and Gerard Alberts (eds), *Computers en hun gebruikers, een halve eeuw computergeschiedenis in Nederland* (special issue) *Studium* 1–2:1–16.

[36] Bogaard, A. van den, H. Lintsen, F. Veraart en O. de Wit. 2008d. *De eeuw van de computer. Geschiedenis van de informatietechnologie in Nederland* Deventer: Kluwer/Stichting Historie der Techniek.

[37] Bruijn, W.K. de. 1964. Computers in de Benelux. *Informatie* 30:2–3.

[38] Bruijn, Nicolaas G. de. 1967. Additional comments on a problem in concurrent programming control. *Communications ACM* 10(3):137–138.

[39] Chomsky, Noam. 1957. *Syntactic structures*. Mouton: The Hague.

[40] Coopey, Richard, ed 2004a. *Information technology policy. An international history*. Oxford: Oxford University Press.

[41] Coopey, Richard. 2004b. Empire and technology: Information technology policy in postwar Britain and France. In Coopey (2004a), *Information technology*, 144–168.

[42] Dael, Ruud van. 2001. *'Iets met computers': over beroepsvorming van de informaticus*. Delft: Eburon.

[43] Dantzig, René van, et al. 1967a. Kwantisering van infostromen: draft. Leiden: Archived at the National Museum Boerhaave.

[44] Dantzig, René van, et al. 1967b. Window-processing for on-and off-line data-handling: draft specifications. Leiden: Archived at the National Museum Boerhaave.

[45] Dantzig, René van, et al. 1968a. Recent hardware and software developments for the PDP-8. In *Proceedings of the 4th European DECUS Seminar (1968)*. Leiden and at Nikhef, Amsterdam: Archived at the National Museum Boerhaave. See also https://ub.fnwi.uva.nl/computermuseum/pdfs/RecentHardwSoftwPDP8.pdf.

[46] Dantzig, René van, and Stef Toenbreker. 1968b. Vensterprogrammering. Leiden: Archived at the National Museum Boerhaave.

[47] Dantzig, René van, et al. 1971a. Data acquisition with the BOL nuclear detection system. *Nuclear Instruments and Methods* 92:199–203.

[48] Dantzig, René van, et al. 1971b. Analysis of multidimensional nuclear data (BOL). *Nuclear Instruments and Methods* 92:205–213.

[49] Dantzig, René van, et. al. 1973. Voorstel tot vervanging van de EL-X8 computer configuratie van het IKO. Leiden: Archived at the National Museum Boerhaave. https://ub.fnwi.uva.nl/computermuseum/pdfs/X8vervanging.pdf.

[50] Dantzig, René van. 1980. BOL. *Philips Technisch Tijdschrift* 39/10:286–291 (Dutch, English and French edition).

[51] Dantzig, René van. 2017. Project BOL (1964–1977), Historical overview. https://www.nikhef.nl/history/bol-EN.

[52] Edgar G. Daylight. 2016. De werking van de geest. In *De geest van de computer*, edited Eric Berkers and Edgar G. Daylight, 23–55. Utrecht: Matrijs.

[53] Dijkstra, Edsger W. 1959a. *Communication with an automatic computer*. [PhD Thesis. October 28, 1959. Universiteit van Amsterdam]. Excelsior, Rijswijk.

[54] Dijkstra, E.W. 1959. Verslag van de voordracht door Dr. E.W. Dijkstra, gehouden op 11 december 1959. De faciliteit tot interruptie in de X1. *Mededelingen van het Rekenmachinegenootschap* 2(1):3–8.

[55] Dijkstra, Edsger W. 1961. An ALGOL 60 Translator for the X1. *ALGOL Bulletin Supplement* 10:3–22. Mathematical Centre, Amsterdam.

[56] Dijkstra, Edsger W. 1961. Making a translator for ALGOL 60. *Algol Bulletin Supplement* 10:23–33. Mathematical Centre, Amsterdam.

[57] Dijkstra, Edsger W. 1961. Letter to the editor: Defense of ALGOL 60. *Communications of the ACM* 11(4):502–503.

[58] Dijkstra, Edsger W. 1962. Over de sequentialiteit van procesbeschrijvingen (Dutch 1962–64) [EWD35]. http://www.cs.utexas.edu/users/EWD/ewd00xx/EWD35.PDF English version: About the sequentiality of process descriptions, at http://www.cs.utexas.edu/users/EWD/translations/EWD35-English.html.

[59] Dijkstra, Edsger W. 1963a. An ALGOL 60 translator for the X1. *Annual Review in Automatic Programming* 3:329–345.

[60] Dijkstra, Edsger W. 1963b. Making a translator for ALGOL 60. *Annual Review in Automatic Programming* 3:347–356.

[61] Dijkstra, Edsger W. 1963c. *Objectprogramma, gegenereerd door de M.C. vertaler*. Mathematical Centre report MR 55. Amsterdam: Mathematical Centre.

[62] Dijkstra, Edsger W. 1964. Cooperating sequential processes, [EWD123] http://www.cs.utexas.edu/users/EWD/ewd01xx/EWD123.PDF.

[63] Dijkstra, Edsger W. 1965a. Co-operating sequential processes. In *Programming languages*, edited F. Genuys, 43–112. New York: Academic Press.

[64] Dijkstra, Edsger W. 1965b. Solution of a problem in concurrent programming control. *Communications ACM* 8(9):569.

[65] Dijkstra, Edsger W. 1965c. *Globale beschrijving van de drijvende arithmetiek van de EL X8* [EWD145] Available at https://www.cs.utexas.edu/users/EWD/transcriptions/EWD01xx/EWD145.html.

[66] Dijkstra, Edsger W. 1965d. *Documentatie over de communicatieapparatuur aan de EL X8*. [EWD140] Available at https://www.cs.utexas.edu/users/EWD/transcriptions/EWD01xx/EWD140.html and a revised version

[EWD149] https://www.cs.utexas.edu/users/EWD/transcriptions/EWD01xx/
EWD149.html.

[67] Dijkstra, Edsger W. 1968. The structure of the THE-multiprogramming system. *Communications of the ACM* 11(5):341–346. https://www.cs.utexas.edu/
users/EWD/ewd01xx/EWD196.PDF.

[68] Dijkstra, Edsger W. 1980. A programmer's early memories. In *A history of
computing in the twentieth century*, edited Metropolis, N., J. Howlett en G.
Rota. New York: Academic Press.

[69] Donselaar, P.J. van. 1967. De ontwikkeling van elektronische rekenmachines
in Nederland (Een historisch overzicht van Nederlandse computers), Technical
report (Amsterdam: Stichting Het Nederlands Studiecentrum voor Administratieve Automatisering en Bestuurlijke Informatieverwerking).

[70] Doran, R.W., and L.K. Thomas. 1980. Variants of the software solution to
mutual exclusion. *Information Processing Letters* 10(4):206–208.

[71] Electrologica. 1957. Electrologica, Korte algemene beschrijving van de X-1,
Technical report EL-1-N.

[72] Electrologica. 1958. Korte algemene beschrijving van de elektronische rekenmachine X1 (EL-3) [Brief description of the electronic computer X1], Technical Report EL-3. Electrologica, 's-Gravenhage.

[73] Electrologica. 196xc. Electrologica ELX series. General Description.
Rijswijk. https://web.archive.org/web/20070719094844/http://kmt.hku.nl/
~hans/pdf_files/electrologica-engl.pdf. Accessed 10 February 2022.

[74] Electrologica. 1965a. Electrologica EL elektronische informatieverwerkende
systemen ELX3, ELX5. Den Haag: N.V. Electrologica 1966. Rijksarchief in
Noord-Holland, Archief van de Stichting Mathematisch Centrum, 1946–1980,
inv. nr. 52.

[75] Electrologica. 1965b. Electrologica EL elektronische informatieverwerkende
systemen ELX2, ELX3, ELX4, ELX5. Den Haag: N.V. Electrologica 1966.
Rijksarchief in Noord-Holland, Archief van de Stichting Mathematisch Centrum, 1946–1980, inv. nr. 52.

[76] Electrologica. 1966. *Programmering EL X8*. Den Haag: N.V. Electrologica.

[77] Ellwood, D.W. 2018. The force of american modernity: World war II and the
birth of a soft power superpower. *International Journal For History, Culture
And Modernity* 6(11):1–17.

[78] Ende, J. van den, N. Weinberg, and A. Meijer. 2004. The influence of Dutch
and EU government policies on Philips' information technology product strategy. In Coopey (2004a), *Information technology*, 187–208.

[79] Engen, Pieter G. van, and Rolf Meesters. 1969. WAMMES, een time-sharing
systeem voor de EL-X8: gids voor gebruikers. Archived at the National
Museum Boerhaave, Leiden. https://ub.fnwi.uva.nl/computermuseum/pdfs/
WAMMESgebruikersgids.pdf.

[80] Frielink, Abraham Barend, and J.C.E. van Kollenburg, eds. 2000. *Leerboek
accountantscontrole*. Vols 1–8. Groningen: Noordhoff Uitgevers.

[81] Gales, B.P.A. 1986. *Werken aan zekerheid: een terugblik over de schouder van AEGON op twee eeuwen verzekeringsgeschiedenis*, 238–241. 's-Gravenhage: AEGON Verzekeringen.

[82] Groenman, Bert, ed. 2001. *Van landgoed tot kenniscampus. Lustrumboek ter gelegenheid van het veertigjarig bestaan van de Universiteit Twente in Enschede*. Universiteit Twente, Enschede.

[83] Hartman, W. 1983. De betekenis van Frielink voor de informatica. In Bindenga (1984), 21–31.

[84] Heijne, Erik H.M. 2003. Semiconductor detectors in the low countries. *Nuclear Instruments and Methods in Physics Research* 309:1–16.

[85] Heyn, F.A., and J.J. Burgerjon. 1952. Het synchro-cyclotron te Amsterdam. *Philips Technisch Tijdschrift* 14:291–307.

[86] Hiller, Lejaren, and Isaacson, Leonard M. 1959. *Experimental music: Composition with an electronic computer*. New York: McGraw-Hill.

[87] Hindemith, Paul. 1949. *Aufgaben für Harmonieschüler* (translation to German of the English original "A concentrated course in traditional harmony", 1943), B. Schott's Söhne, Mainz, Edition 3602.

[88] Hove, G. van den. 2019. *New insights form old programs, the structure of the first ALGOL 60 system*. PhD thesis. University of Amsterdam.

[89] Informatie. 1959a. Enkele gegevens met betrekking tot geplaatste en bestelde machines. *Informatie* 2:7–8.

[90] Informatie. 1959b. Enkele gegevens met betrekking tot geplaatste en bestelde machines. *Informatie* 3:11.

[91] Informatie. 1959c. Enkele gegevens met betrekking tot geplaatste en bestelde machines. *Informatie* 5:8–9.

[92] Informatie. 1960. Enkele gegevens met betrekking tot geplaatste en bestelde machines. *Informatie* 8:16.

[93] Informatie. 1961. Overzicht van in Nederland per 1 oktober 1961 geplaatste en in bestelling zijnde computers. *Informatie* 17:16.

[94] JMC46. *Jaarverslag Stichting Mathematisch Centrum* [Annual Report Foundation Mathematical Center] (1946).

[95] JMC47. *Jaarverslag Stichting Mathematisch Centrum* [Annual Report Foundation Mathematical Center] (1947).

[96] JMC52. *Jaarverslag Stichting Mathematisch Centrum* [Annual Report Foundation Mathematical Center] (1952).

[97] JMC56. *Jaarverslag Stichting Mathematisch Centrum* [Annual Report Foundation Mathematical Center] (1956).

[98] JMC57. *Jaarverslag Stichting Mathematisch Centrum* [Annual Report Foundation Mathematical Center] (1957).

[99] JMC58. *Jaarverslag Stichting Mathematisch Centrum* [Annual Report Foundation Mathematical Center] (1958).

[100] JMC59. *Jaarverslag Stichting Mathematisch Centrum* [Annual Report Foundation Mathematical Center] (1959).

[101] JMC62. *Jaarverslag Stichting Mathematisch Centrum* [Annual Report Foundation Mathematical Center] (1962).

[102] Jonkers, H.L., W.T.H. van Oers, and H.R.E. Tjin A Djie. 1964a. Discussie rond huidige en toekomstige behoefte aan rekencapaciteit van het IKO. IKO internal report Interiko 64. Archived at the National Museum Boerhaave, Leiden and at Nikhef, Amsterdam.

[103] Jonkers, H.L. 1964b. A comparison EL-X8 and CDC-3200 for on-line use. IKO internal report Interiko 64/5. Archived at the National Museum Boerhaave, Leiden and at Nikhef, Amsterdam. https://ub.fnwi.uva.nl/computermuseum/pdfs/X8vsCDC3200.pdf.

[104] Jonkers, H.L. 1964c. Computer requirements of the Institute for Nuclear Physics Research. IKO informal report. Archived at the National Museum Boerhaave, Leiden and at Nikhef, Amsterdam.

[105] Kamp, A.F., ed. 1955. *De Technische Hogeschool te Delft 1905–1955*. 's-Gravenhage: SDU. Baudet, H. 1992. *De lange weg naar de Technische Universiteit Delft*. Den Haag: SDU.

[106] Kate, P.U. ten, and E. Kwakkel. 1972. AIDA - An operating system for the PDP-8. II. Hardware. In *Proceedings 8th DECUS Europe Seminar 1972*. Amsterdam: Archived at Nikhef.

[107] Klüver, Per Vingaard. 1999. From research institute to computer company: Regnecentralen 1946–1964. *IEEE Annals of the History of Computing* 21(2):31–43.

[108] Klüver, Per Vingaard. 2003. Technology transfer, modernization, and the welfare state: Regnecentralen and the making of governmental policy on computer technology in Denmark in the 1960s. In *History of nordic computing*, edited Bubenko, Janis, John Impagliazzo, and Arne Sølvberg, 61–77. Boston, MA: Springer.

[109] Knegtmans, P.J. 1998. *Een kwetsbaar centrum van de geest: de Universiteit van Amsterdam tussen 1935 en 1950*. Amsterdam: Amsterdam University Press.

[110] Knuth, Donald E. 1966. Additional comments on a problem in concurrent programming control. *Communications ACM* 9(5):321–322.

[111] Knuth, Donald E. 1966. Semantics of context-free languages. *Mathematical Systems Theory* 2(2):127–145.

[112] Koerts, L.A.Ch., K. Mulder, J.E.J. Oberski, and R. van Dantzig. 1971. The BOL nuclear research project. *Nuclear Instruments and Methods* 92:157–160.

[113] Koster, Cornelis H.A. 1965. *On the construction of Algol-procedures for generating, analyzing and translating sentences in natural languages*. Mathematical Centre report MR 72. Mathematical Centre. Amsterdam.

[114] Koster, Cornelis H.A. 1971. *A Compiler Compiler*. Mathematical Centre report MR 127/71. Mathematical Centre. Amsterdam.

[115] Krige, J. 2006. *American hegemony and the postwar reconstruction of science in Europe*. Cambridge, MA: The MIT Press.

[116] Kruseman Aretz, Frans E.J. 1962. *Moment expansions in the theory of cooperative phenomena, Dissertation*. Amsterdam: Gemeente Universiteit Amsterdam.

[117] Kruseman Aretz, Frans E.J. 1964. ALGOL 60 translation for everybody. *Elektronische Datenverarbeitung* 6:233–244.

[118] Kruseman Aretz, Frans E.J. 1966a. *Het MC-ALGOL 60-systeem voor de X8; Voorlopige programmeurshandleiding*. Report MR 81. Mathematical Centre. Amsterdam.

[119] Kruseman Aretz, Frans E.J. 1966b. *The ELAN source text of the Mathematical Center ALGOL 60 system for the EL X8*. Mathematisch Centrum rapport MR 84, Mathematical Centre. Amsterdam.

[120] Kruseman Aretz, Frans E.J. 1971a. *Het objectprogramma, gegenereerd door de X8-ALGOL-vertaler van het M.C.*. Mathematical Centre report MR 121/71. Mathematical Centre. Amsterdam.

[121] Kruseman Aretz, Frans E.J. 1971b. On the bookkeeping of source-text line numbers during the execution phase of ALGOL 60 programs. In: *MC-25 informatica symposium: [symposium on the occasion of the 25th anniversary of the Mathematical Centre, Amsterdam, 06-07.01.1972]*, edited De Bakker et al. Mathematical Centre tracts 37. Amsterdam: Mathematical Centre.

[122] Kruseman Aretz, Frans E.J., P.J.W. ten Hagen, and H.L. Oudshoorn. 1973. *An ALGOL 60 compiler in ALGOL 60, text of the MC-compiler for the EL X8*. Mathematical Centre tracts 48. Mathematical Centre, Amsterdam.

[123] Kruseman Aretz, Frans E.J. 1974. Doelstellingen en achtergronden van de operating systems PICO, MICRO en MILLI. *Informatie* 16:672–678.

[124] Kruseman Aretz, Frans E.J. 1995. *33 jaar beoefening van de informatica*. Valedictory lecture. Technische Universiteit Eindhoven.

[125] Kruseman Aretz, Frans E.J. 2001. Uit de oude doos van de X1 en de X8 (over de berekening van sinus en cosinus). In *Liber Amicorum Jos Jansen*, edited M.J.H. Anthonisse. Eindhoven: Eindhoven University of Technology.

[126] Kruseman Aretz, Frans E.J. 2003. *The Dijkstra-Zonneveld ALGOL 60 compiler for the Electrologica X1*. CWI Report SEN-N301. Centrum voor Wiskunde en Informatica. Amsterdam, The Netherlands.

[127] Kruseman Aretz, Frans E.J. 2006. Progress in ALGOL 60 implementation: two successive MC systems compared, unpublished note, November 23.

[128] Kruseman Aretz, Frans E.J. 2008. *A comparison between the ALGOL 60 implementations on the Electrologica X1 and the Electrologica X8*. CWI report SEN-E0801, Centrum Wiskunde & Informatica, Amsterdam.

[129] Kruseman Aretz, Frans E.J. 2013. *On the design of two small batch operating systems 1965–1970*. CWI report SwAT, Centrum Wiskunde & Informatica, Amsterdam.

[130] Laarschot, Piet J.J. van de, and Jan Nederkoorn. 1963. *Text of the second ALGOL 60 translator for the X1*. Technical Report MR 61. Mathematisch Centrum, Amsterdam.

[131] Lamport, Leslie. 1974. A new solution of Dijkstra's concurrent programming problem. *Communications ACM* 17(8):453–455.

[132] Lavington, Simon. 1980. *Early British computers: The story of vintage computers and the people who built them*. Bedford: Manchester University Press.

[133] Lavington, Simon. 2011. Moving targets. *Elliott-automation and the dawn of the computer age in Britain, 1947–1967*. London: Springer.

[134] Lavington, Simon. 2019. *Early computing in Britain: Ferranti Ltd. and government funding, 1948–1958*. Cham: Springer.

[135] Linneaus, Carl. 1753. *Species plantarum*. Sweden: Laurentius Salvius.

[136] Loopstra, B.J. 1959a. Input and output in the X-1 system. In *Information Processing: Proceedings of the International Conference on Information Processing, Unesco, Paris 15–20 June 1959*, 342–344. München: Oldenbourg Verlag.

[137] Loopstra, B.J. 1959b. The X-1 computer. *The Computer Journal* 2(1):39–43.

[138] Lopes Cardozo, M. 1958. Verslag van de Quo Vadis Numerieke Informatietechniek 8/1/'58, 18 Jan. 1958. Philips Company Archives folder 814.8 Map 1.

[139] Luijckx, Guy. 1980. Het cyclotron. *Philips Technisch Tijdschrift* 39(10):274–276.

[140] Lugt, Ch. 1958. Toepassing van numerieke informatietechniek in industriële processen [A note on Numerical Information Technology in Industrial Processes to the Philips division Product for Industrial Applications], Notitie Philips PIT, 3 januari 1958.

[141] Dick Manuel. 2004. Caleidoscoop van de informatietechnologie in Nederland, 1946–2004, In *Ondernemen in netwerken. Nieuwe en groeiende bedrijven in de informatiesamenleving*, edited Wim Hulsink, Dick Manuel en Erik Stam, 35–51. Van Gorcum.

[142] Mars, Anton J., J.L. Visschers, and R.F. van Wijk. 1972. AIDA—an operating system for the PDP-8. I. Software. In *Proceedings of the 8th DECUS Europe Seminar 1972*. Archived at Nikhcf, Amsterdam.

[143] Meertens, Lambert G.L.T. 1962. Kunstmatige intelligentie, een programma voor het optimaal oplossen van een klasse van problemen (Artificial intelligence, a program for optimally solving a class of problems). *Mededelingen van het Nederlands Rekenmachine Genootschap* 4:6–13. (*In Dutch*).

[144] Meertens, Lambert G.L.T. 1968. *Quartet No. 1 in C Major for 2 Violins, Viola and Violoncello*. Mathematical Centre Report MR 96. Mathematical Centre. Amsterdam.

[145] Meertens, Lambert G.L.T. 1968. Componeren met de computer. *Informatie* 10:418–421.

[146] Meertens, Lambert G.L.T. 1969. The imitation of musical styles by a computer. In *Information Processing 68*, Proc. IFIP Congress 1968, Vol. 1, xxv–xxvi. Amsterdam: North-Holland Publishing Company.

[147] Miert, Dirk van. 2005. *Illuster onderwijs: het Amsterdamse Athenaeum in de Gouden Eeuw 1632–1704*. Amsterdam: Bakker.

[148] Mori, Elisabetta. 2019. Coping with the "American Giants". *IEEE Annals of the History of Computing* 41(4):83–96.

[149] Mounier-Kuhn, Pierre-Eric. 2010. *l'Informatique en France; de la seconde guerre mondiale au Plan Calcul*. Paris: PUBS.

[150] Naur, Peter, ed. 1960. J.W. Backus, F.L. Bauer, J. Green, C. Katz, J. McCarthy, A.J. Perlis, H. Rutishauser, K. Samelson, B. Vauquois, J.H. Wegstein, A. van Wijngaarden, M. Woodger, Report on the algorithmic language ALGOL 60. *Num. Mathematik* 2:106–136.

[151] Nieuwe Giessen, D. van de. 1996. *Onderzoek en ontwikkeling bij KPN. Een geschiedenis van de eerste honderd jaar.* Leidschendam: KPN Research.

[152] David Nofre. 2010. Unraveling Algol: US, Europe, and the creation of a programming language, *Annals for the History of Computing* 32(2):58–68.

[153] Nofre, D., M. Priestley, and G. Alberts. 2014. When technology became language: the origins of the linguistic conception of computer programming, 1950–1960. *Technology and Culture* 55(1):40–75.

[154] David Nofre. 2021. The politics of early programming languages: IBM and the algol project. *Historical Studies in the Natural Sciences* 51(3):379–413.

[155] Oberski, Jona E.J., R. van Dantzig, K. Mulder, L.A.Ch. Koerts, and F. van Hall. 1965. IKOB, koppeling van PDP8 en X8. IKO Internal report. Archived at Nikhef, Amsterdam.

[156] Oberski, Jona E.J, L.A.Ch. Koerts, R. van Dantzig, and K. Mulder. 1967. Toelichting op de computers in BOL. IKO internal report Interiko 67/9. Archived at the National Museum Boerhaave, Leiden and at Nikhef, Amsterdam. https://ub.fnwi.uva.nl/computermuseum/pdfs/computersBOL.pdf.

[157] Oberski, Jona E.J., et al. 1971a. Electronics of the BOL system. *Nuclear Instruments and Methods* 92:177–187.

[158] Oberski, Jona E.J. et al. 1971b. The BOL computer hardware configuration. *Nuclear Instruments and Methods* 92:189–191.

[159] R.J. Ord-Smith. 1988. Memories of forty years with computers. In *Vooruitgang, bit voor bit. Liber Amicorum ac Collegarum bij het afscheid van Prof.dr.ir. W.L. van der Poel 26 oktober 1988*, edited Pronk, C. and W.J. Toetenel, 30–34. Delft: Delftse Universitaire Pers.

[160] Paju, Petri, and Helena Durnova. 2009. Computing close to the iron curtain. Inter/national computing practices in Czechoslovakia and Finland, 1945–1970. *Comparative Technology Transfer and Society* 7(3):303–322.

[161] Paju, Petri, and Thomas Haigh. 2016. IBM rebuilds Europe: The curious case of the transnational typewriter. *Enterprise & Society* 17(2):265–300.

[162] Paju, Petri and Thomas Haigh. 2018. IBM's tiny peripheral: Finland and the tensions of transnationality. *Business History Review* 92:3–28.

[163] Philips Company Archives folder 81 'Mechanisatie 1'.

[164] Philips Company Archives folder 81 Map 2, 'Mechanisatie/Automatisering (Numerieke Informatietechnique) 1960–1961'.

[165] Philips Company Archives folder 814.9 'Numerieke besturing'.

[166] Peterson, G.L. 1981. Myths about the mutual exclusion problem. *Information Processing Letters* 12(3):115–116.

[167] Petersson, Tom. 2005. Facit and the besk boys: Sweden's computer industry (1956–1962). *IEEE Annals of the History of Computing* 27(4):23–30.

[168] Petersson, Tom. 2008. Private and public interests in the development of the early swedish computer industry. Royal Institute of Technology, CESIS –

Centre of Excellence for Science and Innovation Studies. In *Working Paper Series in Economics and Institutions of Innovation* 1.

[169] Petzold, Hartmut. 1992. *Moderne Rechenkünstler. Die Industrialisierung der Rechentechnik in Deutschland*. München: Beck.

[170] Poel, W.L. van der, H.H. Clement, and J. Rice. 1958. Patent Specification GB802,745: Improvements in or relating to Electrical Digital Computers. Submitted December 23, 1955, awarded October 8, 1958.

[171] Poel, Willem L. van der. 1956. *The logical principles of some simple computers*. Dissertation, Gemeente Universiteit Amsterdam.

[172] Poel, Willem L. van der. 1989. De ontwikkeling van de computer in Nederland. *Histechnicon* 15(1):2–9.

[173] Poel, Willem L. van der. 2019. Gerrit Anne Blaauw 17 juli 1924–21 maart 2018, *Levensberichten en herdenkingen 2019*, Koninklijke Nederlandse Akademie van Wetenschappen, Amsterdam, 22–25. https://www.knaw.nl/nl/actueel/publicaties/levensberichten-en-herdenkingen-2019/.

[174] Pouls, M.P. 1969. Programma documentatie Associatief tellen. Electrologica report CS.69/64/582. Archived at the National Museum Boerhaave, Leiden.

[175] Raynal, M. 1986. *Algorithms for mutual exclusion*. Oxford: North Oxford Academic.

[176] Reinoud, H. 1956. Over de produktie en toepassing van elektronische administratiemachines. *Economisch-statistische berichten* 41(2020):193–196.

[177] Reinoud, H. 1957a. De recente ontwikkeling van elektronische administratiemachines. *Economisch-statistische berichten* 42(2098):728–732.

[178] Reinoud, H. 1957b. Een Nederlandse industrie van elektronische reken- en administratiemachines? *Economisch-statistische berichten* 42(2103):843–845.

[179] Rem, Martin, and Hans Schippers. 2006. Operating Systems; Edsger W. Dijkstra en zijn THE systeem. In *Gedreven door nieuwsgierigheid; een selectie uit 50 jaar TU/e onderzoek*, edited Lintsen, Harry, and Hans Schippers, 225–231. Stichting Historie der Techniek en Technische Universiteit Eindhoven, Eindhoven.

[180] Theo F. de Ridder. 1972. LISI, een LISP-SIMPLEX systeem met display faciliteiten, Informal IKO report. Archived at the National Museum Boerhaave, Leiden.

[181] Schoonderbeek, J.W. 1980. A.B. Frielink Eredoctor. *De Accountant* 1980(3):140–142. Hen, P.E. de (1995) Aartsvaders van het Nederlandse accountantsberoep. In: Hen, P.E. de (1995) *Hoofdstukken uit de geschiedenis van het Nederlandse accountantsberoep na 1935*. NIVRA, Amsterdam, pp. 247–262.

[182] Sorgdrager, Winnie. 1981. *Een experiment in het bos. De eerste jaren van de Technische Hogeschool Twente 1961–1972*. Alphen aan de Rijn: Samsom.

[183] Staff of Computation Dept. 1964. *Prolegomena to X8 ALGOL*. Internal report MCCD 64 R-989. Mathematisch Centrum, Amsterdam.

[184] Toenbreker, S.J.A.M., P.G. van Engen, R. van Dantzig, L.A.Ch. Koerts, K. Mulder, and J.E.J. Oberski. 1965. De toepassing van een EL X-8 op het IKO. IKO internal report Interiko 65/9. Archived at the National Mu-

seum Boerhaave, Leiden and at Nikhef, Amsterdam. https://ub.fnwi.uva.nl/computermuseum/pdfs/X8opIKO.pdf.

[185] Udekem-Gevers, Marie d'. 2011. *La machine mathématique IRSIA-FNRS (1946–1962)*. Bruxelles: Académie Royale de Belgique.

[186] Vries, Marc de., and Kees Boersma. 2005. *80 Years of Research at the Philips Natuurkundig Laboratorium (1914–1994); the Role of the Nat.Lab. at Philips.* Amsterdam: Pallas Publications.

[187] Waalwijk, J.M., N. Wiedenhof, G. Luijckx, G.A. Brinkman, W.K. Hofker, R. van Dantzig, H.J. Akkerman, P. Bakker. 1980. 35 jaar samenwerking met IKO. *Philips Technisch Tijdschrift* 39(10):269–312 (English, French and Dutch edition).

[188] Wapstra, A.H., H.L. Jonkers, and L.A.Ch. Koerts. 1964. Internal note 'Rekenmachine'. https://ub.fnwi.uva.nl/computermuseum/pdfs/Wapstra.pdf.

[189] Wapstra, A.H., H.L. Jonkers, et al. 1965. Voorstel tot aanschaffing van een electronische rekenautomaat ten behoeve van het fysisch werk op het Instituut voor Kernfysisch Onderzoek. Internal report IKO-2168. https://ub.fnwi.uva.nl/computermuseum/pdfs/X8aanschafvoorstel.pdf.

[190] Whyte, W.H. 1956. *The organisation man*. New York: Simon and Schuster.

[191] Wielinga, B.J., J.E.J. Oberski, R. van Dantzig et al. 1973. Toelichting op de aanvraag voor vervanging van de rekenmachine van het Instituut voor Kernphysisch Onderzoek (IKO) te Amsterdam. IKO informal report. Archived at the National Museum Boerhaave, Leiden. https://ub.fnwi.uva.nl/computermuseum/pdfs/vervanging1973.pdf.

[192] Wijngaarden, Adriaan van. 1948. Principes der Electronische Rekenmachines, Mathematisch Centrum, Rekenafdeling, CR 3, Cursus Februari 1948.

[193] Wijngaarden, Adriaan van. 1949a. Algemeen overzicht moderne rekenmachines. *Nederlands Tijdschrift voor Natuurkunde* 15:243–254.

[194] Wijngaarden, Adriaan van. 1949b. Practisch rekenen. In *Eerste Nederlandse Systematisch Ingerichte Encyclopaedie*, Vol IV, 104–112. Amsterdam: ENSIE.

[195] Wijngaarden, Adriaan van. 1965. Orthogonal Design and Description of a Formal Language. *Reports Stichting Mathematisch Centrum* MR 76. Mathematisch Centrum, Amsterdam. [https://ir.cwi.nl/pub/9208] cf. https://en.wikipedia.org/wiki/Van_Wijngaarden_grammar.

[196] Wijngaarden, Adriaan van. 1969. Peck, John E.L., Mailloux, Barry J., and Koster, Cornelis H.A. (eds). Report on the algorithmic language ALGOL 68. *Num. Mathematik* 14:79–218.

[197] Wit, D. de. 1992. Wat niet te verzekeren valt: Electrologica als casus uit de opbouw van een Nederlandse computerindustrie (1956–1967). *Jaarboek voor de Geschiedenis van Bedrijf en Techniek* 9:261–291.

[198] Wit, D. de. 1994. *The shaping of automation. A historical analysis of the interaction between technology and organization, 1950–1985*, Hilversum: Verloren.

[199] Wit, D. de. 1997. The construction of the Dutch computer industry: The organisational shaping of technology. *Business History* 39(3):81–104.

[200] Wit, O. de, en J. van den Ende. 2000. The emergence of a new regime: Business management and office mechanisation in the Dutch financial sector in the 1920s. *Business History* 42(2):87–118.

[201] Wit, O. de, e.a. 2002. Innovative junctions. Office Technologies in the Netherlands, 1880–1980. *Technology and Culture* 43:50–72.

[202] Zonneveld, Jaap A., and Frans E.J. Kruseman Aretz. 2016. *The NatLab computer center WAA, 1967–1983. Some photos*. Philips Research Technical Note TN-2016/00026, Eindhoven.

[203] Zutphen, Luc van. 1998. Ter nagedachtenis aan Abraham Barend Frielink Registeraccountant. *De Accountant* 1998(7):430.

A Note on the Contributors

Gerard Alberts (1954) is an historian of digital cultures. He is a retired associate professor at the Korteweg—de Vries Institute for Mathematics at the University of Amsterdam. Alberts jumped into history, writing on the founding of the Mathematical Centre in the context of postwar culture, Zij mogen uiteraard daarbij de zuivere wiskunde niet verwaarloozen (1987) and took his PhD in history cum laude on Calculative years (1998). His publications cover history of computing from early computations to hacking and the internet. He extends particular care to the heritage of DDS, the Amsterdam Digital City. Alberts is editor of the Springer series in History of Computing.

Huub de Beer (1981) has worked as an educational researcher, historian, programmer, and computer science teacher. In 2007, he joined the University of Amsterdam as a historian to investigate the history of Dutch computer science in the 1950s and early 1960s. Three years later, while working as a high school computer science teacher, Huub started his PhD project to investigate innovative mathematics education in elementary school at Eindhoven University of Technology (TU/e). After receiving his doctorate in 2016, Huub worked as a programmer in industry before becoming a lecturer in computer science at TU/e in 2019.

René van Dantzig (1937) worked for more than 40 years as an experimental physicist in Amsterdam at the National Institute for Subatomic Physics (Nikhef) and the former Nuclear Physics Institute (IKO). He led research teams, first internally at the in-house accelerators, later in international collaborations at CERN (Geneva), the European Laboratory of Particle Physics. Subsequently, he performed research in nuclear, intermediate-energy, high-energy, particle, and computational physics. Before retiring in 2002, he helped set up an international astro-particle physics experiment located in the depth of the Mediterranean Sea.

Dirk Dekker (1927–2021) steered his career from a PhD in pure mathematics, topology, to a leading position in the numerical side of computer science. Numerical algorithms in ALGOL 68 are at the core of his contributions to the field, first as a work for the Mathematical Center, next as Volume 5 in NUMAL. Dirk Dekker

© The Author(s), under exclusive license to Springer Nature Switzerland AG 2022   189
G. Alberts, J. F. Groote (eds.), *Tales of Electrologica*, History of Computing,
https://doi.org/10.1007/978-3-031-13033-5

served the University of Amsterdam as a full professor in Numerical Mathematics 1971–1992. Dekker was the author of Dekker's algorithm for mutual exclusion, answering to a problem posed to him over lunch by Edsger Dijkstra in 1959. He enjoyed the irony of publishing on this incidental pearl of his intellect here for the first time. Dirk Dekker passed away, November 25, 2021. We are saddened that he did not live to see this result in print.

Jan Friso Groote (1965) is a full professor in Formal Methods at Eindhoven University of Technology. His interest is in efficiently proving the correctness of the software in computer controlled systems. This, for instance, led to the book, Modeling and Analysis of Communicating Systems, The MIT Press 2014. Before commencing in Eindhoven, in 1997, he studied Computer Science at Twente University and wrote a PhD on process algebra at CWI, Amsterdam (1991), where he later became a leader of the research group SEN2.

Paul Klint (1948) is research fellow at the Centrum Wiskunde & Informatica in Amsterdam and professor emeritus at the University of Amsterdam. He is member of ACICT (https://www.adviescollegeicttoetsing.nl), the advisory board that advises the Dutch government on large ICT projects. He is co-founder of several companies including Software Improvement Group (https://www.softwareimprovementgroup.com), Solid Sands (https://solidsands.com), and Swat.engineering (https://www.swat.engineering). His research interests include generic language technology, domain-specific languages, software analysis and renovation, technology transfer and intellectual property rights. He is an active open source contributor and is currently working on a compiler for the meta-programming language Rascal (http://www.rascal-mpl.org/).

Frans Kruseman Aretz (1933) was educated as a physicist. After his PhD he switched to Computer Science, starting his career in that field at the Mathematical Center in Amsterdam, where he became responsible for the software for the Electrologica X1 and X8. In 1969 he moved to Philips Research Laboratories Eindhoven, where he worked until his retirement in 1993. From 1966 until 1971 he was professor by special appointment at Amsterdam University and from 1971 until 1996 part-time professor at the Eindhoven University of Technology. His interests are parsing theory, operating systems, and program development.

Lambert Meertens (1944) became fascinated with the potential of computers while leafing through a brochure on the then new ZEBRA computer exhibited in 1959 at the Tenth FIRATO in Amsterdam and discovering a conditional branch instruction. After a stint as nightshift computer operator of the Electrologica X1 at the Mathematical Centre, he took a job as programmer before joining the scientific staff, eventually heading the Department of Algorithmics and Architecture of then CWI. Meertens has held professorships at New York University, Delft University of Technology and Utrecht University. His research interests have ranged from Artificial Intelligence and Computer Arts to programming language design and "correct by construction" program development formalisms.

Provenance of the Pictures

Fig. 1: Picture Gerard Alberts.
Fig. 2: Picture Jan Friso Groote.
Fig. 1.1: *Statistica* 14(4), p. 276, 1960, picture Gerard Alberts.
Fig. 1.2: Collection & picture Gerard Alberts.
Fig. 1.3: Picture Jaap Zonneveld.
Fig. 2.1: Machines zonder werklieden, Philips Company Archives PCA folder 81 "Mechanisatie 1."
Fig. 2.2a–c: Archives CWI.
Fig. 2.2d: Engelfriet family.
Fig. 2.3: Brochure, Archives CWI.
Fig. 3.1, 3.2: Rijksarchief Noord-Holland (RAHN, SMC, inv. nr. 51).
Fig. 3.3, 3.6: Hans Kulk.
Fig. 3.4, 3.5: Rijksarchief Noord-Holland (RAHN, SMC, inv. nr. 50).
Fig. 3.7: Rijksarchief Noord-Holland (RAHN, SMC, inv. nr. 52).
Fig. 4.1, 4.3, 4.4, 4.6: Pictures Paul Klint.
Fig. 4.2a: Frielink family.
Fig. 4.2b: Archives CWI.
Fig. 4.2c: Blaauw family.
Fig. 4.2d: Lambert Meertens.
Fig. 4.2e: Hamilton Richards.
Fig. 4.2f: Frans Kruseman Aretz.
Fig. 4.5: Jaap Zonneveld.
Fig. 5.1, 5.2: Archives CWI.
Fig. 5.3: Picture Jaap Zonneveld.
Fig. 5.5: Computermuseum UvA.
Fig. 6.1, 6.2: Dekker family.
Fig. 7.1, 7.2, 7.3, 7.4, 7.9, 7.10: Picture Hans Arnold, collection NIKHEF in Archives Boerhaave.
Fig 7.5, 7.8, 7.11, 7.12: René van Dantzig.
Fig 8.1–8.6: Lambert Meertens.

Index

© The Author(s), under exclusive license to Springer Nature Switzerland AG 2022
G. Alberts, J. F. Groote (eds.), *Tales of Electrologica*, History of Computing,
https://doi.org/10.1007/978-3-031-13033-5

Printed in the United States
by Baker & Taylor Publisher Services